Mathematics

Teacher's Guide 1 and 2

R. Chikwakwa
J. Suffolk

MACMILLAN
MALAŴI

First edition 2000 by
MACMILLAN EDUCATION LTD
London and Oxford
Companies and representatives throughout the world

www.macmillan-africa.com

ISBN 99908-44-48-8

9 8 7 6 5 4 3 2
08 07 06 05 04 03 02 01

This book is printed on paper suitable for recycling and made from fully managed and sustained forest sources

Printed and bound in Malaysia

A catalogue record of this book is available in the British Library.

Contents

Preface			v
Book 1	1	Sets	1
	2	Number systems	10
	3	Number bases	19
	4	Coordinates	22
	5	Algebraic expressions	27
	6	Graphs	32
	7	Graphs and gradients	39
	8	Geometry	47
	9	Number patterns	56
	10	Approximations and estimation	61
	11	Commercial and social arithmetic	66
	12	Polygons	71
	13	Statistics	78
	14	More algebra	87
	15	Geometric figures	96
	16	Symmetry	104
Book 2	1	Algebra – equations and formulae	107
	2	Number patterns	111
	3	Numerical concepts	115
	4	Vectors	122
	5	Geometry: plane figures and Pythagoras	129
	6	Travel graphs	137
	7	Indices and logarithms	141
	8	Algebraic variables – linear equations	147
	9	Simultaneous equations	150
	10	Successive translations	158
	11	Inequalities and regions	160
	12	Geometrical constructions	169
	13	Algebra – expansion, factorisation and algebraic equations	177
	14	Ratio and proportion	185

15 Similarity 190
16 Probability 196
17 Mensuration 199
18 Density and mixtures 204
19 Applied arithmetic – miscellaneous applications 207
20 Rotation 214

Preface

The Malaŵi Secondary Mathematics Series has been written to meet the needs of students learning mathematics in forms 1 and 2 in Malaŵi. It includes and explains all the methods, properties and vocabulary that are included in the syllabus for the two years.

The writers have attempted to keep the language used as simple and as easy to understand as they can. The examples used to explain ideas have as much as possible been taken from the experience of the students.

Mathematics is more interesting and more enjoyable and is learnt more effectively if the students understand what they are learning about. Students who build up an understanding of what they have learnt are better equipped to solve problems than students who have learnt mathematics as a mysterious collection of procedures and results without understanding.

In the book all the methods and properties are fully justified. Students are encouraged to find out results for themselves before they are described in the text. For example, students should not just be told what the angle sum of a triangle is. They should find out for themselves by drawing a triangle, measuring each of its angles and finding the sum.

There are numerous worked examples in the text. The working for these examples is carefully explained so that students reading the book by themselves can understand. There are also numerous exercises so that students can have enough practice. Mathematics is largely concerned with the solving of problems so it is important that students have plenty of opportunities to do this.

It is hoped that as a result learning mathematics becomes an enjoyable and successful experience for many students.

This Teacher's Guide has been written to accompany *Malaŵi Junior Secondary Mathematics* Student's Books 1 and 2.

Contained within this Teacher's Guide are comments and helpful hints for the classroom teacher and further explanation of some of the most difficult ideas introduced in the Student's Books. Some suggestions for extending the work of the more able students are also included, as well as the answers to the exercises in the Student's Books.

1 Sets

• Aim of chapter

The aim of the chapter is to introduce students to the basic notation and concepts of sets.

• Objectives

By the end of the chapter the students will be able to:

1 Use set notation to list members of sets and to show membership of sets
2 Identify and use the notations { } and ∅ for the empty set
3 Draw Venn diagrams to illustrate sets
4 Determine whether or not a set is a subset of another set
5 Determine whether two sets are equal
6 Find the number of elements of a set and use the notation n(A)
7 Find and use set notation for the intersection of two sets
8 Find and use set notation for the union of two sets
9 Find the relationship between the number of elements in the union of two sets and the sum of the number of elements in each set.

• What is a set?

This first section introduces the concept of a set by looking at sets of common things. The teacher should discuss with the students the things that they have listed from the three sets. It is important that students are able to say whether a particular object belongs to a set or not. In other words, all sets have to be well defined.

Activity: The aim of this activity is to encourage students to look at sets from a practical point of view. The teacher should take the role of facilitator in this case.

• Set language

The teacher should use common objects in the classroom such as pencils, pens, pins, strings, money (notes of different values), text books (mathematics, geography, history, biology, etc.), mathematical sets and so on. These and other objects can be used to explain the concepts discussed in this chapter. Strings can be used very effectively to illustrate Venn diagrams.

The first section introduces the idea of a set and membership of a set. In mathematics a set has to be 'well-defined'. This means that it must be possible to decide whether or not any object is in the set. For example 'a set of pupils' is not well-defined as it is too vague. We do not know which set is being discussed. 'The set of pupils in room 27' is well-defined as we can easily decide whether a person is or is not a member of this set. Is the person a pupil? Is the person in room 27? Only if the answer to both those questions is 'Yes' is the person a member of the set.

In the book the words 'member' and 'element' are both used.

EXERCISE 1A

1 a The set of the three biggest rivers in Malaŵi.
  b The set of the days of the week.
  c The set of the measures of time.
  d The set of vowels.
  e A set of districts in Malaŵi.
  f The set of the even numbers less than 11.
  g The set of the months with 30 days.

2 a Black, red, green.
  b The answer depends on the school. No letter is written twice. For example, the set of letters of Masongola School is {M, A, S, O, N, G, L}.
  c Saturday, Sunday.
  d May, June, July.
  e Mathematics, English, Chichewa, and so on.
  f The answer depends on the pupil. Remember that no letters are written twice.
  g Tanzania, Zambia, Mozambique.

3 a T b F c T d F e T f F g F

4 Many answers are possible. Students only have to give three in each part of the question. Possible answers include:
  a Lakes Malaŵi, Malombe, Chuita, Chilwa, Kazuni.
  b Coffee, tea, cotton, tobacco.
  c Maize, cassava, sorghum, millet.
  d Pacific, Atlantic, Indian, Antarctic (Southern), Arctic.
  e Malaŵi, Mozambique, Zambia, Zimbabwe, Lesotho, Botswana, South Africa, Swaziland, Angola, Namibia.

5 c e

6 a c

7 a $\text{S} \in C$ b $5 \in P$ c $24 \in E$
  d $\text{J} \in M$ e $\text{M} \in P$ f $24 \in M$

8 a $5 \in A$ b $5 \notin B$ c $5 \in C$ d $6 \in B$
e $13 \notin B$ f $9 \notin C$ g $2 \notin A$ h $17 \notin A$

• The empty set

There is only one empty set, so we say **the** empty set. The teacher should give many different examples which lead to the empty set. These can be amusing: the set of pupils in your class over three metres tall or the set of good football players in a rival football team, for example. Teach pupils both symbols used for the empty set, { } and ∅. The empty set is called the null set.

• Venn diagrams

Venn diagrams are a very useful way of illustrating sets. String and objects can be used to develop Venn diagrams. Put a piece of string round a group of objects and it looks just like a Venn diagram.

EXERCISE 1B

1 a
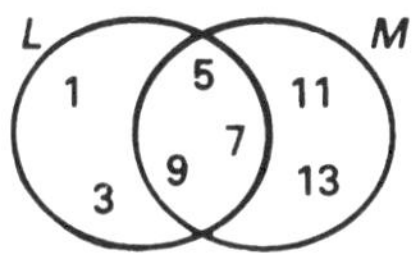

b
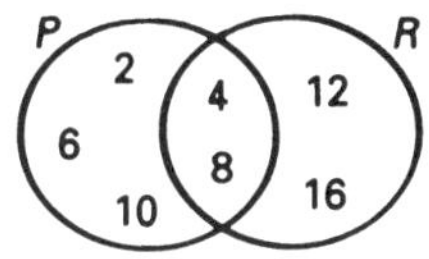

c
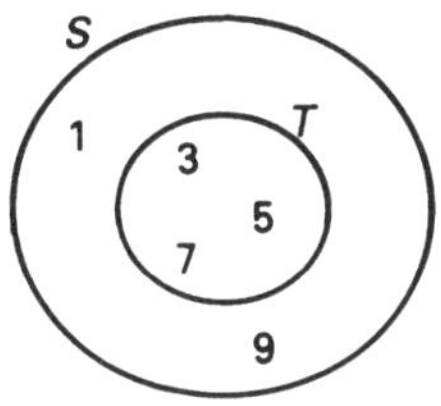

d
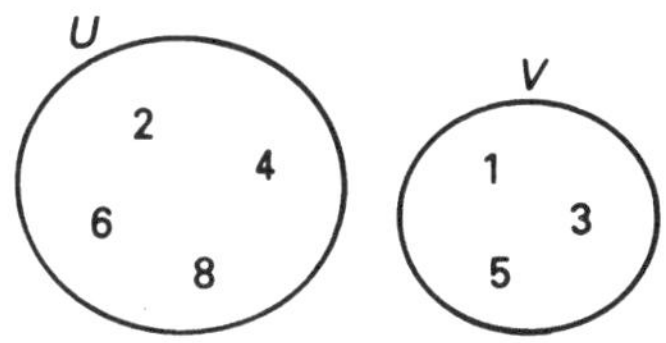

2 a $X = \{0, 2, 4, 6, 12\}$ $Y = \{6, 8, 10, 12\}$
b $X = \{4, 8, 12, 16, 18\}$ $Y = \{4, 5, 8, 10, 20\}$

3 a
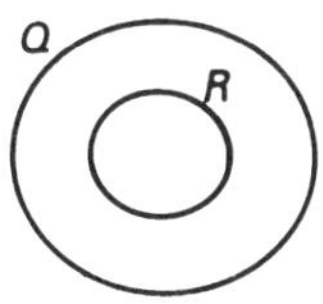

b
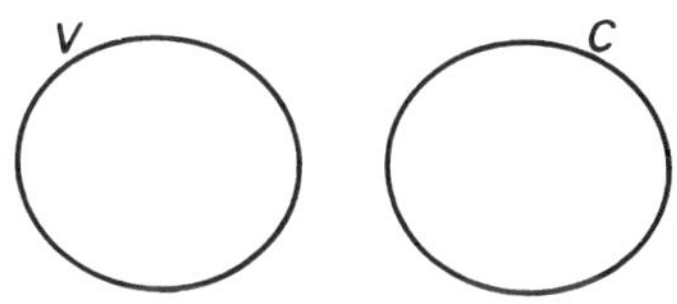

c
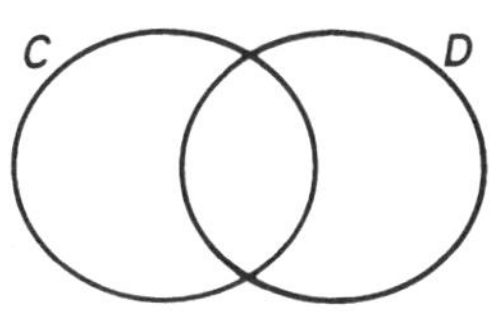

d
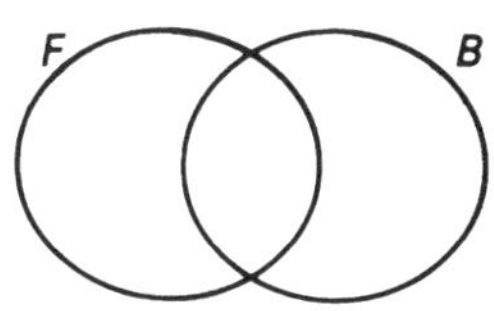

• Subsets

Set A is a subset of set B if every element of A is also in B.
We write $A \subset B$.

Notice that $A \subset A$ because every element of A is in A. The empty set is defined to be a subset of all sets. The reason for this is that it makes the formula for the number of subsets of a set simpler.

The number of subsets of a set is asked about in exercise 1C number **1**.

More able pupils may be able to investigate the number of subsets of a set. They can discover the formula for themselves if they prepare a table like this (they can choose their own sets with 1, 2, 3, ... members):

Set	Number of elements	Subsets	Number of subsets
{a}	1	{a} ∅	$2=2^1$
{a, b}	2	{a} {b} {a, b} ∅	$4=2^2$
{a, b, c}	3	{a} {b} {c} {a, b} {a, c} {b, c} {a, b, c} ∅	$8=2^3$
{a, b, c, d}	4	{a} {b} {c} {d} {a, b} {a, c} {a, d} {b, c} {b, d} {c, d} {a, b, c} {a, b, d} {a, c, d} {b, c, d} {a, b, c, d} ∅	$16=2^4$

The pupils should be able to see the rule for themselves: a set with n elements has 2^n subsets. The set for which $n=0$, the empty set, also satisfies this formula; ∅ has one subset which is itself. When $n=0$, $2^n=2^0=1$.

• Equal sets

Equal sets are sets with the same members. Give examples of equal sets and discuss them with the class.

For example $A=$ {book, pencil, pen} and $B=$ {pencil, book, pen}. $A=B$ because they have the same members.

EXERCISE 1C

1 **a** {a} {b} {c} {a, b} {a, c} {b, c} {a, b, c} ∅ **b** 8

2 **a** {Aida} {Betty} {Grace} {Musa}
{Aida, Betty} {Aida, Grace} {Aida, Musa} {Betty, Grace}
{Betty, Musa} {Grace, Musa}

{Aida, Betty, Grace} {Aida, Betty, Musa} {Aida, Grace, Musa} {Betty, Grace, Musa}
{Aida, Betty, Grace, Musa}
$\varnothing$

b {a} {b} {c} {d} {a, b} {a, c} {a, d} {b, c} {b, d} {c, d}
{a, b, c} {a, b, d} {a, c, d} {b, c, d} {a, b, c, d}
$\varnothing$

c {2} {3} {5} {2, 3} {2, 5} {3, 5} {2, 3, 5} $\varnothing$

d {1} {0} {1, 0} $\varnothing$
Notice that {0} and the empty set { } are different sets.

e {8} { }

f $\varnothing$. The empty set has one subset, the empty set itself.

3 a True b False c True
d False e False f False

4 a $A \subset B$, A is a subset of B
b $A \subset B$, A is a subset of B
c A is not a subset of B and B is not a subset of A
d $A \subset B$, A is a subset of B
e $A \subset B$, A is a subset of B
f A is a subset of B and B is a subset of A

5 $P = Q$

• The number of members of a set

Emphasise the notation of the number of elements in set A, denoted by $n(A)$. Students often find this notation difficult. Give adequate examples to discover the number of elements in given sets.

• Universal sets

The set which contains all the elements under discussion is called the universal set and is given the symbol **ℰ** (**ℰ** is an abbreviation for *ensemble*, the French word for together) or U. The teacher should give many different examples of universal sets.

For example: All the members of a family (mother, father, daughters, sons) when talking about a family.
All the students in a school (Forms 1, 2, 3, 4) when talking about some of the pupils in different classes.
All the students in a class when talking about some of them.

EXERCISE 1D

1 a $n(A) = 7$ b $n(B) = 4$ c $n(C) = 4$
d $D = \{1, 2, 3, \dots, 16\}$ so $n(D) = 16$
e $E = \{4, 5, 6, 7, 8\}$ so $n(E) = 5$

2 a $n(A) = 7$ b $n(B) = 6$ c $n(A) + n(B) = 13$
d $n(A) - n(B) = 1$

• Intersection of sets

Use classroom objects to demonstrate the intersection of two sets. For example, if $A = \{\text{book, pen, pencil}\}$ and $B = \{\text{paper, pen, rubber}\}$, then $A \cap B = \{\text{pen}\}$

The intersection of A and B is double shaded. It consists of the elements that are in both sets. At this stage we are only concerned with the intersection of two sets.

• Union of sets

The union of two sets consists of all the members of the two sets. In the diagram the union of sets A and B is shaded.

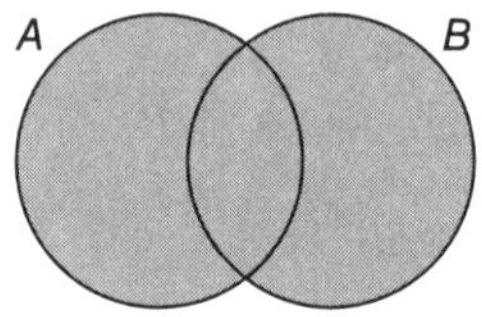

At this stage we are only looking at the union of two sets.

• Disjoint sets

Disjoint sets are have no members in common. They are 'not joined'. A simple example is the even and odd numbers:

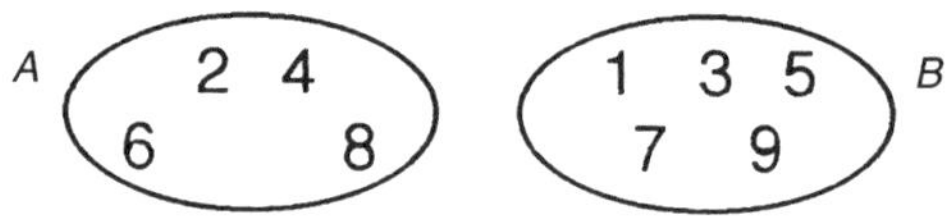

Sets A and B are disjoint.

EXERCISE 1E

1 a {0, 1, 2, 3, 4, 5, 6, 9, 13, 14} b {1, 3}

2 a {0, 1, 2, 3, 5, 6, 7, 9, 11, 12, 13, 14} b { }

3 a {0, 1, 2, 3, 4, 5, 7, 9, 11} b {1, 7, 11}

4 a {0, 1, 2, 3, 4, 6, 8, 9, 10, 12, 13, 14} b {6}

5 a {1, 2, 3, 5, 7, 9, 11, 12} b {5, 7, 11}

6 a {0, 1, 2, 3, 4, 7, 9, 11, 13, 14} b {0, 1}

7 a {1, 2, 3, 4, 5, 6, 7, 8, 9, 10, 11, 12} b { }

8 a {1, 2, 3, 4, 5, 7, 9, 11} b {1, 3, 5}

9 a $P \cup S = \{1, 2, 3, 4, 5, 7, 11, 12\}$
b $P \cap S = \{2, 5\}$ c $n(P) = 5$
d $n(S) = 5$ e $n(P \cup S) = 8$
f $n(P \cap S) = 2$ g $n(P) + n(S) = 10$
h $n(P) - n(S) = 0$

10 a $T \cup Q = \{0, 1, 3, 5, 6, 7, 9, 11, 13, 14\}$
b $T \cup Q = \{1, 3, 9\}$ c $n(T) = 6$
d $n(Q) = 7$ e $n(T \cup Q) = 10$
f $n(T \cap Q) = 3$ g $n(T) + n(Q) = 13$
h $n(T) - n(Q) = -1$

11 a $R \cup U = \{0, 1, 2, 4, 6, 7, 8, 10, 11, 12\}$
b $R \cap U = \{2, 4\}$ c $n(R) = 6$
d $n(U) = 6$ e $n(R \cup U) = 10$
f $n(R \cap U) = 2$ g $n(R) + n(U) = 12$
h $n(R) - n(U) = 0$

12

Question no.	Answer g	Answer e	Answer f
9	$n(P) + n(S) = 10$	$n(P \cup S) = 8$	$n(P \cap S) = 2$
10	$n(T) + n(Q) = 13$	$n(T \cup Q) = 10$	$n(T \cap Q) = 3$
11	$n(R) + n(U) = 12$	$n(R \cup U) = 10$	$n(R \cap U) = 2$

In each case, answer **g** = answer **e** + answer **f**.
$n(A) + n(B) = n(A \cup B) + n(A \cap B)$
These questions are a good preparation for the next section.

• Number of members of union of sets

This is quite a difficult section, especially for the less able pupils.

If two sets are disjoint, then $n(X \cup Y) = n(X) + n(Y)$.

If two sets overlap and have some members in common, then $n(X \cup Y)$ is less than $n(X) + n(Y)$ because $n(X) + n(Y)$ counts the common elements twice. In $(X \cup Y)$ these common elements are only counted once.

The number of elements counted twice in $n(X) + n(Y)$ is the number of common elements, that is the number of elements in $n(X \cap Y)$. So $n(X \cup Y) = n(X) + n(Y) - n(X \cap Y)$

EXERCISE 1F

1 a

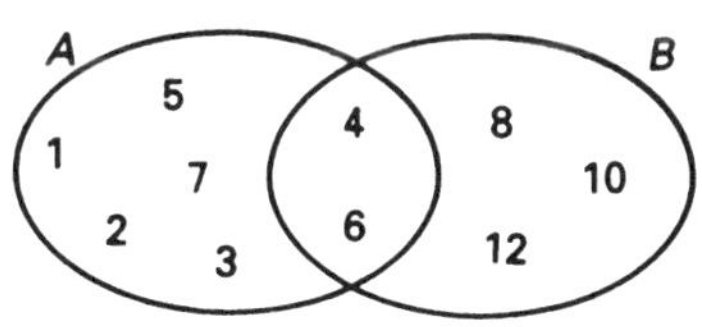

$n(A) = 7 \qquad n(B) = 5$

$n(A \cup B) = 10 \qquad n(A \cap B) = 2$

$$\begin{aligned} n(A) + n(B) - n(A \cap B) &= 7 + 5 - 2 \\ &= 10 \\ &= n(A \cup B) \end{aligned}$$

b

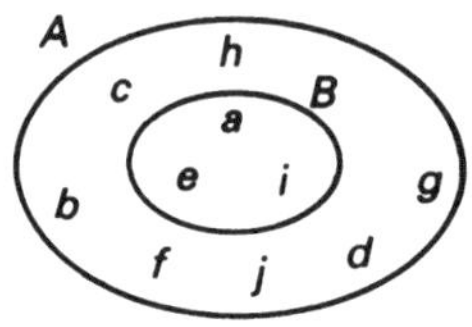

$n(A) = 10 \qquad n(B) = 3$

$n(A \cup B) = 10 \qquad n(A \cap B) = 3$

$$\begin{aligned} n(A) + n(B) - n(A \cap B) &= 10 + 3 - 3 \\ &= 10 \\ &= n(A \cap B) \end{aligned}$$

c

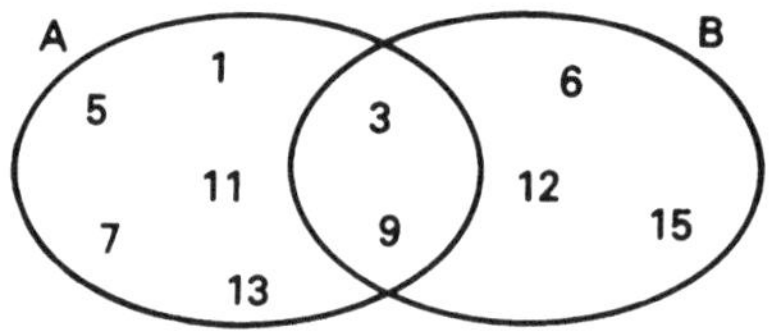

$n(A) = 7 \qquad n(B) = 5$

$n(A \cup B) = 10 \qquad n(A \cap B) = 2$

$$\begin{aligned} n(A) + n(B) - n(A \cap B) &= 7 + 5 - 2 \\ &= 10 \\ &= n(A \cup B) \end{aligned}$$

d

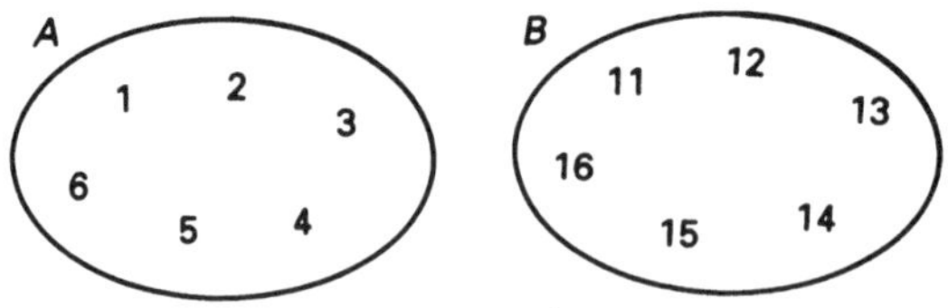

$n(A) = 6 \qquad n(B) = 6$

$n(A \cup B) = 12 \qquad n(A \cap B) = 0$

$$\begin{aligned} n(A) + n(B) - n(A \cap B) &= 6 + 6 - 0 \\ &= 12 \\ &= n(A \cup B) \end{aligned}$$

e
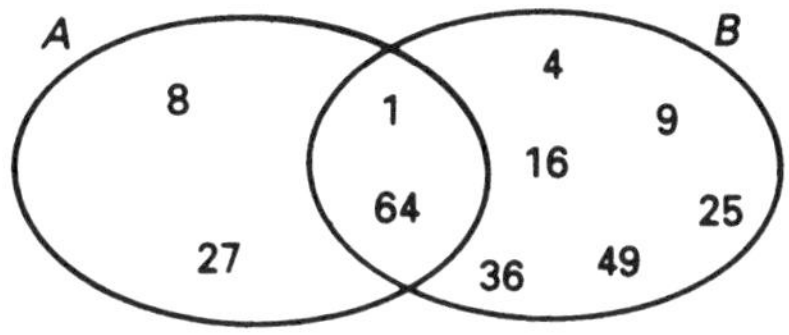

$n(A) = 4$ $n(B) = 8$
$n(A \cup B) = 10$ $n(A \cap B) = 2$
$n(A) + n(B) - n(A \cap B) = 8 + 4 - 2$
$= 10$
$= n(A \cup B)$

f
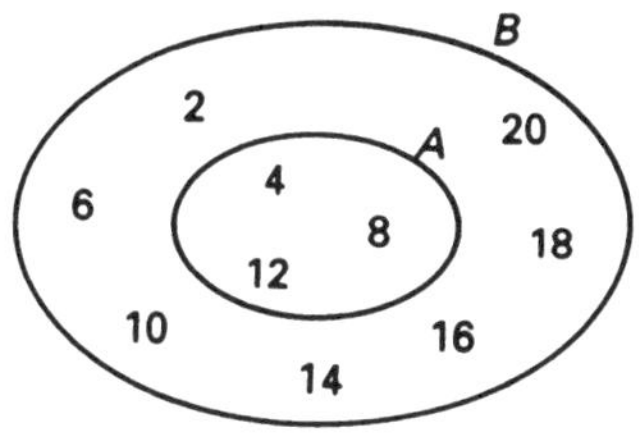

$n(A) = 3$ $n(B) = 10$
$n(A \cup B) = 10$ $n(A \cap B) = 3$
$n(A) + n(B) - n(A \cap B) = 3 + 10 - 3$
$= 10$
$= n(A \cup B)$

g
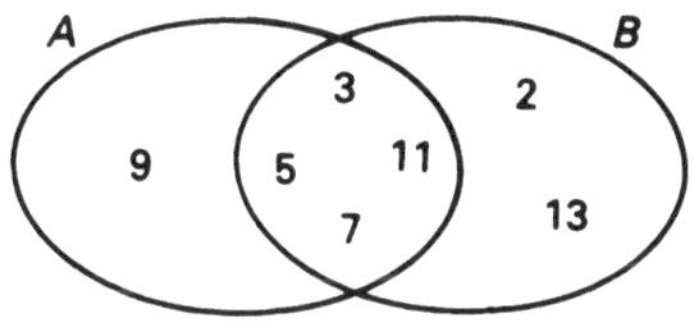

$n(A) = 5$ $n(B) = 6$
$n(A \cup B) = 7$ $n(A \cap B) = 4$
$n(A) + n(B) - n(A \cap B) = 5 + 6 - 4$
$= 7$
$= n(A \cup B)$

2 **a** $n(A) = 5$
b $A \cup \varnothing = A$ so $n(A \cup \varnothing) = 5$
c $A \cap \varnothing = \varnothing$ so $n(A \cap \varnothing) = 0$
d $A \cup A = A$ so $n(A \cup A) = 5$
e $A \cap A = A$ so $n(A \cap A) = 5$

2 Number systems

• Aim of chapter

The aim of the chapter is to review basic arithmetic and to teach students how to carry out operations with integers.

• Objectives

By the end of the chapter the student will be able to:

1. Use place value for large numbers
2. Solve practical arithmetical problems with whole numbers using the four operations
3. Carry out long multiplication
4. Find the lowest common multiple of two or more whole numbers
5. Identify even, odd and square numbers
6. Carry out long division
7. Find the highest common factor of two or more whole numbers
8. Express a number as the product of its prime factors
9. Find the square root of a perfect square
10. Show integers on the number line
11. Order numbers on the number line
12. Add, subtract, multiply and divide integers.

• Natural and whole numbers

There are several important sets of numbers that students need to be familiar with. These are:

The set of **natural numbers**, $N=\{1, 2, 3, 4, 5, \ldots\}$
The set of **whole numbers**, $W=\{0, 1, 2, 3, 4, \ldots\}$
The set of **integers**, $Z=\{\ldots -4, -3, -2, -1, 0, 1, 2, 3, \ldots\}$

The set of **rational numbers**, $Q=\{\frac{p}{q}: p, q \in Z, q \neq 0\}$
The set of **real numbers**, R consists of rational and irrational numbers.

The number line is an important and effective aid when teaching the properties of various types of numbers.

• Place value

The chapter begins with a quick review of place value.

EXERCISE 2A

1 The numbers are:
   a Twelve thousand seven hundred and fifty-six
   b Six hundred and four thousand, eight hundred
   c Three hundred and eighty-four thousand
   d Three hundred thousand
   e Fifteen million, nine hundred thousand; nineteen eighty-seven
   f Nineteen eighty-nine; two hundred and thirty-nine thousand, three hundred and seventy-six

2 a Four thousand six hundred and twenty-eight
   b Ten thousand, five hundred and eighty
   c Eighteen thousand and five
   d Twenty-nine thousand, four hundred
   e One hundred and eighty thousand, two hundred and fifty
   f Twelve million, five hundred thousand

• Addition

This section is largely revision. All the calculations in this and subsequent sections can be done very easily with calculators. The ability to use a calculator is important as it relieves most of the tedium of complex calculations, but the ability to carry out arithmetical computations quickly and independently of a calculator is still important.

EXERCISE 2B

1 a 462 b 1215 c 4999 d 441
   e 21 733 f 92 203

2 a 48, 52 b 52, 63 c 48, 84 d 84, 92
   e 52, 63, 84 f 48, 63, 92 g 63, 84, 92

3 605 km

4 8400

5 K148

• Subtraction

It is particularly important when subtracting large numbers to write them in columns correctly.

EXERCISE 2C

1 a 420 b 280 c 71 d 127
   e 573 f 3031 g 4581

2 The answers will depend on the date the question is answered. On 4 May 1995 (for example) the answers should be:
   a 95 b 33 c 22 d 16 e 48 f 8

3 a 52 and 84 b 48 and 92 c 84 and 92 d 48 and 63

4 175 km

5 42 million kilometres

6 a $\begin{array}{r} 586 \\ -234 \\ \hline 352 \end{array}$ b $\begin{array}{r} 1554 \\ -289 \\ \hline 1265 \end{array}$ c $\begin{array}{r} 4456 \\ -3587 \\ \hline 869 \end{array}$ d $\begin{array}{r} 2084 \\ -816 \\ \hline 1268 \end{array}$

• Multiplication In order to use long multiplication the student has to first learn about multiplying by multiples of ten. Associated with multiplication are multiples, lowest common multiples, even and square numbers.

• Multiples 66 is a multiple of 6 and 11 because $66=11\times 6$.

• Lowest common multiple The lowest common multiple of two or more numbers is the smallest number that is a multiple of both of them. The LCM of two numbers can also be found by writing out their multiples and finding the common multiples.

For example, 12 has multiples 12, 24, 36, 48, 60, 72, 84,…
and 18 has multiples 18, 36, 54, 72, 90,…

The lowest common multiple of 12 and 18 is 36.

This method is simpler than that in the book, but if often takes more time as the list of multiples needed can be quite long.

• Even numbers Even numbers are multiples of 2.
They can be arranged in pairs:

2	4	6	8	10
X	XX	XXX	XXXX	XXXXX
X	XX	XXX	XXXX	XXXXX

• Odd numbers Odd numbers are not even.
They cannot be arranged in pairs:

1	3	5	7	9	11
X	XX	XXX	XXXX	XXXXX	XXXXXX
	X	XX	XXX	XXXX	XXXXX

• Square numbers Any square number is the result of multiplying a whole number by itself.

Project The sum of the first n odd numbers is n^2. We can illustrate this diagrammatically:

1 3	1 3 5	1 3 5 7	1 3 5 7 9
x o	x o x	x o x o	x o x o x
o o	o o x	o o x o	o o x o x
	x x x	x x x o	x x x o x
		o o o o	o o o o x
			x x x x x

$1+3=2^2$ $1+3+5=3^2$ $1+3+5+7=4^2$ $1+3+5+7+9=5^2$

EXERCISE 2D

1 a 630 b 6800 c 18 000
d 15 000 e 21 000 f 67 200

2 a 25, 30, 35, 40, 45, 50, 55, 60
b 24, 32, 40, 48, 56, 64
c 24, 36, 48, 60, 72, 84
d 90, 180, 270, 360

3 a 7, 14, 21, 28, 35, 42, 49
b 9, 27, 45
c 1, 4, 9, 16, 25, 36, 49
d 10, 20, 30, 40, 50
e 9, 18, 27, 36, 45
f 1, 3, 5, 7, 9, 11, 13, 15, 17, 19
g 21, 23, 25, 27, 29
h 42, 44, 46, 48, 50
i 1, 16 ($16=4^2$ and $4=2^2$)

4 a 16, 34, 36, 68 b 3, 5, 11, 15, 27, 45, 59, 121
c 36, 121

5 a 36 b 45 c 60
d 120 e 120 f 210

6 510

7 K435 000

8 Yes, $22\times14=308$

9 245 km

10 280

11 420

• Division

Long division is quite difficult. Many students are confused by examples such as $6452\div31=208$, giving the answer wrongly as 28.

• Factors

If a whole number divides exactly into another whole number then the smaller number is a factor of the larger number.

Since $66\div6=11$, 6 is a factor of 66. 11 is also a factor of 66.

• Highest common factor

The highest common factor of two or more numbers is the largest number that divides into all of them.

For example, 66 has factors 1, 2, 3, 6, 11, 22, 33, 66

and 44 has factors 1, 2, 4, 11, 22, 44.

The *common* factors are 1, 2, 11, 22 and the highest common factor is 22.

• Prime numbers

A prime number has exactly two factors. They are 1 and itself. Students often think that 1 is a prime number. It is not a prime number. It has only one divisor, namely itself. Prime factors have exactly 2 factors.

• Prime factors Prime factors are factors that are prime. 66 has factors 1, 2, 3, 6, 11, 22, 33 and 66. The prime numbers in this list are 2 and 3 so the prime factors of 66 are 2 and 3.

• Square roots Do not teach the definition – it is not easy to follow. Instead use examples: $\sqrt{25} \times \sqrt{25} = 25$ $\sqrt{427} \times \sqrt{427} = 427$

Project The Sieve of Eratosthenes is a well known means for finding all the prime numbers less than 100. Eratosthenes was a Greek mathematician who lived 2200 years ago and spent much of his life in Alexandria in Egypt.

EXERCISE 2E

1 a 56 b 41 c 43 d 44
e 31 rem 2 f 37 rem 1 g 163 rem 20 h 162
i 203 j 208

2 a {1, 2, 7, 14} b {1, 2, 3, 4, 6, 8, 9, 12, 18, 24, 36, 72}
c {1, 2, 3, 4, 6, 7, 12, 21, 28, 42, 84} d {1, 3, 29, 87}
e {1, 7, 49} f {1, 5, 19, 95}
g {1, 3, 19, 57} h {1, 11}

3 a 6 b 12 c 9 d 3
e 15 f 4 g 10 h 14

4 a $2 \times 3 \times 3$ b $2 \times 2 \times 2 \times 3$ c $2 \times 2 \times 2 \times 5$
d $2 \times 3 \times 11$ e $2 \times 2 \times 2 \times 2 \times 5$ f $2 \times 2 \times 2 \times 3 \times 3$
g $2 \times 2 \times 5 \times 5$ h $2 \times 2 \times 2 \times 2 \times 2 \times 2$

5 a 7 b 9 c 10 d 12 e 4

6 25 rows ($52 \div 21 = 24.76$)

7 33 litres

8 27 bags ($660 \div 25 = 26.5$)

9 83.375

10 $23 \times 8 + 7 = 191$
$191 \div 7 = 27$ remainder 2

• Integers There are many other ways of introducing integers (also called 'directed numbers') apart from temperature. Possible examples are:

i altitude
ii balance of account in bank
iii time before or after an event

Whatever you use to introduce the idea of integers, it is important that you stress the need for a starting point, O, and some idea of opposites: up/down, left/right, credit/debit or before/after. All of these examples can be illustrated on a number line with origin O and negative and positive numbers.

• Order on the number line

Students often find it strange that, for example, 1 is greater than −20 000. They are used to thinking of 'is greater than' as comparing size, not order. Stress that the number to the right is always greater than the number to the left. Use as your introductory examples:
−1° is warmer than −20 000°, K1 in the bank is more than an overdraft of K20 000 and so on.

EXERCISE 2F

1 a +3 b −1 c −1 d +4
  e 0 f −1 g +3 h −3

2 a T b F c F d F
  e T f T g F h F

3 a 4, 2, −3, −5 b −1, −3, −4, −6, −8
  c 3, 1, 0, −10 d 5, 3, −2, −4, −6

4 a −3 is greater than −10 b −5 is less than 1
  c −3 is greater than −7 d 6 is greater than −4
  e −15 is less than 10 f −100 is less than 0
  g −5.2 is greater than −5.3 h −2 is greater than −3.5

• Adding integers

Students often find adding integers difficult because there is not a simple rule like there is for multiplication. The approach in the book attempts to help students to work these problems in their heads, as they will have to in examinations or later work.

If you ask teachers to work out (+104)+(−107) they will straightaway give the answer −3. They work it out thus:
the difference between 104 and 107 is 3, the larger number is negative so the answer is negative. The book leads on to this: (+4)+(−7) is 4 steps to the right then 7 steps to the left, the net result being 3 steps to the left, −3. When using the number line the book deliberately starts from 0, then moves 4 steps right, then 7 steps left. If you start from +4, the cancelling out effect is lost.

Another way of introducing this is through cards. You need some cards each labelled +1 and some cards each labelled −1. A +1 and a −1 card cancel each other out, for +1+(−1)=0. (+4)+(−7) is illustrated thus:

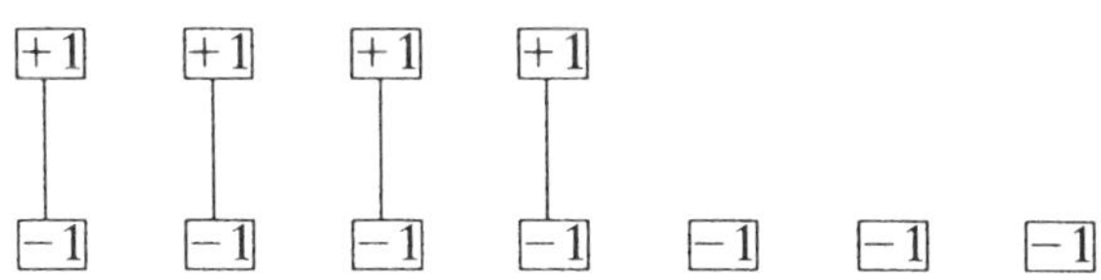

Four pairs of cards cancel each other out, leaving three negative one cards (= −3) as the answer.

EXERCISE 2G

1	a −9	b −5	c −2	d 0
	e −17	f +4	g −6	h 0
	i −29	j +4	k +8	l 0
2	a 3	b 5	c −4	d 0
	e −1	f 22	g 30	h −3
3	a −1049	b −5	c −2	d 0
	e −200	f +4	g −4	h 0

• Subtracting integers

It is much simpler to treat all subtractions of integers as additions of the inverse than to try to find effective and easy to use illustrative examples. Subtracting an integer has the same effect as adding its inverse. This is demonstrated in the book with a few examples.

EXERCISE 2H

1	a −1	b −21	c 16	d −10
	e −1	f −8	g 28	h −13
	i 3	j −6	k 22	l −2.8
2	a 7	b 21	c 18	d 36
	e −17	f −32	g −52	h −92
3	a 21°C	b 5°C	c 44°C	d 21°C
4	16 metres			
5	K12 000			

• Multiplying integers

The four rules are developed from examples in this section. The most difficult to find an example for in everyday life is negative×negative.

EXERCISE 2I

1	a +20	b −104	c −63	d −25
	e +72	f −12	g −187	h −36
	i + 208	j −5	k −105	l −1
2	a −10	b −104	c −77	d −324
	e −72	f − 120	g −451	h −162
3	K1 050 000	K150 000		
4	K510 000	K870 000		

• Dividing integers

The rules for the division of integers follow immediately from the rules for multiplication.

EXERCISE 2J

1 a −5 b −6 c −3 d −1
e +8 f +6 g −5 h −9
i − 30 j − 4 k +19 l +2
m −5 n −3 o −4 p −1
q +12 r 37

• Rational numbers

The bottom number in a fraction is called the denominator; it tells us how many parts the whole is divided into. The top number in a fraction is called the numerator which tells us how many of the parts have been taken.

Rational numbers are numbers which can be written in the form $\frac{a}{b}$ where a and b are both integers and $b \neq 0$. (We cannot divide by 0.) Rational numbers can be put in order, added, subtracted, multiplied and divided.

• Ordering rational numbers

Equivalent fractions are used to change all the rational numbers to have the same denominator. They can then be ordered using the numerators.

EXERCISE 2K

1 a Equivalent b Equivalent
c Not equivalent d Not equivalent

2 a $\frac{3}{4}$ b $\frac{2}{9}$ c $\frac{10}{14}$ d $\frac{5}{8}$

3 a $\frac{3}{8}, \frac{5}{8}, \frac{7}{8}$ b $\frac{2}{3}, \frac{3}{4}, \frac{5}{6}$ c $\frac{1}{4}, \frac{1}{3}, \frac{1}{2}$ d $\frac{1}{2}, \frac{2}{3}, \frac{3}{4}$

4 a $\frac{1}{8}$ is less than $\frac{5}{8}$ b $\frac{9}{10}$ is greater than $\frac{3}{10}$
c $\frac{1}{2}$ is less than $\frac{3}{4}$ d $\frac{2}{3}$ is less than $\frac{3}{4}$
e $\frac{5}{6}$ is greater than $\frac{7}{9}$ f $\frac{15}{20}$ is greater than $\frac{2}{3}$

• The four operations on rational numbers

This section reviews the addition, subtraction, multiplication and division of and by fractions.

EXERCISE 2L

1 a $5\frac{3}{8}$ b $12\frac{1}{4}$ c $7\frac{2}{5}$

2 a $2\frac{5}{24}$ b $2\frac{11}{12}$ c $7\frac{7}{20}$

3 a $2\frac{1}{8}$ b $7\frac{4}{9}$ c $3\frac{9}{20}$

4 **a** 24 **b** 270 **c** 24

5 Christine eats more cake, by $\frac{1}{12}$.

6 $3\frac{5}{8}$

7 41 years

8 360

9 $31\frac{1}{2}$

10 9 cakes

3 Number bases

• Aim of chapter

The aim of the chapter is to introduce students to basic operations with numbers in different bases.

• Objectives

By the end of the chapter the students will be able to:

1 Change numbers from base ten to another base, including base eight
2 Add and subtract in different bases
3 Multiply and divide in different bases (simple examples only).

• Base eight

This is a short chapter. The topic is included in order to increase the understanding of our counting system. Do not spend too long on it. The topic is not developed much further than the material included in this chapter.

We count in base ten, because we have ten fingers. If we had eight fingers then presumably we would use base eight as the basis of our numeration system. In base eight there are eight numerals which are 0, 1, 2, 3, 4, 5, 6 and 7. In base six there are six numerals: 0, 1, 2, 3, 4 and 5.

The first section teaches students how to change numbers from a base into 'ordinary' numbers in base ten.

EXERCISE 3A

1 a 17_{ten} b 59_{ten} c 38_{ten} d 133_{ten}
e 273_{ten} f 64_{ten} g 11_{ten} h 259_{ten}

2 123_{seven}

3 a 3×8 b 3×6 c $3 \times (5 \times 5)$ d 3
e $3 \times (4 \times 4 \times 4)$ f 3×9 g $3 \times (8 \times 8)$ h 3

4 a 31_{eight} b 61_{eight} c 47_{eight}

5 a 24_{five} b 42_{five} c 114_{five}

6 57_{eight}

• Adding and subtracting in different bases

Adding and subtracting in different number bases can be found interesting because it is rather different from ordinary addition and subtraction. $6+6=14$, which is correct in base eight, looks different. It may be helpful to build up an addition table in various bases. Here is the addition table for base eight:

+	0	1	2	3	4	5	6	7
0	0	1	2	3	4	5	6	7
1	1	2	3	4	5	6	7	10
2	2	3	4	5	6	7	10	11
3	3	4	5	6	7	10	11	12
4	4	5	6	7	10	11	12	13
5	5	6	7	10	11	12	13	14

There are two ways of carrying out addition problems in a base other than base ten. You can carry out the calculation in the base, using an addition table like that given above. Alternatively, you can change the numbers into base ten, carry out the calculation, and change your answer back into the base in which the calculation is set. (You can use both methods as a check; it is very easy to make careless mistakes when working with an unfamiliar base.)

• Changing from base ten to other bases

Changing from base ten to other bases is more difficult than going the other way. The method is explained fully in the text. The technique will be useful in the next section. Try to keep your examples simple. Long and complicated examples are not very useful or interesting.

EXERCISE 3B

1 a 762_{eight} b 1471_{eight} c 1473_{eight} d 2503_{eight}

2 a 202_{four} b 1130_{four} c 1022_{four} d 2201_{four}

3 a 21_{four} b 64_{eight} c 55_{eight}
d 55_{seven} e 236_{eight} f 162_{nine}

4 b is correct

5 a 410_{eight} b 1524_{six} c 721_{eight} d 466_{eight}
e 122_{four}

• Multiplying and dividing in different bases

Multiplication tables are very helpful in handling these rather tricky problems.

EXERCISE 3C

1 a 322_{eight} b 322_{eight} c 1433_{eight}
d 421_{eight} e 107_{eight} f 65_{eight}
g 72_{eight} rem 1 h 220_{eight} rem 4

2

×	0	1	2	3	4	5
0	0	0	0	0	0	0
1	0	1	2	3	4	5
2	0	2	4	10	12	14
3	0	3	10	13	20	23
4	0	4	12	20	24	32
5	0	5	14	23	32	41

a 423_{six} b 2143_{six} c 1132_{six}
d 152_{six} e 33_{six} f 205_{six}

4 Coordinates

• Aim of chapter

The aim of the chapter is to use coordinates to describe the position of a point.

• Objectives

By the end of the chapter the students will be able to:

1 Describe the position of a desk in a classroom using a number pair
2 Describe the position of a point in relation to an origin using coordinate axes
3 Give the coordinates of any point, whether the coordinates are negative or positive.

• Position in class

The introduction of coordinates can be used to tidy up the classroom. Before beginning this topic, the pupils need to be sitting in neat rows, in straight lines. The teacher then asks pupils how to describe the position of their desks to someone who is not in the room. From this discussion the idea of coordinates can develop.

It is a convention that the column number (the x-coordinate) is given first before the row number (the y-coordinate). We have to have this convention, otherwise a coordinate pair like (4,5) would be ambiguous. In the diagram, the number of rows is different from the number of columns. This is deliberate, because it is easy to confuse rows and columns.

This first section looks merely at describing class position. The idea of origin and of x and y axes comes in the next section.

EXERCISE 4A

1 a Jo b Grace c Alice
  d Ali e May f Bill

2 a (6, 1) b (4, 3) c (2, 3)
  d (5, 4) e (2, 2) f (4, 5)

3 Practical activity

4 (2, 3), (4, 3) and (6, 3). The row numbers are all 3. (All the desks are in the 3rd row.)

5 (2, 3), (2, 2) and (2, 5). The common numbers are all 2. (All the desks are in the 2nd column.)

6 a They all add up to 7. The desks are in the same diagonal line.
b They all add up to 9. They are also in a diagonal line.
c They are in a diagonal line through Alice's desk.

• Coordinate axes

A knowledge of the description of the position of desks in the classroom leads on to the use of coordinate x and y axes. The column number becomes the x-coordinate, and the row number becomes the y-coordinate. The x-coordinate is the number along, while the y-coordinate is the number up from the origin. The origin is important when using coordinates; it and the axes should always be marked on pictures of coordinates.

At this stage the coordinates, like the desk positions, only use positive numbers. The number line has been extended from one dimension to two dimensions.

EXERCISE 4B

1	a W	b X	c Z	d Y	e M	f N
2	a (2, 1)	b (1, 4)	c (6, 1)	d (3, 3)	e (4, 4)	f (6, 6)

• Negative coordinates

With negative coordinates we can now move along left (negative) as well as right and down (negative) as well as up on our coordinate axes. In the exercise points are plotted to create geometrical shapes.

EXERCISE 4C

1

A(1, 2)	B(2, 4)	C(4, 1)	D(3, 0)
E(−3, 2)	F(−5, −3)	G(2, −3)	H(5, −1)
I(0, 4)	J(−6, 0)	K(−2, 5)	L(−3, −3)
M(0, −5)	N(−2, 0)	P(3, −1)	Q(4, 3)
R(−5, 4)	S(5, −5)	T(−6, 5)	

2

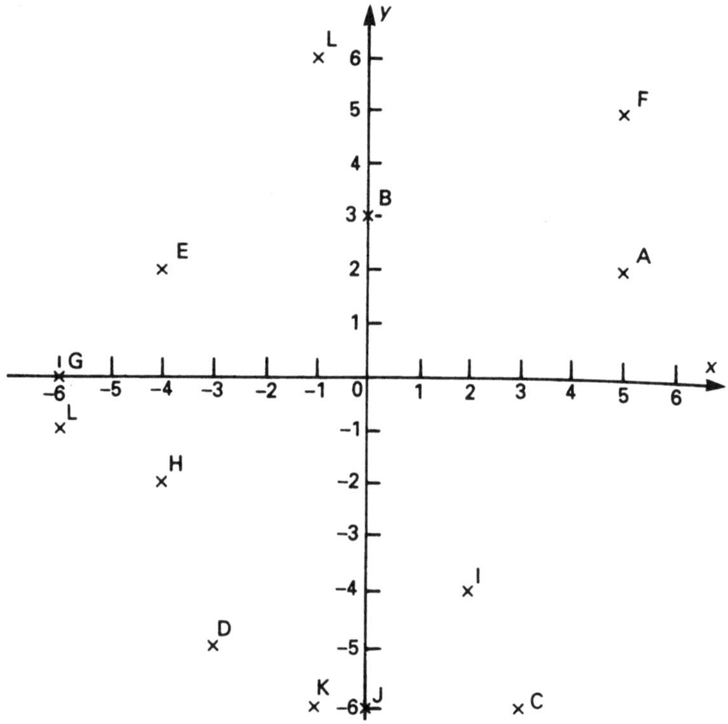

3

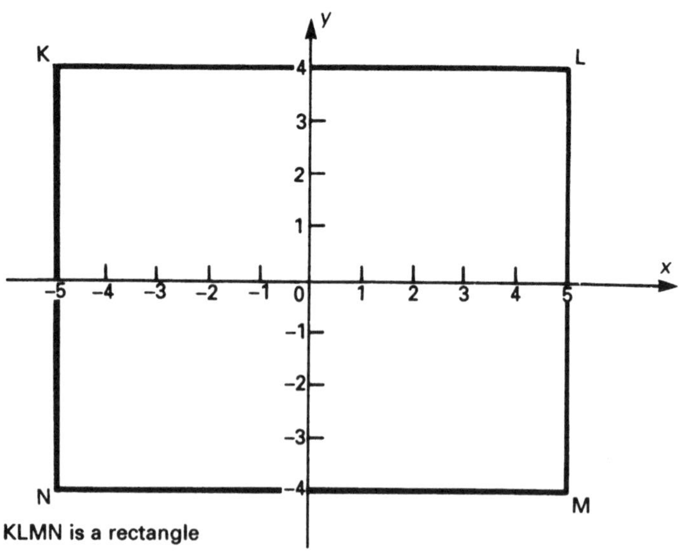

KLMN is a rectangle

4

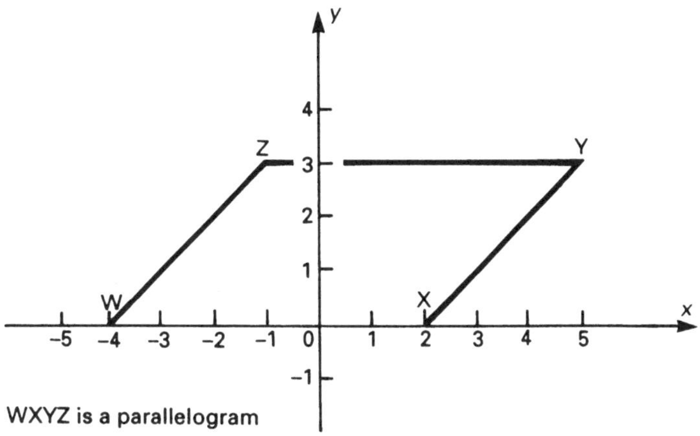

WXYZ is a parallelogram

5

a

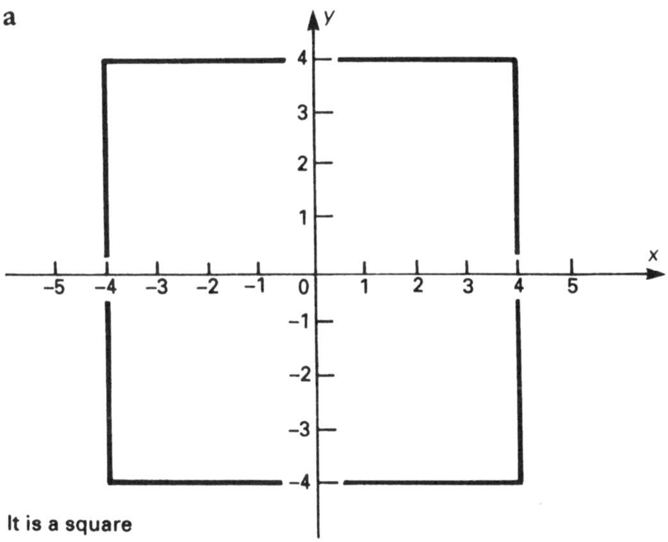

It is a square

b

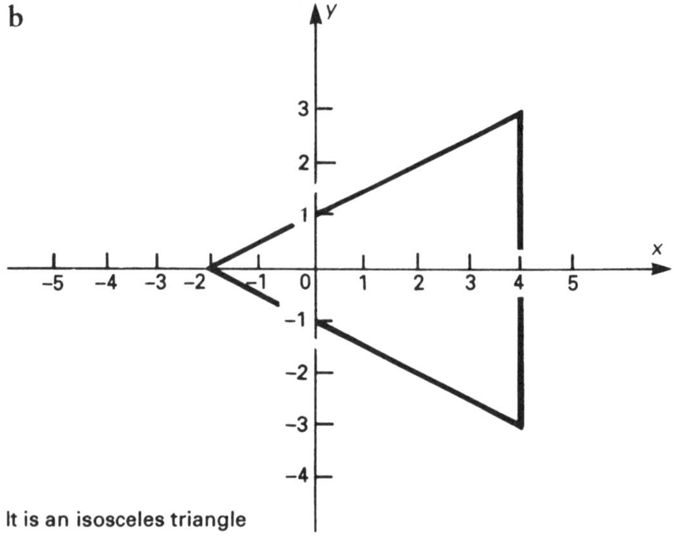

It is an isosceles triangle

c

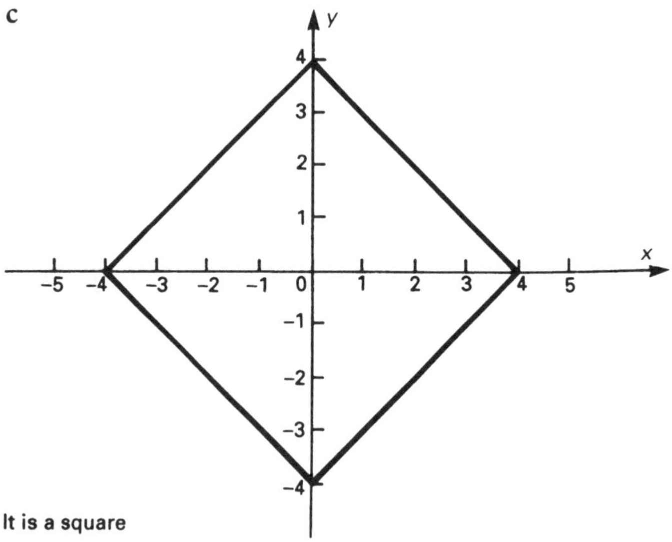

It is a square

5 Algebraic expressions

- **Aim of chapter** The aim of the chapter is to introduce students to the use of algebra to express situations, the evaluation of expressions and formulas, the simplification of expressions and the use of indices.

- **Objectives** By the end of the chapter the students will be able to:
  1. Find mathematical rules in sentences and use them to solve problems
  2. Express mathematical rules as formulas
  3. Find mathematical expressions to describe situations
  4. Evaluate expressions and formulas
  5. Simplify expressions involving like and unlike terms
  6. Use indices as a short-hand for repeated multiplication of numbers and letters.

This chapter introduces the use of letters to stand for numbers, which is one of the most important features of mathematics.

Many students have difficulty with the use of letters. They do not understand how letters are used. A letter in algebra stands for an unknown number or numbers in a variety of ways.

a In an equation like $3x+5=47$, the x stands for a number we do not yet know. Finding this number is called 'solving' the equation.

b In equations such as $x^2+4x=3$ or $x^3-3x^2-8x-12=0$, the x stands for more than one unknown number.

c In an equation like $y=4x+3$, a relationship between two numbers is described. x can take any value we like; the value of y **depends** on the value of x.

d With a formula like $P=2(a+b)$, for the perimeter of a rectangle, the perimeter can be calculated once the length and the breadth are known.

e In an identity like $x^2-y^2=(x+y)(x-y)$, we are told that x^2-y^2 can be expressed in another, but equivalent way. This relationship is true no matter what values x and y have.

In all these cases, the letters **stand for** numbers. There is a tendency for students to think of letters as standing for things. It is important to emphasise that letters are replacements for numbers.

• Mathematical rules

In this section, mathematical rules are developed from simple situations. In this first section, all the rules are expressed in words. No letters or formulas are used in this section. Students often have a lot of difficulty understanding the symbolism used in algebra; by first asking students to express rules in words it is hoped that problems caused by the letters will be avoided.

EXERCISE 5A

1 a The age of the daughter is 18 years less than the age of her mother
  b 34 years old
  c 44 years old
  d 18 years old

2 a Number *B* is 3 more than number *A*
  b 19
  c 28

3 a Number *D* is found by multiplying number *C* by 5
  b 80
  c 12

4 a We multiply *E* by 5 and add 1
  b 81
  c 12

5 a We multiply the number of bars purchased by 800 tambala
  b 12 000 tambala
  c 7

• Formulas

The rules that were expressed in words in the previous section are now written more briefly using letters. The conventions for writing algebraic expressions are discussed in this section. It is important not to overlook them. It is too easy to assume that what is obvious to us is obvious to the student. For example, that $2x$ means the same as $2 \times x$ is not at all obvious to the student. It could mean twenty-something. After all, 25 means 'twenty + five', so $2x$ might reasonably be thought to mean 'twenty plus x'. The conventions of algebraic usage need to be gone through and understood by the students.

• Coefficients

The numerical coefficient of a term is the number in front of, and thus multiplying, the letter or group of letters in the term. These numbers can be whole numbers or fractions, positive or negative.

EXERCISE 5B

1 $d = w - 18$ 2 $A + 3 = B$
3 $5C = D$ 4 $5E + 1 = F$
5 $800n = c$

• Algebraic expressions

This section gives the students practice in writing algebraic expressions.

EXERCISE 5C

1 $(a + 20)$ marbles

2 $(x - 3)$ km

3 K$\frac{n}{6}$

4 $c + 6$

5 $2x$ years

6 $b = g + 9$

7 Suppose my age is x years old
a My brother is $(x + 3)$ years old
b My sister is $(x - 2)$ years old

8 Let the number of goats be g and the number of sheep be s
a $g = s + 12$
b $s = g - 12$

9 If the number is t, the result is $(6t + 4)$

10 Let the number be n

Dividing by 5 gives $\frac{n}{5}$

Taking away 3 gives $\frac{n}{5} - 3$

• Evaluating expressions and formulas

In this section there is a lot of practice substituting values for letters in expressions.

EXERCISE 5D

1 a 32 b 18 c 37 d 25
e 29 f 9 g 11 h 44

2	a 24	b 0	c −2	d 16
	e 17	f 60	g 20	h −2
3	a 21.5	b 10	c 16.3	d 14.7
	e 16.1	f 0.4	g 405	h 9
4	a 6	b 3	c $2\frac{1}{6}$	d $-\frac{3}{4}$
	e 3	f 0	g 4	h 3
5	a 22	b 48	c 24	
	d 138	e 22	f $1\frac{1}{2}$	
6	a 19	b 34	c 6	
	d −5	e −8	f 4	
7	a 17	b 57	c 1	
	d −13	e −23	f −3	
8	a 2	b −2	c 3	
	d 10	e 12	f 4	
9	a 16	b 2	c 4	
	d 4	e −1	f 89	

• Like and unlike terms

This section looks at how algebraic expressions can be simplified. The first examples consist of like terms which can be combined but cannot be evaluated until we know what numbers to put instead of the letters.

Expressions like $4b+3a$ which contain unlike terms cannot be added together **until we know the numerical values that the letters have**. Suggesting that a stands for apples and b for bananas and $4a+3b$ cannot be combined is misleading. It gives the impression that the a and b stand for things, but they stand for numbers. If $4a$ and $3b$ cannot be added for this sort of reason, how can we multiply them together, as in $4\text{a} \times 3\text{b} = 12ab$? It seems very peculiar to be talking about multiplying apples and bananas. We cannot add unlike terms until we know what numbers to replace them by.

EXERCISE 5E

1	a 19	b 40	c 61	
	d 68	e 12	f 5	
2	a $13x$	b $3a$	c $14p$	d $j+8$
	e $5k-9$	f $12+3m$	g $16y-15$	h $12n+2$
	i $10q-10$	j $6w-5$	k $3r+4$	l $22-7s$
3	a $8a+b$	b $11x+6y$	c $4p+2q$	d $2a+14b$
	e $6s-5t$	f $15m$	g $7p+10q$	h $5m+5n$
	i $3u+4v$	j 0		

4 a $8+11d$ b $14+3q$ c $17-17g$
d $9a-8$ e $7b-3e+7$ f $9z-3y-11$
g $15r+2s-5$ h $15-10t+10p$

• Indices

Before we can look at quadratic expressions like x^2+4x-3, we need to introduce indices. They are introduced with numbers, before moving on to letters. Students must learn the difference between base and index.

EXERCISE 5F

1 a 12^3 b 8^4 c 5^5 d 3^8

2 a 59 049 b 729 000 c 7776 d 1 000 000

3 a 4 b 5 c 3 d 6
e 2 f 2 g 8 h 3

4 a (i) 4 (ii) 9 (iii) 25 (iv) 64
b (i) 32 (ii) 243 (iii) 1024 (iv) 7776
c (i) 2^n (ii) 5^n (iii) 7^n (iv) 10^n

EXERCISE 5G

1 a 10^{10} b -8^5 c $(-3)^7=-3^7$

2 a $\frac{1}{16}$ b 2401 c -729 d 625

3 a a^6 b $2y^5$ c a^4b^2 d p^3q e $2r^5$

6 Graphs

• Aim of chapter

The aim of the chapter is to introduce students to the drawing of straight line graphs.

• Objectives

By the end of the chapter the students will be able to:

1 Find the equations of vertical and horizontal lines
2 Draw the graph of any equation of the form $y = mx + c$
3 Find the x and y intercepts of the graphs of lines with equations of the form $y = mx + c$
4 Identify parallel straight line graphs from the coefficient of x in their equations.

• Vertical and horizontal lines

By plotting points in a vertical line on graph paper and writing down their coordinates, students will see that all the points on the line have the same x-coordinate, and that it is reasonable to call the line "$x =$ the coordinate". In the same way, all the points on a horizontal line have the same y coordinate and the line is named "$y =$ that coordinate".

• Equation of a straight line

The students now draw graphs that are not vertical or horizontal. All the graphs at this stage are of the form $y = mx + c$ and are straight line graphs.

It is important to prepare a table of values before plotting the points. As the graphs are all straight, it is only necessary to plot two points of the graph and join them with a straight line, but it is easy to make arithmetical errors and so it is prudent to find and plot at least three points. If they are not in a straight line then it is clear that there is an error somewhere. The points that are plotted should be far apart. This will make any small errors in placing a point on the right spot less important.

In the exercise the students are asked to plot the values of x from -2 to $+6$ each time. You may wish to reduce the number of points they plot, but be careful that the points of intersection with the x and y axes are included.

EXERCISE 6A

1 $y=2x+1$

(This graph could be drawn for values of x from -2 to $+2$ and it would still cut both axes.)

x	-2	-1	0	1	2	3	4	5	6
$2x$ $+1$	-4 $+1$	-2 $+1$	0 $+1$	2 $+1$	4 $+1$	6 $+1$	8 $+1$	10 $+1$	12 $+1$
$2x+1$	-3	-1	1	3	5	7	9	11	13

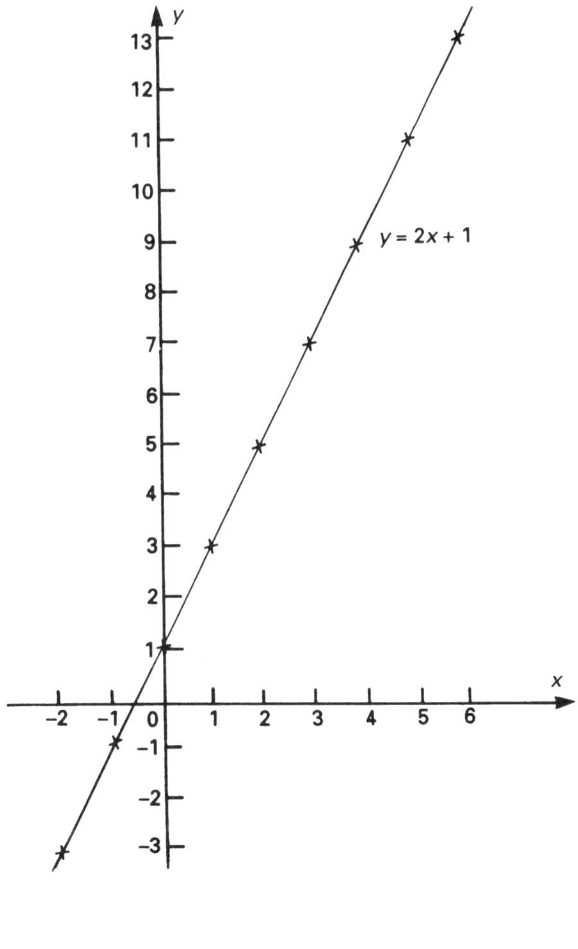

2 $y=x-1$

x -1	-2 -1	-1 -1	0 -1	1 -1	2 -1	3 -1	4 -1	5 -1	6 -1
$x-1$	-3	-2	-1	0	1	2	3	4	5

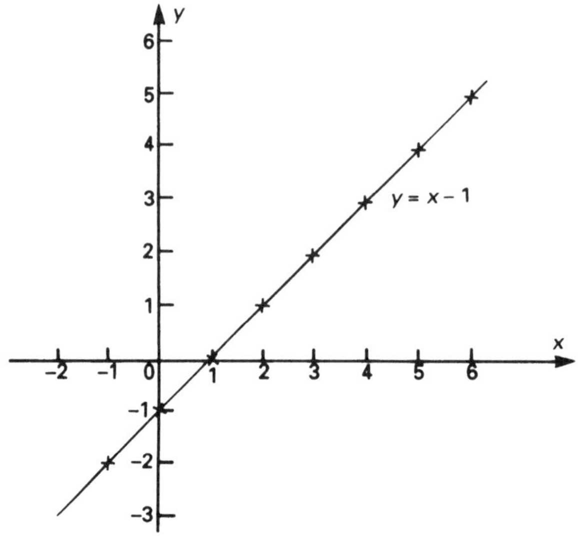

3 $y=5-x$

x	-2	-1	0	1	2	3	4	5	6
5 $-x$	5 2	5 1	5 0	5 -1	5 -2	5 -3	5 -4	5 -5	5 -6
$5-x$	7	6	5	4	3	2	1	0	-1

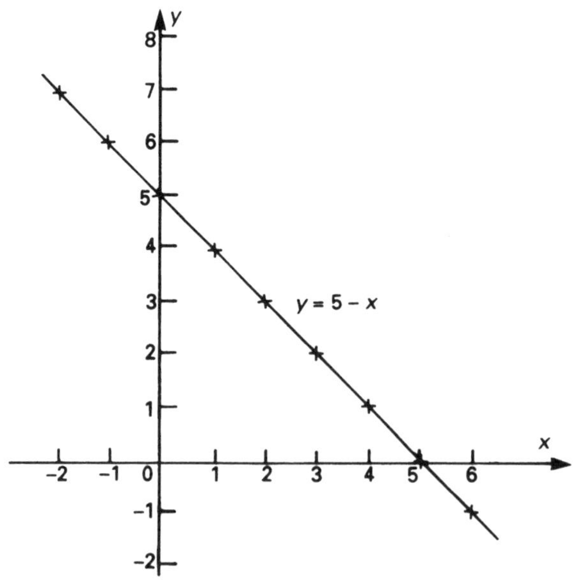

4 $y = 6 - 2x$

x	-2	-1	0	1	2	3	4	5	6
6 $-2x$	6 4	6 2	6 0	6 -2	6 -4	6 -6	6 -8	6 -10	6 -12
$6-2x$	10	8	6	4	2	0	-2	-4	-6

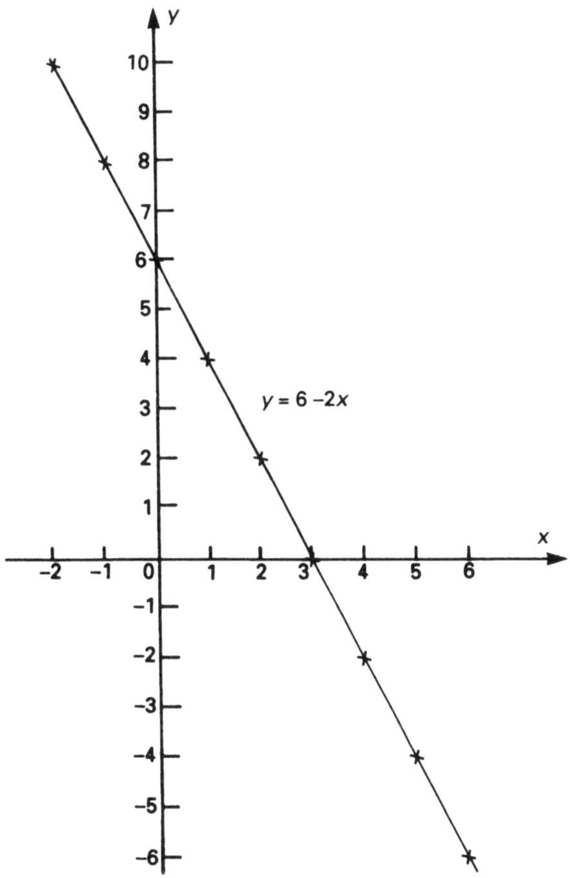

5

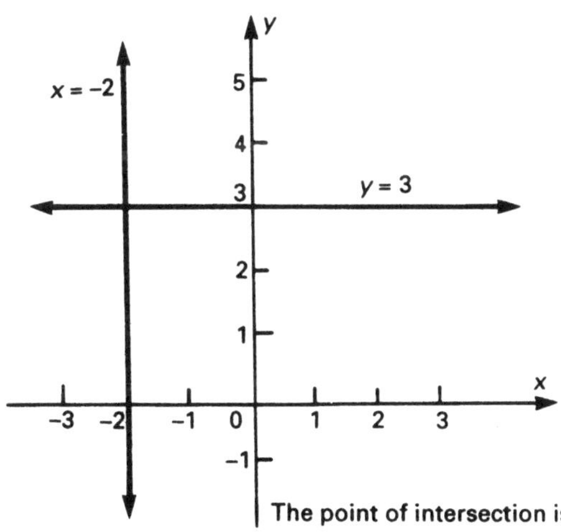

The point of intersection is (−2, 3)

6

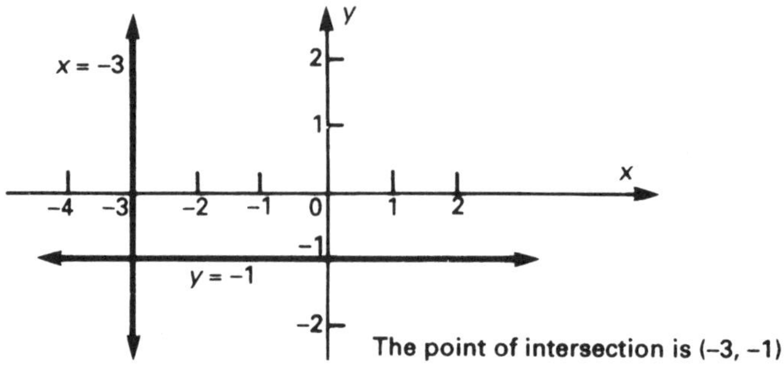

7

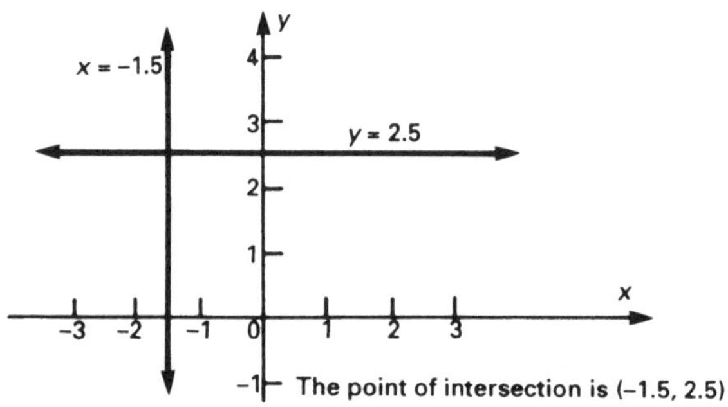

• Intersection with the axes

The point where a graph cuts the y-axis is called its y-intercept.
The y-intercept of the equation $y=mx+c$ is c.
The point where a graph cuts the x-axis is called its x-intercept.
At the x-intercept, $y=0=mx+c$ and $x=\frac{c}{m}$

EXERCISE 6B

1

x	-1	0	1	2	3	4
$2x$	-2	0	2	4	6	8
$2x-5$	-7	-5	-3	-1	1	3

y-intercept -5. Graph crosses y-axis at $(-5, 0)$.

x-intercept $\frac{5}{2}$. Graph crosses x-axis at $(\frac{5}{2}, 0)$.

2

x	-3	-2	-1	0	1	2	3
$\frac{1}{2}x$	-1.5	-1	-0.5	0	0.5	1	1.5
$+1$	$+1$	$+1$	$+1$	$+1$	$+1$	$+1$	$+1$
$\frac{1}{2}x+1$	-0.5	0	0.5	1	1.5	2	2.5

y-intercept 1. Graph crosses y-axis at (0, 1).
x-intercept -2. Graph crosses x-axis at (-2, 0).

3

x	-1	0	1	2	3	4
3	3	3	3	3	3	3
$-x$	1	0	-1	-2	-3	-4
$3-x$	4	3	2	1	0	-1

y-intercept 3. Graph crosses y-axis at (0, 3).
x-intercept 3. Graph crosses x-axis at (3, 0).

4

x	-1	0	1	2	3	4
6	6	6	6	6	6	6
$-2x$	2	0	-2	-4	-6	-8
$6-2x$	8	6	4	2	0	-2

y-intercept 6. Graph crosses y-axis at (0, 6).
x-intercept 3. Graph crosses x-axis at (3, 0).

5

x	-3	-2	-1	0	1
$3x$	-9	-6	-3	0	3
4	4	4	4	4	4
$3x+4$	-5	-2	1	4	7

y-intercept 4. Graph crosses y-axis at (0, 4).

x-intercept $-1\frac{1}{3}$. Graph crosses x-axis at ($-1\frac{1}{3}$, 0).

6

x	-1	0	1	2	3	4	5	6
-4	-4	-4	-4	-4	-4	-4	-4	-4
$x-4$	-5	-4	-3	-2	-1	0	1	2

y-intercept -4. Graph crosses y-axis at (0, -4).
x-intercept 4. Graph crosses x-axis at (4, 0).

7

x	-2	-1	0	1	2
$2x$	-4	-2	0	2	4

x-intercept 0. Graph crosses x-axis at (0, 0).

• Parallel lines

In the equation $y=mx+c$ the gradient is m. So equations with the same coefficient of x, such as $y=5x$, $y=5x+3$, $y=5x-13$, are parallel.

EXERCISE 6C

1 a 7 b 9 c -1 d 1

e -6 f $\frac{1}{8}$ g 1.5 h $\frac{1}{8}$

2 Yes 3 Yes 4 Yes

7 Graphs and gradients

- **Aim of chapter** The aim of the chapter is to teach students about the gradient and y-intercept of a straight line graph and how they can be found from the equation of the graph.

- **Objectives** By the end of the chapter the students will be able to:
  1 Find the gradient of the straight line through two points on the coordinate axes
  2 Draw the graphs of equations of the form $y = mx + c$
  3 State the gradient and y-intercept of an equation of the form $y = mx + c$ where m is the gradient and c is the y-intercept
  4 Find the equation of a straight line when given the coordinates of two points through which it passes.

- **Gradient** Students sometimes think that the gradient is the length of the hypotenuse divided by the horizontal displacement.

$$\text{In fact the gradient} = \frac{\text{vertical rise}}{\text{horizontal displacement}}$$

EXERCISE 7A

1

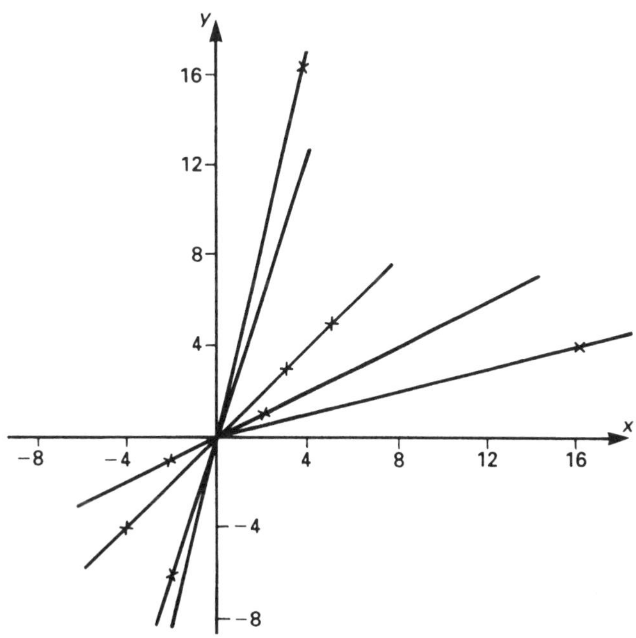

2 a $\frac{1}{2}$ b 1 c 1 d 4

e $\frac{1}{4}$ f $\frac{1}{2}$ g 1 h 3

3 The ladder with slope $\frac{3}{1}$

4 The hill with slope 600 m/3 km

• Gradient through any two points

The formula for the gradient of the straight line between two points is most effectively introduced by some numerical examples. The first examples should be in the first quadrant with all the coordinates positive as the arithmetic in these cases is much simpler. Consequently, the lines in the first exercise only have gradients which are positive.

EXERCISE 7B

1 a 3 b $\frac{3}{2}$ c 2 d 4 e $\frac{5}{8}$ f $\frac{6}{5}$

• Negative gradient

In the next exercise all of the gradients are negative.

EXERCISE 7C

1

a
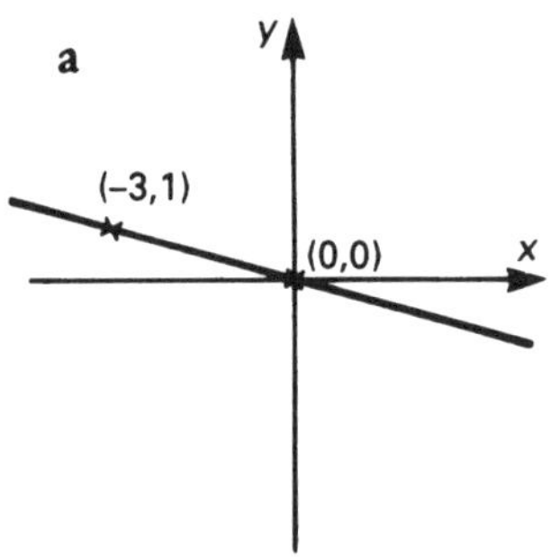

b
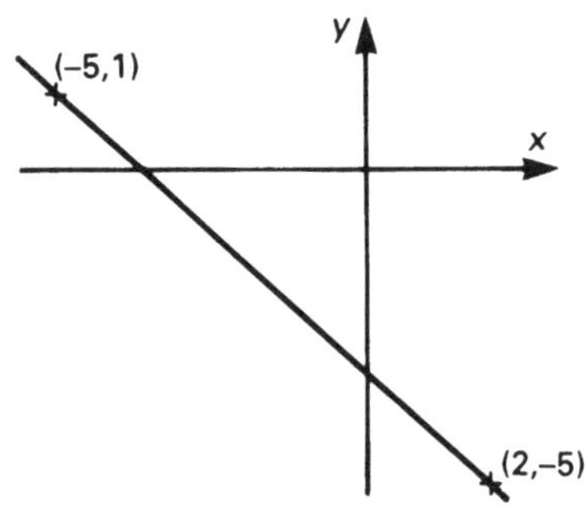

c
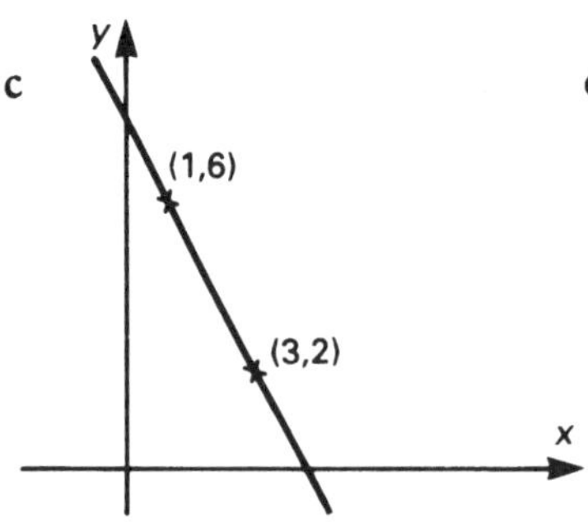

d
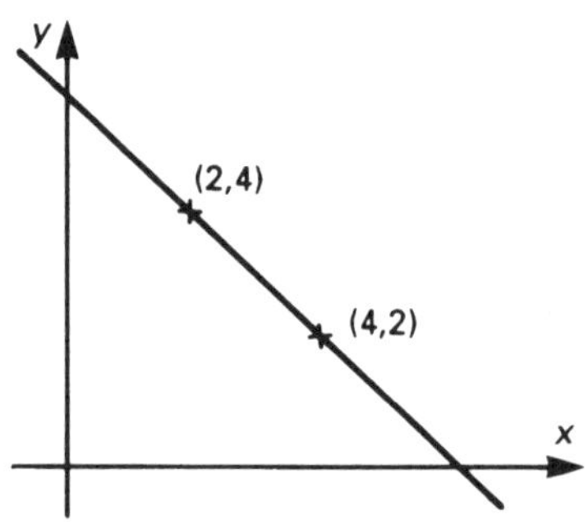

2 a $-\frac{1}{3}$ b $-\frac{6}{7}$ c -2 d -1

• Equation of a straight line

In this section the students learn how to draw up a table of values and draw a straight line graph. When drawing a straight line graph we only need to plot two points, but it is prudent to plot more than two points to check that a careless error in the computation has not been made. Such an error will be noticed as soon as it is found that not all the points are on a straight line.

EXERCISE 7D

1

x	-2	-1	0	1	2	3	4	5	6
$3x$ -1	-6 -1	-3 -1	0 -1	3 -1	6 -1	9 -1	12 -1	15 -1	18 -1
$3x-1$	-7	-4	-1	2	5	8	11	14	17

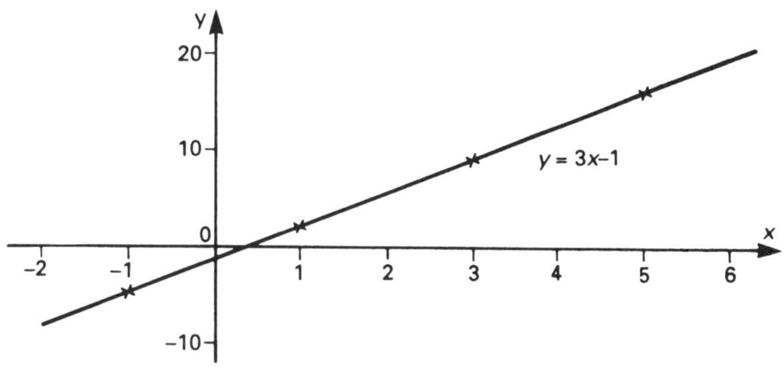

2

x 1	-2 1	-1 1	0 1	1 1	2 1	3 1	4 1	5 1	6 1
$x+1$	-1	0	1	2	3	4	5	6	7

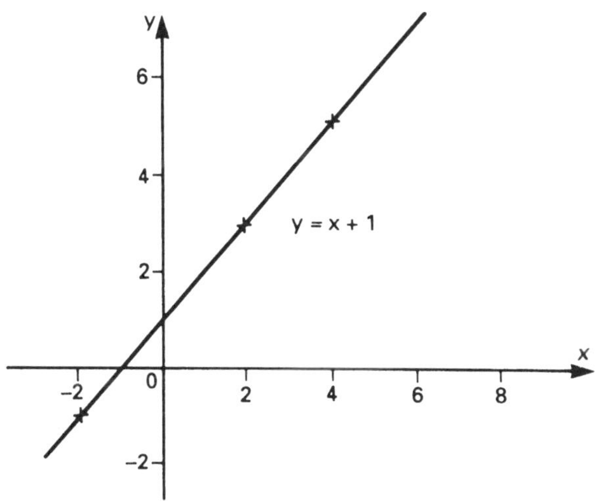

3

x	-2	-1	0	1	2	3	4	5	6
$4x$	-8	-4	0	4	8	12	16	20	24
-2	-2	-2	-2	-2	-2	-2	-2	-2	-2
$4x-2$	-10	-6	-2	2	6	10	14	18	22

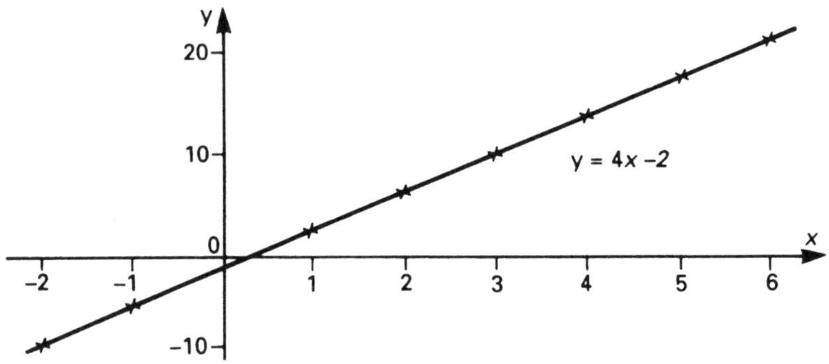

4

x	-2	-1	0	1	2	3	4	5	6
$-2x$	4	2	0	-2	-4	-6	-8	-10	-12
8	8	8	8	8	8	8	8	8	8
$8-2x$	12	10	8	6	4	2	0	-2	-4

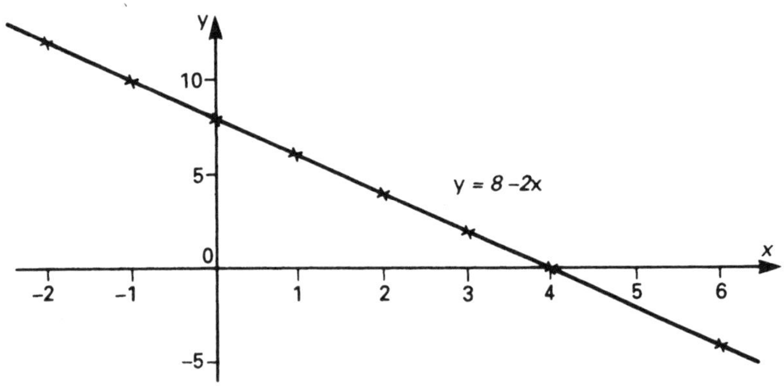

5 $y=3x-1$ has gradient 3
$y=x+1$ has gradient 1
$y=4x-2$ has gradient 4
$y=8-2x$ has gradient -2

The next section emphasises the gradient and y-intercept. If we know both of these then we know the direction of the line and where it crosses the y-axis.

EXERCISE 7E

1 a gradient 1, y-intercept 0
b gradient 5, y-intercept 0
c gradient 3, y-intercept 0
d gradient $\frac{1}{4}$, y-intercept 0
e gradient -1, y-intercept 0
f gradient -3, y-intercept 0
g gradient $-\frac{2}{3}$, y-intercept 0
h gradient 2, y-intercept 5
j gradient $\frac{1}{2}$, y-intercept 3
k gradient 3, y-intercept -7
l gradient $\frac{3}{5}$, y-intercept 8
m gradient -7, y-intercept 2
n gradient -3, y-intercept -8
o gradient $3\frac{3}{8}$, y-intercept -2

2 a $y=4x$ gradient 4, y-intercept 0
b $y=\frac{1}{3}x$ gradient $\frac{1}{3}$, y-intercept 0
c $y=4x-6$ gradient 4, y-intercept -6
d $y=4x+\frac{2}{3}$ gradient 4, y-intercept $\frac{2}{3}$
e $y=-3x-\frac{5}{2}$ gradient -3, y-intercept $-\frac{5}{2}$
f $y=-x+\frac{4}{3}$ gradient -1, y-intercept $\frac{4}{3}$
g $y=-\frac{1}{2}x+7$ gradient $-\frac{1}{2}$, y-intercept 7
h $y=-\frac{8}{3}x+\frac{20}{5}$ gradient $-\frac{8}{3}$, y-intercept $\frac{20}{3}$
i $y=\frac{3}{5}x+3$ gradient $\frac{3}{5}$, y-intercept 3
j $y=-8x+7$ gradient -8, y-intercept 7
k $y=-\frac{1}{2}x+3$ gradient $-\frac{1}{2}$, y-intercept 3
l $y=\frac{4}{5}x+4$ gradient $\frac{4}{5}$, y-intercept 4

3 $y=2x$

4 $y=3x-11$

5 $y=\frac{3}{5}x+\frac{24}{3}$ or $5y=3x+24$

6 $y=\frac{1}{2}x+6$

EXERCISE 7F

1 a

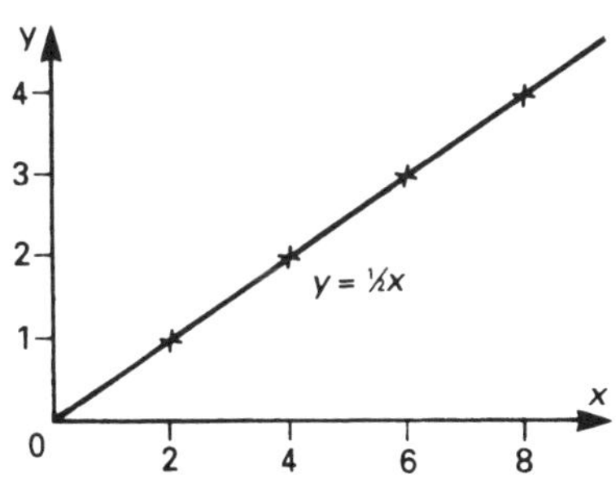

b

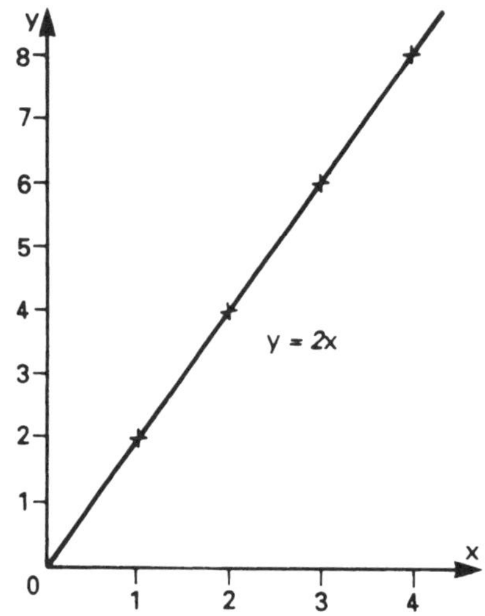

c

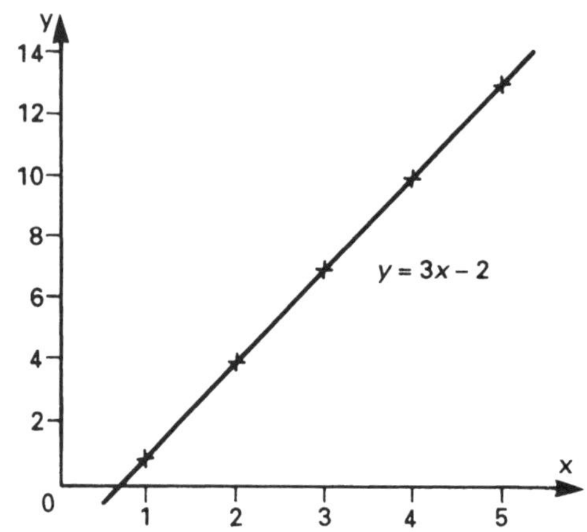

2 a $y=\frac{1}{2}x$ b $y=2x$ c $y=3x-2$

3 a gradient 3, y-intercept 0, equation $y=3x$

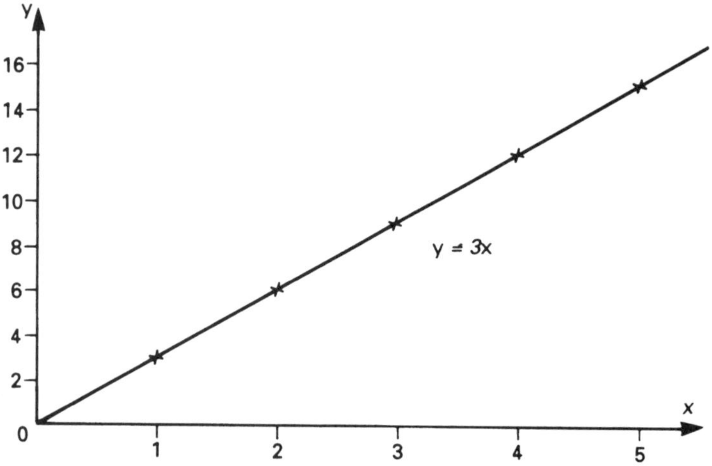

b gradient $\frac{5}{2}$, y-intercept 0
equation $y=\frac{5}{2}x$

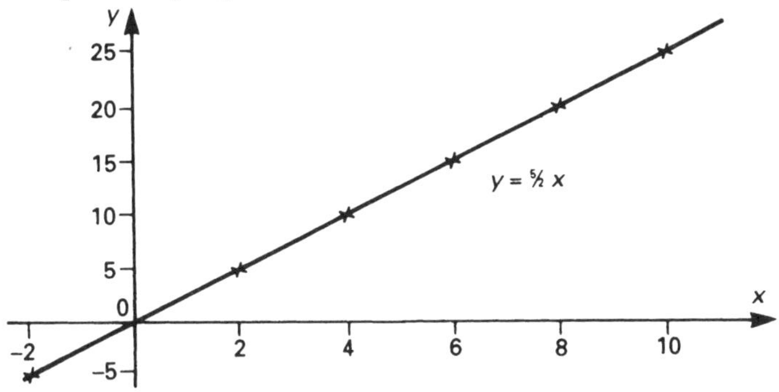

c gradient -2, y-intercept 12
equation $y=12-2x$

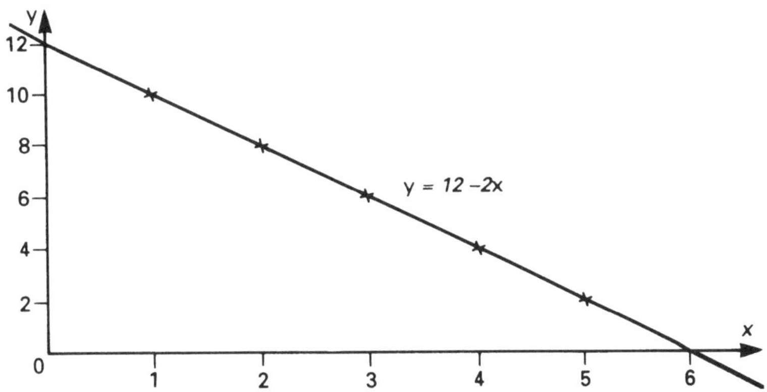

d gradient $\frac{1}{3}$, y-intercept $4\frac{1}{3}$
equation $y=\frac{1}{3}x+4\frac{1}{3}$

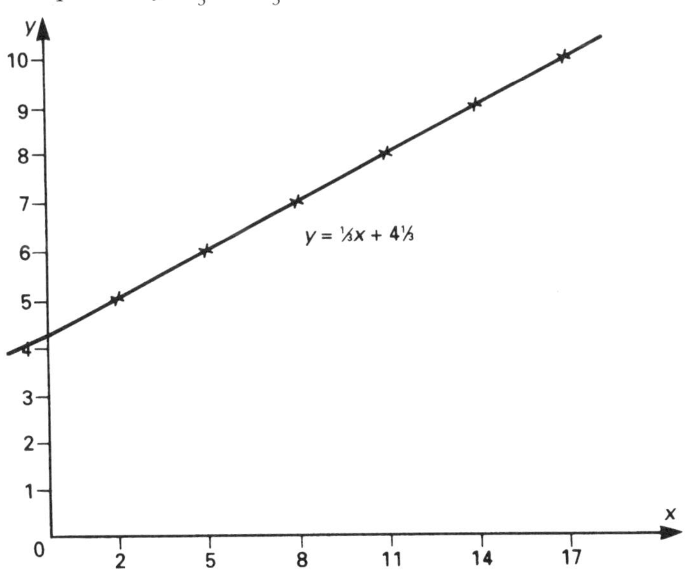

4 a (3, 14) does not fit. The equation of the line is $y = 5x$

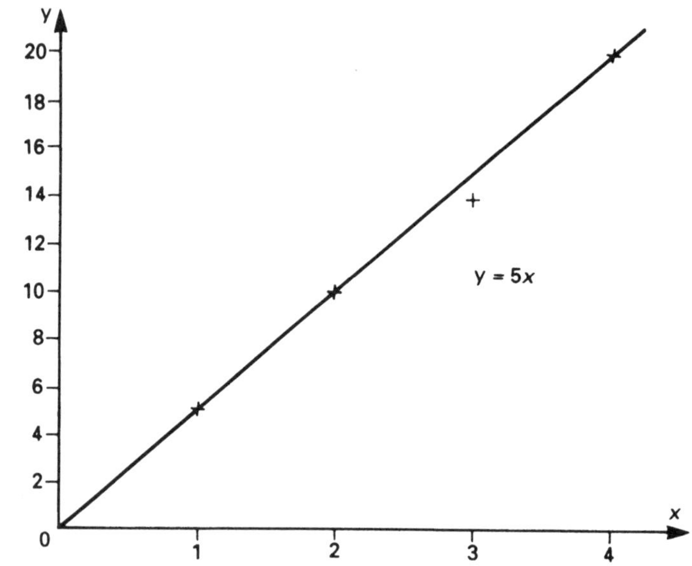

b (0, 0) does not fit. The equation of the line is $y = 2x - 1$

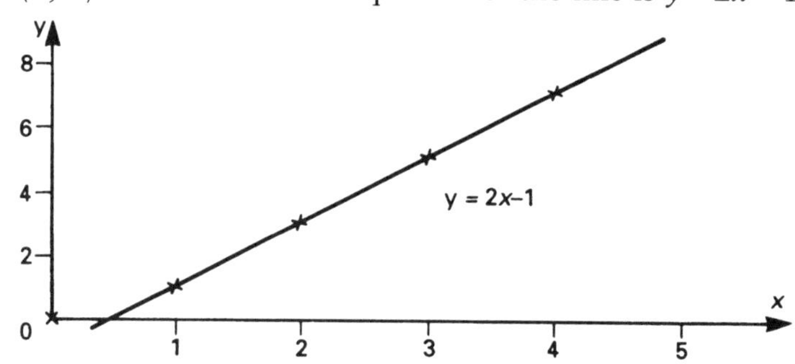

c (2, 10) does not fit. The equation of the line is $y = 3x + 3$

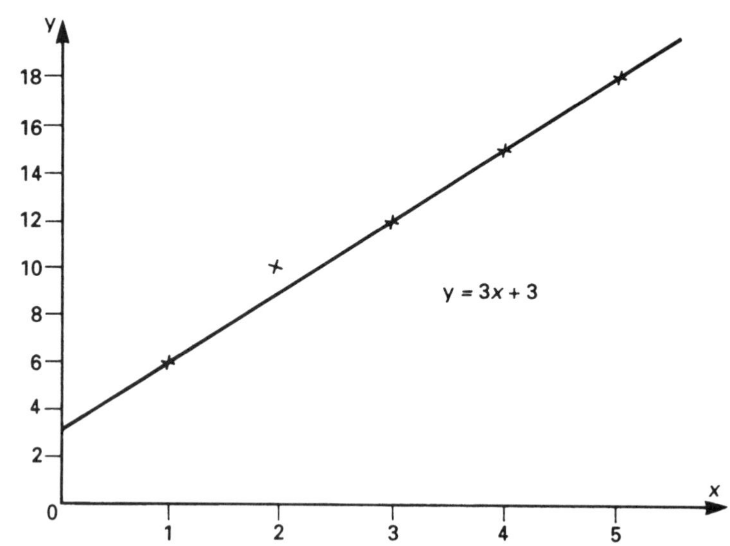

8 Geometry

• Aim of chapter

The aim of the chapter is to introduce students to the measuring and drawing of angles, to the solution of simple angle problems and to compass and ruler constructions.

• Objectives

By the end of the chapter the students will be able to:

1. Identify parallel lines
2. Measure the length of straight lines
3. Identify angles as acute, right, obtuse, straight or reflex
4. Use a protractor to measure and draw any angle in degrees
5. Identify complementary and supplementary angles
6. Use the properties of angles on a straight line to solve problems
7. Use the properties of angles at a point and vertically opposite angles to solve problems
8. Construct the perpendicular bisector of a line using compass and ruler only
9. Construct the perpendicular from a point to a line using compass and ruler only
10. Construct the bisector of a given angle using compass and ruler only
11. Construct the bisector of angles of 45° and 60° using compass and ruler only
12. Identify corresponding, alternate and allied angles when two lines are cut by a transversal.

• Do you remember?

This section reminds students of some of the basic ideas of plane figures. Plane figures are so called because they can be drawn on a flat surface or plane. Do not spend too much time talking about the idea of a point and a line. The labelling of a line segment as AB, for example, is important. Normally, the end-points of this line segment are A and B.

Points on the same line are collinear. Lines which meet at the same point are concurrent.

• Parallel lines

If two lines **in the same plane** never meet, no matter how far they are extended, then those two lines are parallel. Good examples that illustrate the idea of parallel lines are the opposite sides of the face of a brick or exercise book, the two rails on a railway line, the two sides of a road, and wires on a telephone pole. There are many others. Use some of these to help the students to understand what parallel lines are.

• Measuring lines

It is important that students learn to measure the length of a line both in centimetres and in millimetres. It is also important that they learn to measure quickly and accurately to the nearest millimetre. This section and exercise give plenty of practice in drawing lines of a given length and measuring given lengths in centimetres and millimetres.

EXERCISE 8A

1 5.6 cm, 4.1 cm, 2.3 cm, 4.5 cm, 6.4 cm

2 **a** 7.7 cm **b** 51 mm **c** 51 mm **d** 3.5 cm

3 The students' answers will need to be checked with a ruler.

4 AD = 3.8 cm AC = 3.5 cm BD = 3.5 cm

5 The students' lines will need to be checked with a ruler to see that they are 5 cm apart. Their diagrams should look like this (not drawn accurately):

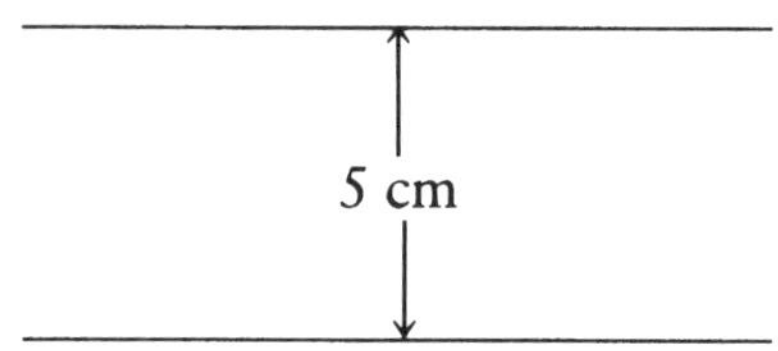

6 HG//JI; EF//CD//AB

• Drawing parallel lines

The two sides of a ruler can also be used to draw two parallel lines quickly.

• Angles and lines

Angles can be thought of in two ways. They can be thought of in terms of the sharpness of a point made by two lines when they meet. This is the approach used in this brief introduction. They can also be thought of in terms of an amount of turning, which idea is used in the next section to develop angles. Students should be familiar with both.

• Angles

Turns are introduced as clockwise or anti-clockwise. Later on students will learn that the convention is to regard a clockwise turn as negative and an anti-clockwise turn as positive which is rather confusing. The turn we start from is a whole turn, also described as a full turn or a revolution. This is divided into a quarter turn and a half turn.

A full turn is divided into 360 degrees. The use of the curious number 360 is due to the ancient Babylonians, as written about in the Old Testament, who counted in 60s. (They also are responsible for 60 seconds = 1 minute, 60 minutes = 1 hour.)

The right angle is the most important angle. The method of making a right angle by folding a piece of paper as described in the text-book can be carried out using any old piece of paper and is a most useful exercise.

The section introduces some important words that the students will need to remember: perpendicular, acute angle, obtuse angle and reflex angle.

• Using a protractor

This section teaches students how to use a protractor. The protractor causes two difficulties. Firstly, it has two scales and the students have to learn which to use. The approach in the book is to suggest that pupils measuring or drawing an angle first decide whether the angle is acute or obtuse. They then choose a scale which gives them an angle between 0° and 90° (if it is an acute angle) or between 90° and 180° (if the angle is obtuse).

Secondly, the vertex of the angle is not placed at the edge of the protractor. On most wooden board protractors (which are not transparent) the vertex is placed next to the mid-point of the diameter of the semi-circle. On transparent small protractors the mid-point of the diameter is not at the edge. They have to be careful to put the protractor in the correct place, or else all their answers will be slightly wrong.

EXERCISE 8B

1 a n, z b t c q, u, x d p, r, s, v, w, y

2 a 30°   b 70°   c 90°
d 130°   e 170°   f 20°

3 Check the students' answers for accuracy. An error of 1° is acceptable. If the angle should be 30°, accept 29° – 31°.

EXERCISE 8C

The angles to be drawn and measured now are reflex angles.

1 a 240°   b 200°   c 300°
d 265°   e 215°   f 340°

2 $n = 20°$ $p = 340°$ $q = 150°$ $r = 210°$
$s = 270°$ $t = 90°$ $u = 175°$ $v = 185°$
$w = 254°$ $x = 106°$ $y = 325°$ $z = 35°$

3 Measure the students' angles; accept as sufficiently accurate angles that are 1° too big or too small.

• Angles on a straight line

Here for the first time are some calculations using angles. We know that a straight line has an angle of 180°. If this angle is divided up into some smaller angles, then the sum of all those angles is 180°.

• Angles at a point

The equality of vertically opposite angles can be demonstrated using a pair of scissors or two crossed sticks. It is easy to see that the opposite angles are equal, no matter how much we open the scissors.

EXERCISE 8D

1 Angle AXD = 67°, angle AXB = 113°

2 $P\hat{Q}R = 129°$

3 $A\hat{O}B = 90°$

4 59°, 121°, 59°

5 a 113° b 23°

6 a 143° b 82° c 4°

7 a 53° b 32° c 14°

• Constructing perpendiculars

It was the ancient Greeks who were the first to attempt to draw figures using a compass and 'straight edge' only and this has been part of mathematics ever since. Some people argue that this activity has no real use and should be abandoned. It does, however, encourage students to draw neatly and accurately. Some constructions are educationally useful; the information needed to construct a triangle is the same as the minimum information needed to be sure two triangles are congruent. This should not be surprising: the information sufficient to be confident that two triangles are congruent would be enough to enable them to be drawn accurately as well.

Too often constructions are taught as tricks, and are easily forgotten. If the reason why a construction works is understood, then it is very much easier to remember what to do. The construction of a perpendicular uses the fact that the diagonals of a rhombus are at right angles.

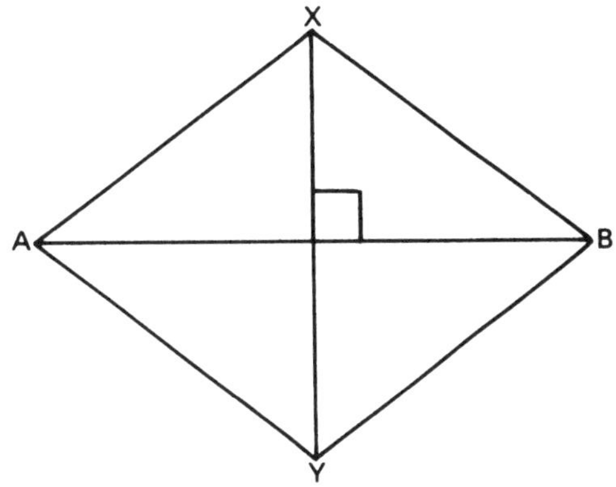

If equal length arcs are drawn from A and B, they will cut at X above AB and at Y below AB. AX, XB, BY and YA will all be the same length. The figure AXBY is a rhombus. This is what is drawn in exercise 8E.

The construction of the perpendicular from a point to a line in exercise 8F depends on the properties of isosceles triangles. Teachers may prefer to postpone the teaching of each of the constructions in this chapter to the time when they teach the properties of the figures whose properties make the construction work.

EXERCISE 8E

a–d Construct and label: as illustrated in the diagram in the text-book.
e Both angles are right angles.
f AP = PB

To construct the perpendicular from a point to a straight line, we make an isosceles triangle. The altitude of an isosceles triangle is perpendicular to its base.

In the figure, MCD is an isosceles triangle with MC = MD.

P is the midpoint of CD so PC = PD and MP is perpendicular to CD.

In the construction, the two equal arcs give PC = PD. Equal arcs from C and D meeting at M mean that MC = MD and the figure is an isosceles triangle.

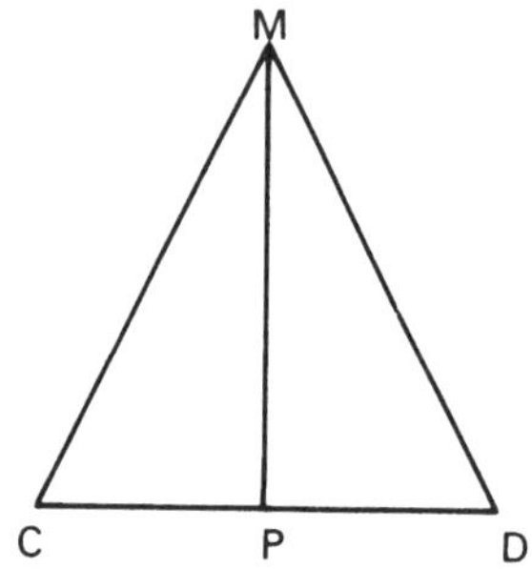

EXERCISE 8F

a–e Construct and label: as in the text-book.

f Yes

The radius has to be more than half the length of the line so that the arcs cut each other.

• Formal constructions

This section introduces the conventional way in which constructions are presented.

EXERCISE 8G

The students practise the constructions developed in exercises 8E and 8F. They should be encouraged to use different lines. They can drop perpendiculars to vertical lines, for example, or to lines of 6 cm or 8 cm long.

• Constructing angles

The first construction is of the angle bisector. This construction also uses a property of a rhombus. This time the property used is that the angles of a rhombus are bisected by its diagonals.

We start with angle PQR. At Q equal arcs are drawn cutting PQ and QR at A and B, so QA = QB. Then equal arcs are drawn from A and B cutting at K, so QA = QB = AK = BK, and QBKA is a rhombus.

QK is a diagonal of the rhombus so it bisects angle PQR.

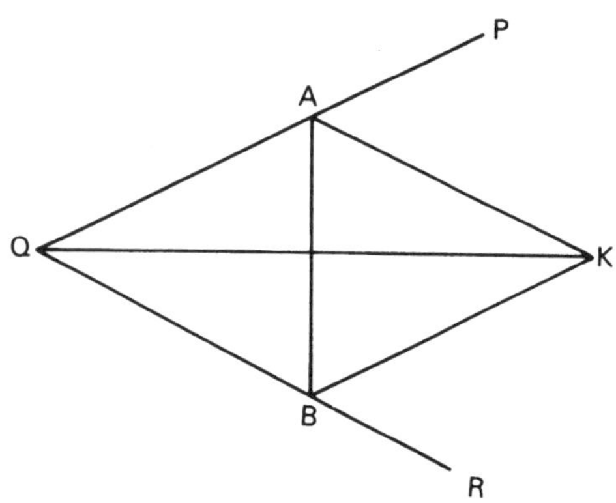

This technique makes it possible to construct other angles. We have already learnt how to construct an angle of 90° (a perpendicular). Bisecting an angle of 90° gives us an angle of 45°. We can repeat the bisecting, getting angles of 22.5 °, 11.25 ° and so on.

To construct an angle of 60° we make an equilateral triangle, as explained in the text. Successive bisections give us angles of 30°, 15°, $7\frac{1}{2}$° and so on.

• Copying a given angle without measuring it

This section goes through the traditional steps for carrying out this procedure.

As with other constructions, it is important that students learn to work neatly and accurately.

EXERCISE 8H

1 The students should follow the procedure for constructing angles of 60° (pages 95–96) and then bisect the angle of 60° three times to construct angles of 30°, 15° and 7.5°

2 The students should follow the procedure for constructing angles of 90° and 45° (page 95) and then bisect the angle of 45° to construct the angle of 22.5°

3

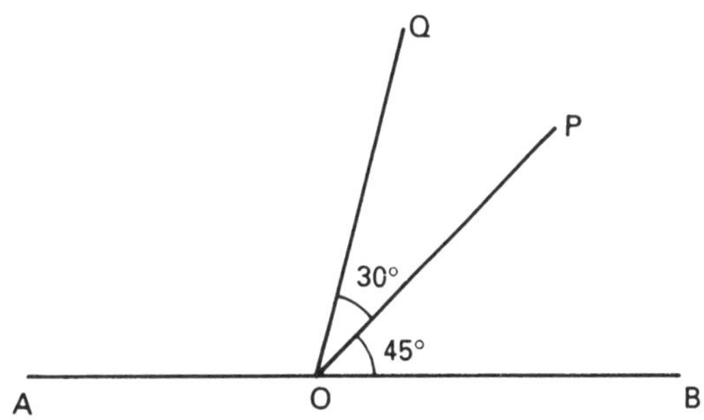

First construct angle of BOP = 45 °. Then construct angle POQ = 30°.
Angle BOQ = 75°

4 105° = 60° + 45°

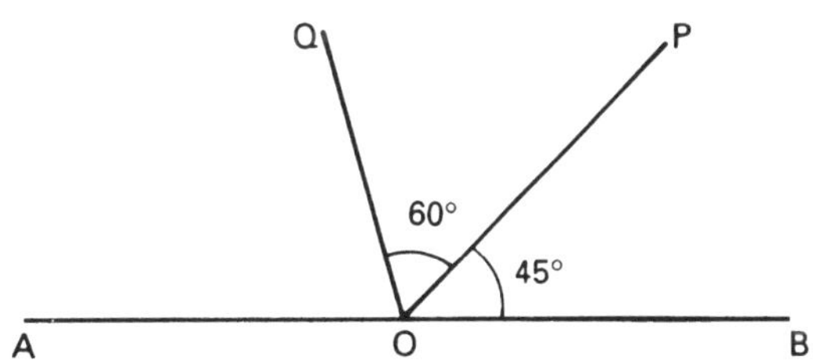

First construct angle BOP = 45°. Then construct angle POQ = 60°.
Angle BOQ = 45° + 60° = 105°

5 $135° = 90° + 45°$. To construct an angle of $135°$, we construct angles of $90°$ and $45°$.

6

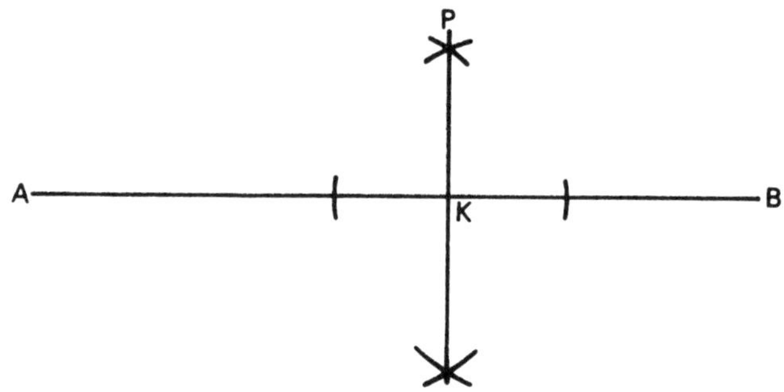

7 a

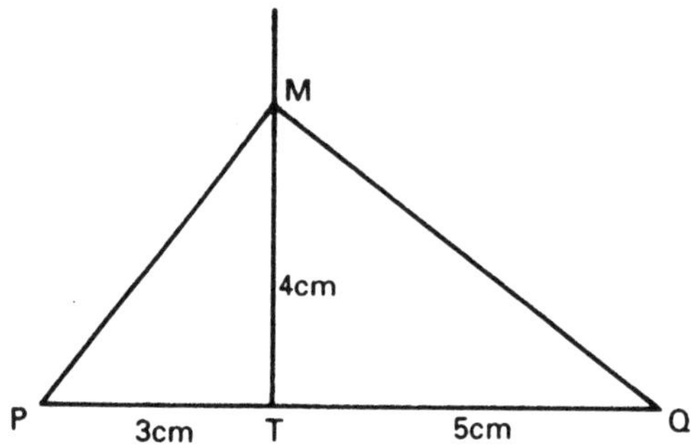

b i PM = 5 cm   ii MQ = 6.4 cm

• Angles and parallel lines

This section introduces corresponding, alternate and allied angles formed when two lines are cut by a transversal. The teacher should be aware and emphasise that these angles are obtained whether or not the two lines are parallel.
For example:

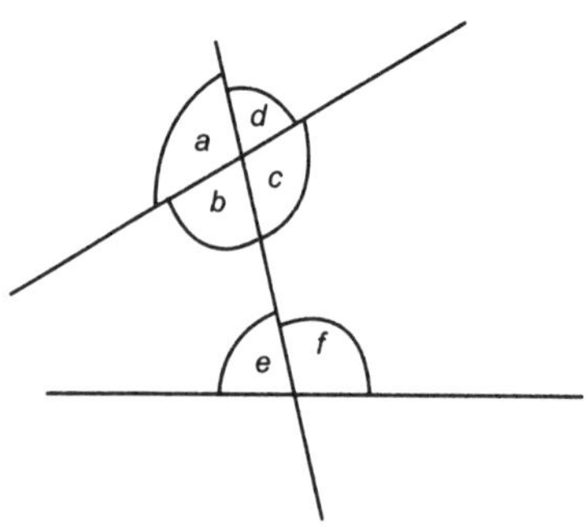

a is corresponding to *e*.
b is alternate to *f*.
b and *e* are allied.

However, the pairs of angles a and e, b and f, and so on, are not equal, and the sum of b and e is not 180°. Only when the lines cut by the transversal are parallel are pairs of alternate and corresponding angles equal and allied angles sum to 180°.

EXERCISE 8I

1 Corresponding angles: $a=e$, $c=g$, $b=f$, $d=h$.
Alternate angles: $c=f$, $d=e$.
Allied angles: c and e, d and f.

2 **a** $a=52°$, $b=128°$, $c=128°$, $d=52°$
b $b=115°$, $c=115°$, $c=115°$
c $a=95°$, $b=125°$
d $c=67°$

9 Number patterns

• Aim of chapter

The aim of the chapter is to introduce students to number patterns, sequences and tests of divisibility.

• Objectives

By the end of the chapter the students will be able to:

1 Identify rectangle, square and triangle numbers
2 Continue sequences of numbers when given the first few terms
3 Apply tests of divisibility by 2, 3, 4, 5, 8, 9 and 10 to numbers.

• Rectangle numbers

Some numbers can be represented by special shapes and some numbers form sequences. Rectangle numbers are natural numbers that can be shown as rectangles. These are the composite numbers which are not prime.
We know $20 = 5 \times 4$.

We can show this as a 5 by 4 rectangle:

x x x x x
x x x x x
x x x x x
x x x x x

We can also show 20 as a 10 by 2 rectangle:

x x x x x x x x x x
x x x x x x x x x x

A square is a rectangle and a square number is also a rectangle number. However, a prime number, for example 11, can only be shown as a rectangle of unit width:

x x x x x x x x x x x

11 is not called a rectangle number. (It is sensible to exclude these numbers, for otherwise all natural numbers would be rectangle numbers and the word would have no useful meaning.)

- **Square numbers**

Some numbers can be shown as squares, as are illustrated in the text-book. These square numbers are 1, 4, 9, 16, 25, 36, 49, …

- **Triangle numbers**

Some numbers can be shown as triangles, as illustrated in the text-book. These numbers are

1, 3, 6, 10, 15, 21, 28, …

They are constructed by adding one new line to the triangle for each term:

$1,\quad 3=1+2,\quad 6=1+2+3,\quad 10=1+2+3+4,$
$15=1+2+3+4+5,\quad 21=1+2+3+4+5+6$
$28=1+2+3+4+5+6+7$

The nth term will be

$1+2+3+4+5+6+7+8+9+\ldots+n=\frac{1}{2}n(n+1)$

This can be demonstrated without algebra by repeating each triangle to make a rectangle; the triangle has half as many members as the rectangle:

1	3	6	10	15	21
x	x x	x x x	x x x x	x x x x x	x x x x x x
o	x o	x x o	x x x o	x x x x o	x x x x x o
	o o	x o o	x x o o	x x x o o	x x x x o o
		o o o	x o o o	x x o o o	x x x o o o
			o o o o	x o o o o	x x o o o o
				o o o o o	x o o o o o
					o o o o o o

The size of each rectangle is

$1\times2\quad 2\times3\quad 3\times4\quad 4\times5\quad 5\times6\quad 6\times7$

The rectangle for the nth triangle number has area $n(n+1)$ and the nth term will be $\frac{1}{2}n(n+1)$.

EXERCISE 9A

1 a

x x x x x x
x x x x x x 6×3
x x x x x x

x x x x x x x x x
x x x x x x x x x 9×2

These can be turned to show 3×6 and 2×9.

b

x x x x x x x
x x x x x x x 7×2

c

x x x x x x x
x x x x x x x
x x x x x x x
x x x x x x x 7×6
x x x x x x x
x x x x x x x

x x x x x x x x x x x x x x
x x x x x x x x x x x x x x 14×3
x x x x x x x x x x x x x x

x x x x x x x x x x x x x x x x x x x x x
x x x x x x x x x x x x x x x x x x x x x 21×2

2 a x x x x x x
x x x x x x
x x x x x x
x x x x x x 6×6
x x x x x x
x x x x x x

x x x x x x x x x x x x x x x x x x
x x x x x x x x x x x x x x x x x x 18×2

x x x x x x x x x x x x
x x x x x x x x x x x x 12×3
x x x x x x x x x x x x

x x x x x x x x x
x x x x x x x x x
x x x x x x x x x 9×4
x x x x x x x x x

b x x x x x
x x x x x
x x x x x 5×5
x x x x x
x x x x x

25 is the square of a prime number, 5

3 Only the abler pupils should do more than parts **a** and **b** of this question. The rest of the question is similar to the discussion before the exercise of the sum of the first 1, 2, 3, 4, ... n triangle numbers.

a 15, 21, 28

b **i** 4 **ii** 9 **iii** 16 **iv** 25

c They are all squares.
The sum of the 1st and 2nd is 2^2.
The sum of the 2nd and 3rd is 3^2.
The sum of the 3rd and 4th is 4^2.
The sum of the 4th and 5th is 5^2.

So the sum of the 10th and 11th is $11^2 = 121$.
The sum of the 99th and 100th is $100^2 = 10\,000$.
The sum of the nth and $(n+1)$th is $(n+1)^2$.

d

x o o o	x x o x o o o o o	
1 + 3	3 + 6	
x x x o x x o o x o o o o o o o	x x x x o x x x o o x x o o o x o o o o o o o o o	x x x x x o x x x x o o x x x o o o x x o o o o x o o o o o o o o o o o
6 + 10	10 + 15	15 + 21

• Sequences

This section looks at some simple sequences and number patterns.

Exercise 9B

Questions **7–9**, **11** and **12** should only be attempted by abler pupils.

1 **a** 6, 10, 14 **b** 27, 25, 23 **c** 10, 40, 160

2 **a** 13, 15, 17 **b** 14, 16, 18 **c** 27, 31, 35
d 243, 729, 2187 **e** 162, 486, 1458 **f** 44, 40, 36
g 13, 18, 16 **h** 26, 34, 43

3 20, 23, 26

4 144, 196, 256, 324, 400

5 **a** 34, 55, 89
This sequence is the Fibonacci sequence. Every term is the sum of the two previous terms.
b 729, 2187, 6561
c 36, 41, 46
d 216, 343, 512

6 **a** 1 234 321 **b** 123 454 321 **c** 1111 **d** 11 111

7 127, 176, 233
The terms given are $2=1^2+1$, $11=3^2+2$, $28=5^2+3$, $53=7^2+4$ and $86=9^2+5$. The next three terms are $11^2+6=127$, $13^2+7=176$ and $15^2+8=233$.

Another way of doing it is to look at the differences. The differences between successive terms are $11-2=9$, $28-11=17$, $53-28=25$, $86-53=33$. The differences increase by 8 each time. The next three differences are 41, 49 and 57. Therefore the next three terms are $86+41=127$, $127+49=176$ and $176+57=233$.

8 a 64 (this is 8^2, notice that $1+2+\ldots+7+8+7+\ldots=8^2$)
b 81 (this is 9^2, notice that $1+2+\ldots+8+9+8+\ldots=9^2$)
c $100^2=10\,000$ (following on from parts **a** and **b**)

9 a 64
b $25^2=625$. Here we are adding up the first 25 odd numbers. In the first part, the sum of the first 8 odd numbers is $64=8^2$.
c $50^2=2500$. These are the first 50 odd numbers.

10 a 123456787654321 b 11 111 111

11 222, 350, 520
The terms are $2=1^3+1$, $10=2^3+2$, $30=3^3+3$, $68=4^3+4$ and $130=5^3+5$. So the next three terms are $6^3+6=222$, $7^3+7=350$ and $8^3+8=520$.

12 15 55 $\frac{1}{2}n(n+1)$
The fifth triangle number is half of $5\times 6=15$.
The tenth triangle number is half of $10\times 11=55$.
The nth triangle number is half of $n\times(n+1)=\frac{1}{2}n(n+1)$.

• Tests of divisibility

Tests for divisibility by 2, 3, 4, 5, 8, 9 and 10 are given. (The test for divisibility by 7 is too difficult to be worth the time needed to learn it.)

EXERCISE 9C

1 a Divisible by 3 and 5 only
b Divisible by 2 and 3 only
c Divisible by 3, 5 and 9 only
d Divisible by 2, 3, 4 and 8 only
e Divisible by 2, 3, 4 and 9
f Divisible by 2, 5 and 10 only
g Divisible by none of them
h Divisible by 3 and 9 only

2 A number is divisible by 15 ($=3\times 5$) if its last digit is 0 or 5 and the sum of the digits is divisible by 3.
a Yes
b Not divisible by 3 (the sum of the digits is not divisible by 3)

3 A number is divisible by 20 ($=4\times 5$) if its last digit is 0 and it is divisible by 4 (another way of expressing this would be to say the last digit is 0 and the second last digit is even)
a No (second last digit is 1) b Yes

10 Approximations and estimation

• Aim of chapter

The aim of the chapter is to introduce students to approximations and the rounding of numbers.

• Objectives

By the end of the chapter the students will be able to:

1 Choose appropriate degrees of accuracy when measuring quantities
2 Round numbers to the nearest hundredth, tenth, unit, ten and hundred
3 Round numbers to any specified number of significant figures
4 Make rough estimates of the answers to calculations.

• Approximations

When we measure the length of a line the answer we give is only an approximation. If we measure a line as 8.0 cm long, we cannot tell whether the line is exactly 8.0 or 8.01 or 7.99 cm long. Normally the length of a line is measured to the nearest millimetre as we can be no more accurate than that with a ruler and our eyes. This is true whatever is measured: the volume of petrol we buy at the garage; the volume of liquid in a can of drink; the weight of a bag of 1 kg sugar and so on.

Students should be able to give many other examples of items that we buy in shops and for which a quantity is stated. This can be compared with the way we buy items in the market.

We can also ask how much accuracy is needed. Suppose a road sign said that the distance between two towns is 58.357 km. How useful would that information be? The sign tells us the distance is 58 km and 357 meters. Do we need to know the number of metres? A road-builder who is tarring the road would need to be that accurate, but for the motorist driving between the two towns a sign saying '58 km' would give sufficient information, so road signs give the distance to the nearest kilometre.

This kind of discussion applies to all sorts of measurements. Appreciating the appropriate degree of approximation is most important.

EXERCISE 10A

There can be more than one answer to some of these questions. As the text-book states, the accuracy depends on the purpose of the measurement. A carpenter making furniture will need to be very accurate so that pieces of wood fit together precisely. The time taken to walk 10 kilometres home need only be given roughly, to the nearest quarter of an hour, but the time to run 10 kilometres in an athletic competition has to be given very accurately indeed to make it possible to compare times athletes take to run the distance in different parts of the world.

1 To the nearest 100 grams
2 To the nearest kilometre
3 To the nearest minute
4 To the nearest metre
5 To the nearest centimetre
6 To the nearest kilometre
7 To the nearest gram
8 To the nearest hour

• Rounding numbers

This section looks at rounding numbers to the nearest ten, to the nearest unit, to two decimal places, to the nearest hundred and so on.

Rounding is an important way of approximating numbers. We can round down or round up to the nearest ten, tenth, hundred, hundredth and so on. There is discussion in the text of the action to be taken when the number to be rounded is a '5'. We always round up in this case: 4.5 = 5 to the nearest whole number.

EXERCISE 10B

1 a (i) 23.4 m (ii) 10.5 cm (iii) 7.3 cm (iv) 103.8 cm
(v) 33.3 m (vi) 1.0 km (vii) 0.1 m (viii) 4.5 mm
b (i) 23 m (ii) 10 cm (iii) 7 cm (iv) 104 cm
(v) 33 m (vi) 1 km (vii) 0 m (viii) 5 mm

2 a (i) 1.26 m (ii) 29.17 kg (iii) 8.56 s
(iv) 0.90 km (v) 54.49 mm (vi) 2.25 m
b (i) 1.3 m (ii) 29.2 kg (iii) 8.6 s
(iv) 0.9 km (v) 54.5 mm (vi) 2.2 m
c (i) 1 m (ii) 29 kg (iii) 9 s
(iv) 1 km (v) 54 mm (vi) 2 m

3 a (i) 128 710 m (ii) 12 350 s
(iii) 934 160 km (iv) 24 400 km
b (i) 128 700 m (ii) 12 300 s
(iii) 934 200 kg (iv) 24 400 km

• Significant figures

Many students have difficulty deciding what figures are significant and what figures are not significant and it is quite hard to explain clearly and simply. The zero is a particular problem and should be avoided in all the early examples the students meet.

That 5.433 to two significant figures is 5.4 is not usually a problem, but what about writing 5.0403 to one decimal place? This has to be written as 5.0. Even worse: 0.0050443 to three significant figures is 0.00504. The first three zeros are not significant: their purpose is to hold the numbers in the correct place. The 0 in between 5 and 4 is significant because it is in the middle of the number. It is not a place holder.

Later on, standard form is useful for showing how to find significant figures. We can illustrate what is happening by comparing our number with 504.43: what is that to the nearest whole number? Answer 504.

EXERCISE 10C

1	a 0.003	b 0.00081	c 77.4	
	d 141	e 888	f 0.011	
2	a 6.05	b 0.03	c 0.88	
	d 50.48	e 1.00	f 7.00	
3	a 130	b 23	c 19	
4	a 200	b 160	c 3.4	d 56
5	a 0.46	b 0.37	c 0.017	d 0.68
6	a 2.0	b 1400	c 0.28	

• Rough estimates

Rough answers are very useful in helping to avoid mistakes when we are carrying out calculations. Careless mistakes can occur when we are working a multiplication, whether we are using long multiplication, logarithms or a calculator. If we make a rough estimate of the answer before the calculation we can ensure that the answer is roughly the right size.

For example, if we want to work out 58.2×9.83 we round the numbers to one significant figure and carry out the calculation:

$58.2 = 60$ and $9.83 = 10$ to one significant figure and
$60 \times 10 = 600$

If we carry out the calculation we find $58.2 \times 9.83 = 572.106$ which is 600 to one significant figure. The estimate for $58.2 \div 9.83$ is $60 \div 10 = 6$. The exact answer is 5.92065... .

Oral calculations of estimates are useful and effective as the calculations are easy to carry out.

EXERCISE 10D

This exercise is ideal for practising the use of a calculator. For example, the answer to question **4a** $6.31 \div 4.17$ is 1.5131894 according to my calculator but we do not need all these decimal places and an answer to two decimal places, which is the accuracy of the numbers in the question, is appropriate. Finding the calculator answer and then giving a sensible approximation is good practice. So often those who use calculators give an answer with large numbers of figures and that tells the teacher that the pupil has been using a calculator, for who would want to work out the answer by long division to so many places of decimals?

In questions **1** and **2**, for each part, the rough answer is given first, followed by the answer to one decimal place.

1	a $3 \times 3 = 9$	8.6	b $4 \times 2 = 8$	8.0
	c $5 \times 2 = 10$	7.8	d $4 \times 2 = 8$	7.6
	e $7 \times 4 = 28$	25.2	f $8 \times 3 = 24$	22.4

2	a $9 \div 3 = 3$	2.5	b $7 \div 3 = 2.3$	2.7
	c $5 \div 2 = 2.5$	2.4	d $10 \div 4 = 2.5$	2.8
	e $80 \div 20 = 4$	3.6	f $100 \div 5 = 20$	20.1

In questions **3** and **4**, for each part, the rough answer is given first, followed by the answer to the accuracy used in the question.

3	a $4 \times 2 = 8$	8.71
	b $300 \times 20 = 6000$	7320
	c $800 \times 600 = 480\,000$	467 000
	d $600 \times 900 = 540\,000$	521 000
	e $80 \times 80 = 6400$	6470
	f $2 \times 70 = 140$	96.4

4	a $6 \div 4 = 1.5$	1.51
	b $60 \div 5 = 12$	7.29
	c $700 \div 200 = 3.5$	3.11
	d $1200 \div 300 = 4$	4.493
	e $\dfrac{400 \div 10}{60} = 0.7$	0.5803
	f $\dfrac{40 \times 60 \times 4}{60 \times 40} = 4$	4.13

• Finding squares using a calculator

This and the next few sections are intended to help students use calculators efficiently.

Most calculators have a key for finding the squares of numbers. Students can also find the square of a number by multiplying the number by itself.

• Finding square roots using a calculator

Most calculators have a square root key $\sqrt{}$ or $\sqrt{x}$ on them. Using this key, the square root of any number can be found directly.

• Finding cubes using a calculator

To cube a number we can use simple multiplication or the power key, labelled x^y or y^x, depending on the calculator. Sometimes the INV button has to be used as well.

• Finding cube roots using a calculator

Cube roots can be found by direct use of the cube root key, $\sqrt[3]{}$ or $\sqrt[3]{x}$. Sometimes the INV button has to be used as well.

EXERCISE 10E

1	a 144	b 225	c 34 077.16	d 84.64
2	a 2.449 49	b 7.615 77	c 0.152 97	d 6.008 33
3	a 8	b 389.017	c 0.004 83	d 1685.159
4	a 2.620 74	b 6	c 0.7	d 3.304 98
5	a 1077.1123	b 558.2905	c 172.7626	d 0.382 88

11 Commercial and social arithmetic

• Aim of chapter

The aim of the chapter is to teach students the use of arithmetic to solve simple practical problems, including household bills, income tax and insurance.

• Objectives

By the end of the chapter the students will be able to:

1 Work out household bills
2 Calculate income tax
3 Calculate insurance rates
4 Calculate commissions.

This chapter looks at arithmetic applied to everyday life. The topics covered are budgeting, shopping economically by comparing prices of different sizes of the item being purchased, taxes, commissions and insurance. There are many other areas of everyday life in which arithmetic plays an important part and a chapter like this cannot cover all of them. The teacher is encouraged to include as many real life examples as possible. In all cases try to use up to date figures and prices. The figures used in this book were reasonably accurate in December 1999 but will quickly become out of date.

• Budgeting

This section looks at planning how to spend money. Examples are given for shopping for groceries and for school equipment purchases. The teacher can make up lots of similar examples, with purchases of items that students themselves want to buy such as music cassettes and so on. In all examples the work should be set out neatly with prices and costs in columns.

• Comparing prices

This section covers one area in which what is learnt at school can be very helpful in everyday life. If we check prices when we shop we can save quite a lot of money. If a 250 g packet of tea costs K31 and a 500 g packet costs K60, it is quite easy to compare prices. Two 250 g packets weigh the same as one 500 g packet, but two 250 g packets cost $2 \times$ K31 = K62, K2 more than the cost of a single 500 g packet.

Other prices may be much harder to compare, such as in the example using biros in the text-book, but it is a useful exercise and when we go shopping we can save money like this. It is not necessarily the largest packet that is the cheapest per unit so it is always a good idea to check.

EXERCISE 11A

1 K116

Item	Unit cost (K)	Number	Cost (K)
Pad of paper	20	3	60
Pens	2	3	6
Exercise book	5	10	50
		Total spent	K116

2 He will have K115 change.
He should bring his mother K35.

Item	Unit cost (K)	Number	Cost (K)
Pineapple	15	1	15
Banana bunch	30	1	30
Oranges	K20 for 10	20	40
		Total spent	K85

3 K19 980

Item	Unit cost (K)	Number	Cost (K)
Netball	1600	3	4800
Football	1400	2	2800
Volleyball net	5000	1	5000
Volleyball	1200	5	6000
Saw	240	2	480
Hammer	300	3	900
		Total spent	K19 980

4 Yes he does have enough money. His change is K145.50.

Item	Unit cost (K)	Number	Cost (K)
Loaf of bread	20	2	40
Tin of margarine	64	2	128
Bar of soap	18	1	18
Maize flour	13 per kg	3 kg	39
Cooking oil	93 per *l*	0.5 *l*	46.50
Pkt of tea leaves	25	1	25
Toothpaste tube	58	1	58
		Total spent	K354.50

5 K27

Item	Unit cost (K)	Number	Cost (K)
Paraffin	11 per litre	3 litres	33
Margarine tin	64	1	64
Maize flour	13 per kg	2	26
		Total spent	K123

6 K212

Item	Unit cost (K)	Number	Cost (K)
Packet of milk	20	3	60
Beans	20 per kg	2 kg	40
Rice	23 per kg	4 kg	92
Loaf of bread	20	1	20
		Total spent	K212

7 K110.30

Item	Unit cost (K)	Number	Cost (K)
Loaf of bread	20	2	40
Maize flour	13 per kg	0.6 kg	7.80
Cooking oil	93 per litre	0.5litre	46.50
Beans	20 per kg	0.8 kg	16
		Total spent	K110.30

8 K2900

Item	Unit cost (K)	Number	Cost (K)
Volleyball	1200	1	1200
Netball	1600	1	1600
Music cassette	50	2	100
		Total spent	K2900

9 K96.25

Item	Unit cost (K)	Number	Cost (K)
Rice	23 per kg	0.5 kg	11.50
Beans	20 per kg	0.75 kg	15.00
Cooking oil	93 per litre	0.75 litre	69.75
		Total spent	K96.25

10 2 kg bags are cheaper (they cost K20.50 per kg).

11 Packets of 10 are cheaper – pencils cost K1.35 each (pencils in the packs of 6 cost K1.50 each).

• Commission

Commissions are a simple application of percentages. This section revises students' previous work on the topic which was covered in the primary school. Use as many realistic examples as possible.

EXERCISE 11B

1 K24.72 2 K4680

3 K4340 4 K1456

• Income tax

There are several different types of tax. This section looks at income tax. The teacher should discuss with students the importance of taxes. The taxes which the government collects help pay for the provision of social services in the community. They help pay for the building and operating of health centres, roads and schools and for providing clean water, amongst other things.

• Value added tax (VAT)

Value added tax (VAT) is charged on many goods that are sold in shops. Food, educational materials and agricultural inputs are not charged VAT. VAT is usually calculated as a percentage of the value of what is being sold.

• Sales tax

Find out the actual rates of sales tax at present when you teach this topic. These rates change from time to time.

EXERCISE 11C

1 K754 2 K336

3 K61 4 K19.80

5 a K9600 b K80 000

• Household bills

This section introduces students to some of the bills urban dwellers have to pay for the services provided by the City Assembly and other organisations like ESCOM, the Water Board and Malaŵi Post and Telecommunications Corporation. Students can bring bills from their homes to use in class. Teachers should contact the organisations concerned to get up-to-date information and leaflets containing details of current services and charges.

EXERCISE 11D

1 a K532.82 b K356.59 c K432.00
2 a 508.88 kWh b 957.48 kWh c 1120.13 kWh
3 a K435.33 b K644.43 c K742.83
d K288.23

• Insurance

This section introduces students to several types of insurance – life, car and home insurance. People insure to guard against the value of a loss. The money is paid to the insurance company each month or each year.

• Life insurance

Wise people insure their lives so that their family has some money if they die when they are young.

EXERCISE 11E

1 a K18.70 b K31.75
2 K1.60

• Car insurance

Car insurance is compulsory in Malaŵi. The law requires that every car is insured. Try to find out actual insurance rates for cars. These rates change from year to year.

EXERCISE 11F

a K311.95 b K279.20

12 Polygons

• Aim of chapter The aim of the chapter is to teach the angle properties of triangles and polygons.

• Objectives By the end of the chapter the students will be able to:

1 Show practically the sum of the angles of a triangle is 180°
2 Show that each exterior angle is equal to the sum of the interior opposite angles
3 Identify and solve angle problems involving right-angled, acute-angled, obtuse-angled, isosceles, equilateral and scalene triangles
4 Construct a triangle using a ruler and compasses when all three sides are known
5 Construct a triangle using a ruler, protractor and compasses when two sides and the angle between them are known
6 Construct a triangle using a ruler, protractor and compasses when one side and two angles are known
7 Identify pentagons, hexagons, octagons and decagons
8 Find the sum of the interior angles of any polygon
9 Show that the sum of the exterior angles of a polygon is 360° and use this to solve problems
10 Find the interior and exterior angles of any regular polygon
11 Draw regular polygons
12 Identify congruent triangles.

• Triangles The two standard methods by which students can discover for themselves the sum of the angles of any triangle are given in the text-book. Both methods should be used. The first method is to measure the angles of a triangle and add them up. Students should all draw different shaped triangles so that they can see that the shape makes no difference. Some pupils should draw obtuse-angled triangles to show that the rule applies to this sort of triangle as well.

The exercise on cutting up triangles is also worth doing. The pupils can draw their triangles on any old piece of rough paper.

If you have no scissors, you can cut the paper by folding along the lines of the triangle and tearing the paper. If you make the fold very firmly the paper should tear in a straight line.

EXERCISE 12A

This exercise is a practical activity designed to enable students to discover the angle sum of any triangle by drawing triangles, measuring the sizes of the angles and adding them together.

1 The length of the longest side is always less than the sum of the lengths of the other two sides.

2 **a** The sum of the angles is always 180°.
b Yes
c Yes

Because the sum of the angles of a triangle and the sum of the angles of a straight line are both 180°, the exterior angle property holds:

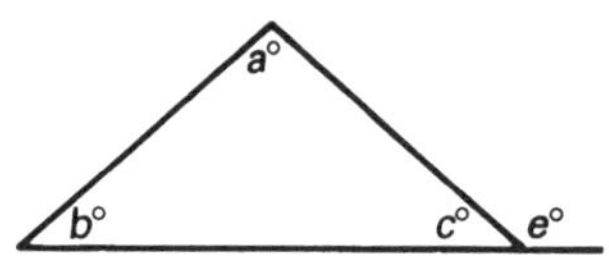

$(a+b)+c=180$
$e+c=180$
So $a+b=e$

EXERCISE 12B

This exercise is a practical activity designed to enable students to find out for themselves that the exterior angles of any triangle are equal to the sum of the two interior opposite angles. They each draw a triangle and find out this result by measurement.

$b+c=i=d \qquad a+b=e=f \qquad c+a=g=h$

EXERCISE 12C

Before students carry out this exercise, do a couple of worked examples on the board.

a	$a=125°$	$b=55°$	$c=150°$	$d=155°$
b	$p=140°$	$q=130°$	$r=90°$	$s=90°$
c	$w=150°$	$x=30°$	$y=100°$	$z=70°$
d	$k=155°$	$l=145°$	$m=10°$	$n=170°$

• Special triangles

In this section, students are introduced to all the different types of triangles. These are right-angled, acute-angled, obtuse-angled, isosceles, equilateral and scalene. They should draw all these triangles and find out their properties practically for themselves.

The easiest way to draw an isosceles triangle is on squared paper, using the fact that the base is bisected by the height at right angles:

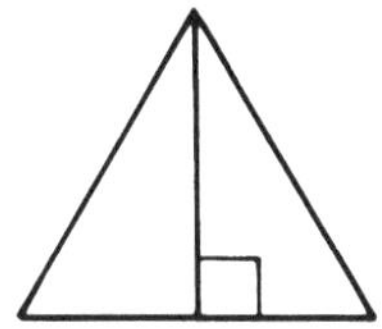

EXERCISE 12D

1 a Obtuse-angled b Equilateral
c Isosceles, acute-angled d Isosceles, right-angled
e Equilateral f Obtuse-angled
g Right-angled

2 a $a=91°$ b $b=59°$ c $c=55°$
d $d=130°$ e $e=100°$ f $f=60°$

• Constructing triangles

This section looks in detail at the construction of triangles using ruler and compass. The emphasis should be on neat and accurate work. There are six pieces of information we could be told about a triangle. We could be told the lengths of three sides and the sizes of three angles, but we do not need all this information in order to draw a triangle. As we shall see, we can draw a triangle accurately with less information than this.

EXERCISE 12E

Different members of the class will have triangles that are different sizes. They will all be the same shape.

• Three sides given

When we know the lengths of all three sides, we can draw the triangle uniquely and accurately and find out the sizes of the angles by measurement.

• Two sides and one angle given

This is the most tricky case. If the angle we are given is the angle between the two sides whose lengths we know then we can draw the triangle:

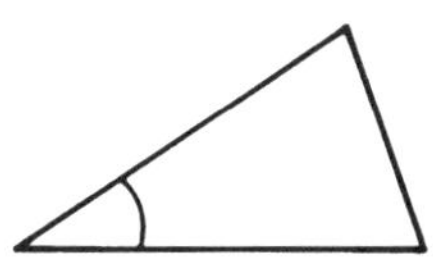

If the angle we are given is not the angle between the two sides whose lengths we know, then we can draw two possible triangles to fit the data:

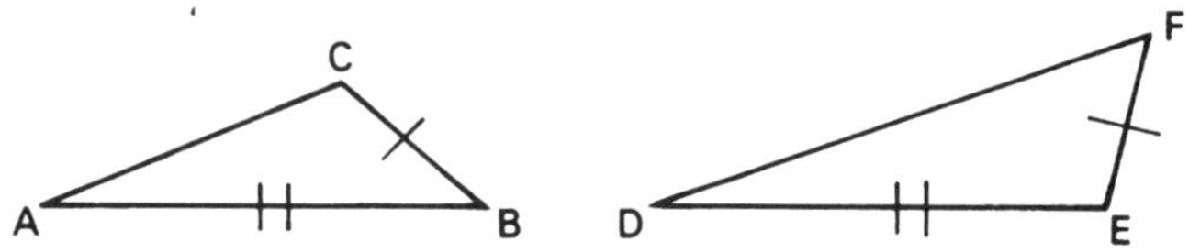

In the two triangles above, AB = DE, angle BAC = angle EDF and BC = EF, but the triangles are not congruent.

• One side and two angles given

When we know two angles of a triangle we also know the third, because the three angles must add up to 180°. When we know the angles, we know the shape of the triangle. If we are also told one side, that is enough for us to know the size of the triangle.

EXERCISE 12F

1, 2, 3 Construct triangles, measure angles and sides as stated in question.

4 a Yes b No c Yes d Yes
 e Yes f Yes

5 Construct triangles.

• Congruency

This section looks in detail at the concept of congruency applied to shapes with three and more sides. Understanding of congruency depends on experiencing real life examples. Discuss such examples with the students.

EXERCISE 12G

1 B and H, D and F

• Congruent triangles

This section looks further at the ideas developed earlier in the sections on constructing triangles. If we know the lengths of the three sides of a triangle, for example, then we know enough to be able to construct the triangle. If we know that two triangles have sides which are the same length then we know enough to be able to say that two triangles which share those measurements are congruent.

This is the reason that the four sets of the minimum information needed to construct a triangle are the same as the four sets of minimum conditions for being able to say that two triangles are congruent:

Side – included angle – side (SAS)
Angle – angle – side (AAS)
Side – side – side (SSS)
Right angle – hypotenuse – side (RHS)

The tricky case – side, side and an angle that is not included – also needs to be discussed.

EXERCISE 12H

1 DEF

2 **a** CXD **b** DXA

3 **a** $K\hat{H}M$ **b** XY **c** KM **d** $Y\hat{X}Z$

EXERCISE 12I

1 All three (AAS) 2 Only GHJ and KLM

3 $A\hat{X}C$ and $P\hat{X}R$; $A\hat{X}B$ and $R\hat{X}Q$; $B\hat{X}C$ and $Q\hat{X}P$

EXERCISE 12J

1 GHJ (RHS), NPQ (RHS), MLK (SAA)

2 **a** No **b** Yes (SAS) **c** Yes (SAS)

• Polygons

The rest of the chapter looks at polygons, their special names and their angle properties.

EXERCISE 12K

1 **a** 5 **b** AC, AD, BE, BD, CE

2 **a** 2 diagonals

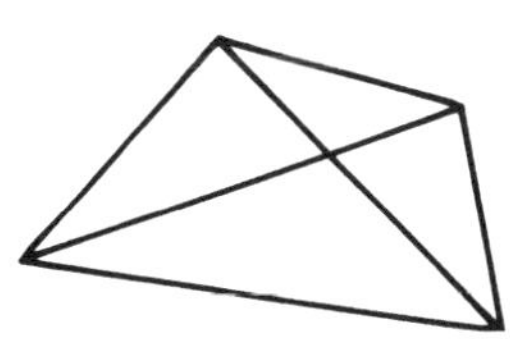

b 9 diagonals

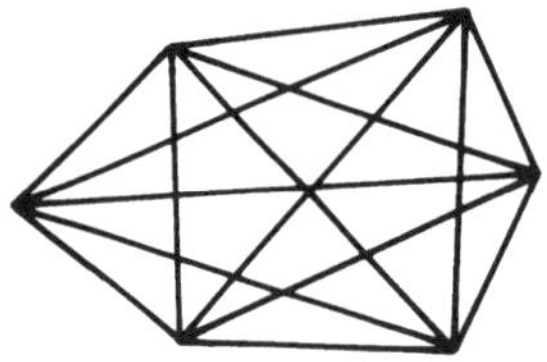

c 0 diagonals

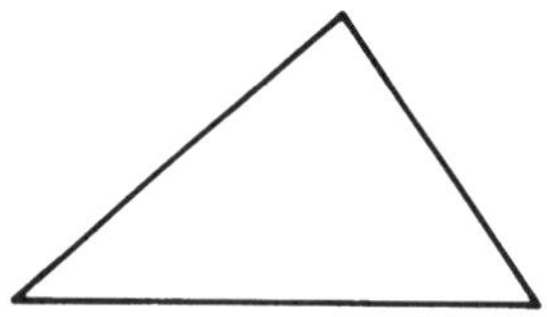

• Interior angles of a polygon

This section uses the previous work on the diagonals of a polygon to divide polygons into triangles and thereby find out the angle sum of a polygon. Notice that the diagonals are all drawn from one vertex. If the diagonals were drawn from more than one vertex the triangles would overlap and we would have angles in the middle of the figure to consider. By drawing all the diagonals from one point there is no overlap and the angles of the triangles are precisely the angles of the polygon.

Since a polygon with n sides can be divided into $(n-2)$ triangles it must have an angle sum of $(n-2) \times 180°$.

• Exterior angles

This section establishes the remarkable fact that the exterior angles of a polygon, taken in order (that means going round the polygon in the same direction taking one exterior angle at each vertex), always add up to 360°, no matter how many sides the polygon has. The justification given derives from a consideration of a journey round a polygon. As we move from one side to the next, we turn through an exterior angle. Going round the polygon means we turn through all the exterior angles, but it also means we make one complete revolution of 360°. We deduce therefore that the sum of the exterior angles is 360°. The greater the number of sides the polygon has, the smaller each exterior angle will be.

EXERCISE 12L

1 a 1440° b 3600° c 2700°
  d 4500° e 3060° f 2160°

2 a 39° b 36° c 120°

3 Seven 900°

4 105°

5 a 12 sides b 20 sides c 30 sides

6 a 180 000° b 180 000 000°

7 $a = 174$. The interior angles are 119°, 108°, 127° and 6°

8 54°

• Regular polygons

The fact that the exterior angles of any polygon add up to 360° is very helpful when calculating the angles of regular polygons. The interior angle at a vertex and the exterior angle there always add up to 180° because they make up a straight line. It is often easier to find the interior angles of a regular polygon by dividing 360° by the number of sides; this gives us the exterior angle which we then subtract from 180° to find the interior angle.

EXERCISE 12M

1 a 20° b 18 sides

2 a 6°, 60 sides
  b 18°, 20 sides
  c 1°, 180 sides

3 a 36°
  b (i) 36° (ii) 72° (iii) 36°

4 a Yes, a 15-sided polygon b No

• Drawing regular polygons

The chapter ends with a practical drawing exercise. The book offers a simple way of constructing regular polygons. For an n-sided regular polygon, the angle subtended by each side at the centre is $360°/n$. Measure out n of these angles. The arms of the angles cut a circle at the vertices of an n-sided regular polygon. The angles are easier to draw if n is a factor of 360.

EXERCISE 12N

The students should draw some attractive neat figures.

13 Statistics

• Aim of chapter

The aim of the chapter is to display information using pictograms, bar and pie charts and line graphs, and to interpret information displayed in these ways.

• Objectives

By the end of the chapter the students will be able to:
1 Use a variety of means to collect data
2 Display and interpret information using pictograms
3 Display and interpret information using pie charts
4 Display and interpret information using bar graphs
5 Display and interpret information using line graphs
6 Find the mean, median and mode of scores
7 Decide which is the best of the mean, median and mode to describe particular sets of data.

• Introducing statistics

This section introduces the students in a simple way to the use of statistics.

• Collecting data

The numbers that are used in statistics have to be collected somehow. Discussion should centre on how statistics are collected sorted, displayed and analysed.

• Pictograms

A pictogram is a way of displaying data using pictures or symbols to represent the data we want to show. Sometimes a picture will stand for one item, as in the first example in the textbook, where one egg stands for one egg laid. Sometimes a picture stands for more than one item; in the example in the text, a picture of a goat stands for five goats.

EXERCISE 13A

1

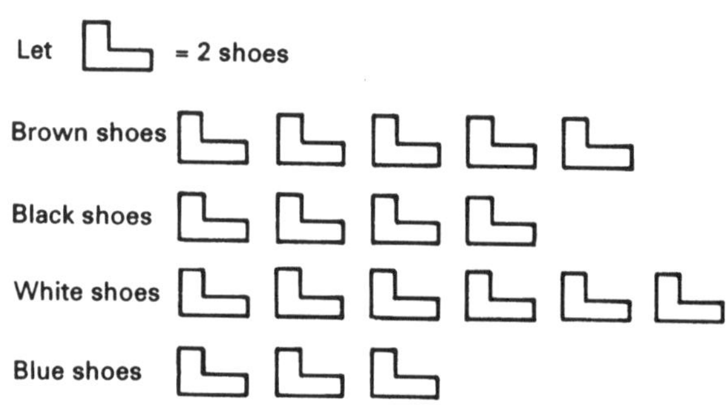

2

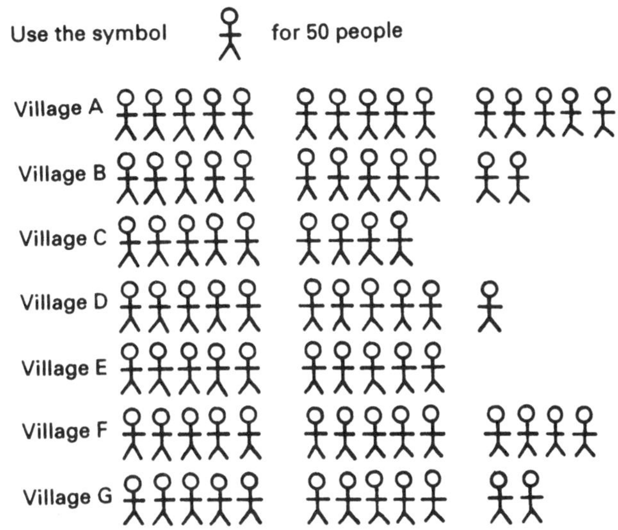

3

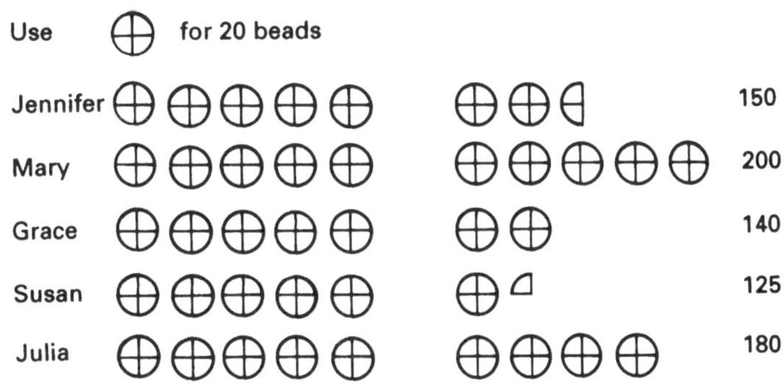

- **Pie charts**

Pie charts are good for illustrating how something is shared. For example in the text-book a farmer divides his land between grazing, corn, cabbages and tomatoes. The pie chart shows the proportion of his land that is being used for each purpose.

When drawing a pie chart, the students should start by drawing a circle with a compass. The sector sizes are calculated so that their areas are in proportion to the number they represent. The size of the area is determined by the angle at the centre of the sector. Make sure that the students label their diagrams and each sector clearly.

EXERCISE 13B

1 The total number of hours is 24.

a Sleeping $\frac{7}{24} \times 360° = 105°$

b Working $\frac{8}{24} \times 360° = 120°$

c Eating $\frac{2}{24} \times 360° = 30°$

d Reading $\frac{1}{24} \times 360° = 15°$

e Travelling $\frac{2}{24} \times 360° = 30°$

f Washing $\frac{1}{24} \times 360° = 15°$

g Talking $\frac{3}{24} \times 360° = 45°$

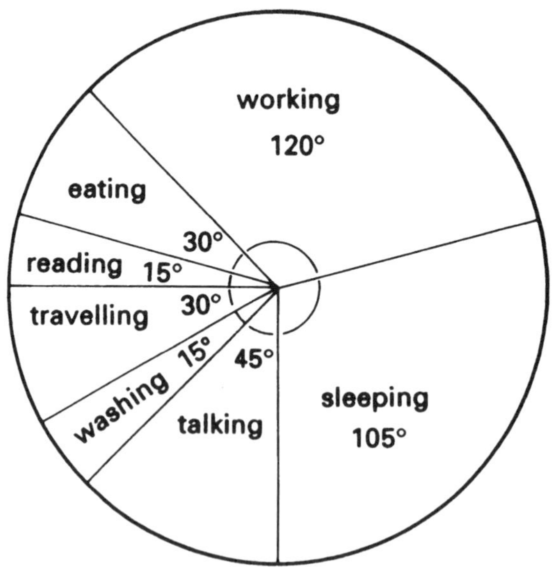

2 The total number of marbles is 720.

a Blue marbles $\frac{120}{720} \times 360° = 60°$

b Red marbles $\frac{180}{720} \times 360° = 90°$

c Green marbles $\frac{90}{720} \times 360° = 45°$

d Yellow marbles $\frac{225}{720} \times 360° = 112.5°$

e White marbles $\frac{105}{720} \times 360° = 52.5°$

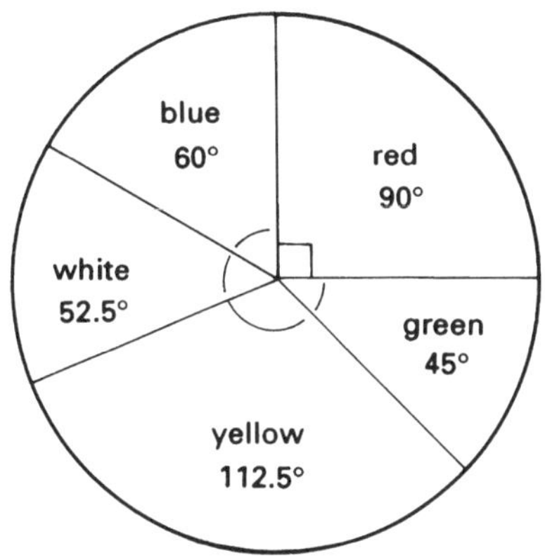

3 The total number of vehicles and other transport is 180.

a Cars $\frac{70}{180} \times 360° = 140°$

b Lorries $\frac{30}{180} \times 360° = 60°$

c Buses $\frac{15}{180} \times 360° = 30°$

d Bicycles $\frac{40}{180} \times 360° = 80°$

e Donkeys $\frac{5}{180} \times 360° = 10°$

f Walkers $\frac{20}{180} \times 360° = 40°$

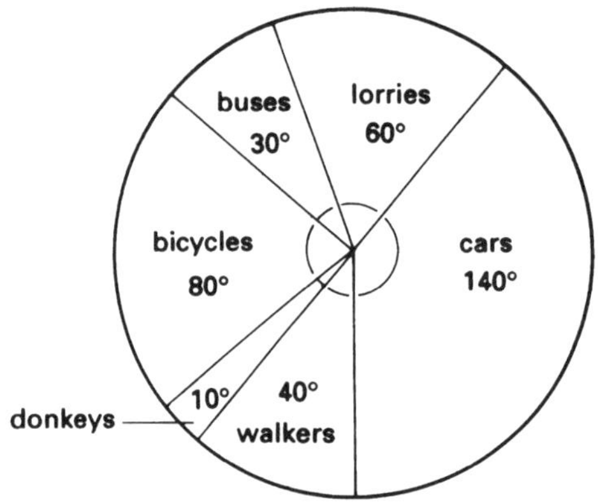

- **Bar graphs** When we use bar graphs to show information, the number or quantity of each item is shown by the height or length of the bar.

All the bars have the same width.

Charts should be drawn on a grid and should be given a title.

EXERCISE 13C

1

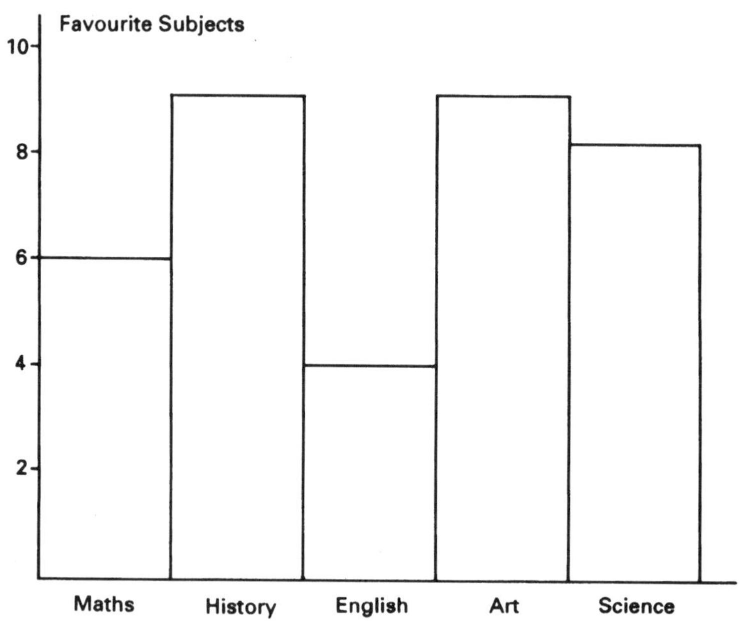

2

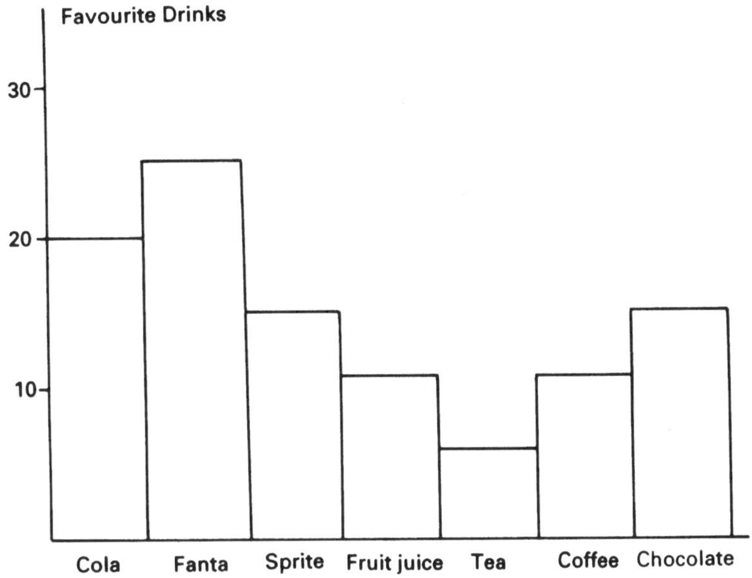

• Line graphs Line graphs are often used to show how quantities, such as the height of a plant or person or the temperature of a patient, change over time.

EXERCISE 13D

1

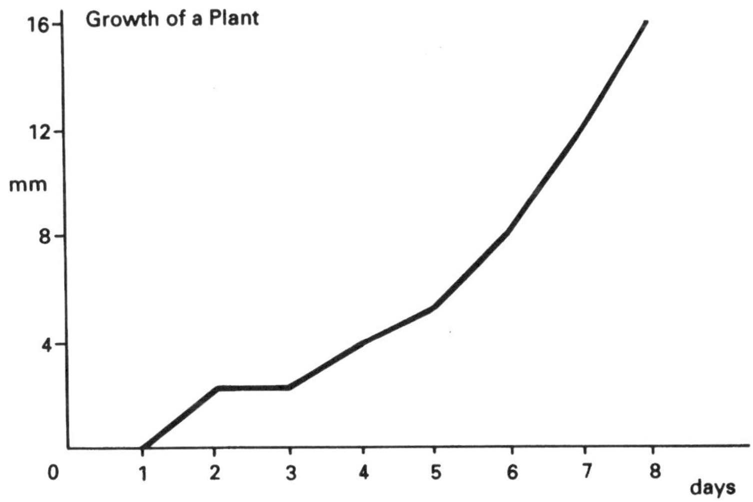

2

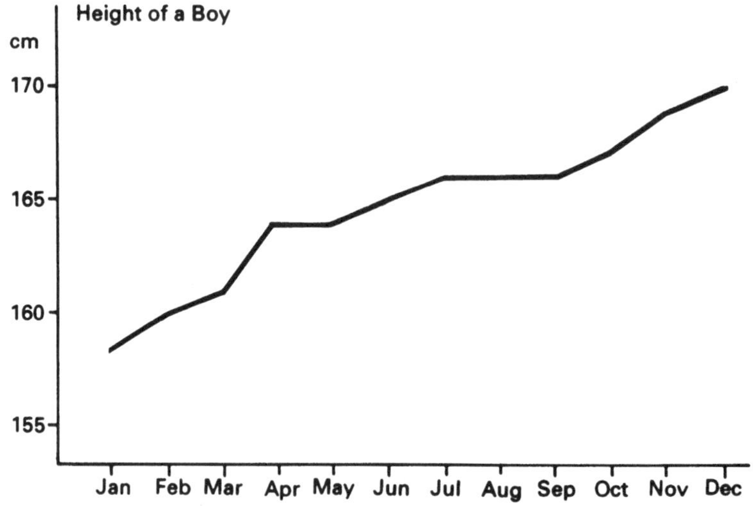

3

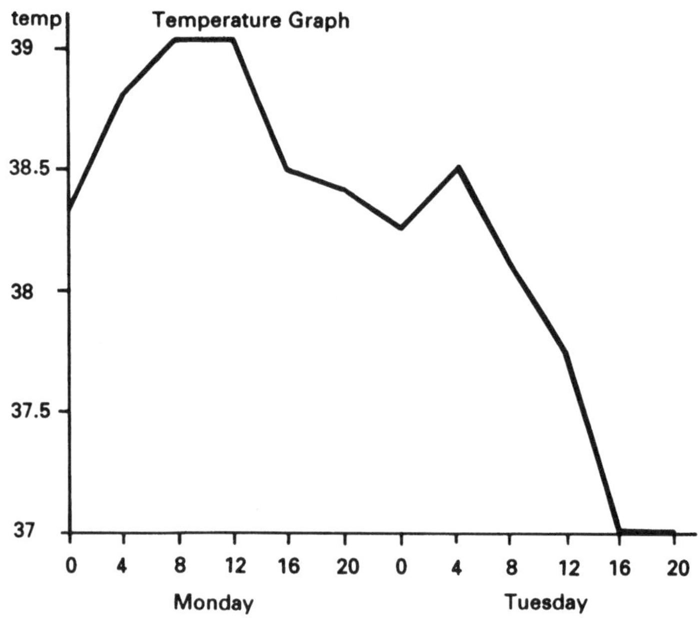

• Averages

We use averages to give an impression of data without having to look at all of it. One number is used as a representative of all the data. It is important that students understand the different types of average (mean, median and mode) and when it is appropriate to use each of them.

• Which average?

Each of the mean, median and mode has its advantages and disadvantages. We now summarise these:

The mean

Advantages of mean	Disadvantages of mean
Easy to work out with a calculator	Can only be used for numbers and measurements
Use all the data	Not always one of the values
This is what most people think of as the average	A few very large or small numbers can affect its size significantly

To illustrate the disadvantage of the way a few very large numbers can affect the mean significantly, consider a shop where the wages paid are K1000, K1000, K1000, K2000 and K100 000. The mean wage is K21 000, very much larger than all the wages except one.

The median

Advantages of median	Disadvantages of median
Easy to find when the values are in order	Can only be used for numbers or measurements
Is one of the values if you have an odd number of measurements	May not be one of the values if you have an even number of measurements
	A lot of values can take a long time to put in order

The mode

Advantages of mode	Disadvantages of mode
Can be found for any kind of data	Not very useful for small numbers
Simple to find by counting, not calculating	There may be more than one mode
Quick, easy to find from a frequency table, bar chart, pictogram or pie chart	

Students often confuse mean, median and mode. When writing test questions choose the numbers in such a way that the mean, median and mode have different values. If the values are the same (as in question 3c in Exercise 13E) the students can get the answers correct without having understood which is which.

EXERCISE 13E

1	Mean = 19	Median = 19.5	Mode = 20
2	Mean = K1.46	Median = K1.46	Mode = K 1.45 and K 1.50
3	a Mean = 7.27	Median = 7	Mode = 7 and 10
	b Mean = 12	Median = 11.5	Mode = 10
	c Mean = 13	Median = 13	Mode = 13
4	a Mean = 13	Median = 13	Mode = 11 and 13
	b Mean = 29.67	Median = 30.5	Mode = 31
	c Mean = 13	Median = 13	Mode = 13
5	Mean = 2.3	Median = 3	Mode = 3
6	Mean = 8.14	Median = 8	Mode = 8

14 More algebra

• Aim of chapter

The aim of the chapter is to introduce and develop the use of brackets and inequalities in algebra.

• Objectives

By the end of the chapter the students will be able to:

1. Use and multiply out algebraic expressions involving brackets
2. Simplify algebraic expressions
3. Solve algebraic equations
4. Express word problems as equations and solve them
5. Evaluate expressions and formulas by substitution
6. Use the inequality symbols $<$, $>$, $\leqslant$ and $\geqslant$
7. Represent inequalities on the number line
8. Solve inequalities involving two inequality symbols
9. Factorise algebraic expressions
10. Find the HCF and LCM of algebraic terms.

• Brackets in algebra

We need brackets to show the order in which operations are to be carried out. Brackets are used whenever we want the expression inside to be treated as a whole. Whenever something is done to a bracket what is done is done to everything inside it. So if a bracket is multiplied or divided by a number then every term inside it is multiplied or divided by that number. The signs inside the bracket are not changed.

It is important that students learn to use brackets properly, because errors with brackets are probably the most common errors made in algebra. The confusion is understandable: 'x add 5 multiply by 2' is written $(x+5)\times 2$ whereas the very similar 'x multiply by 2 add 5' is written $2x+5$, with no brackets involved. The practical examples are most important: teaching brackets as just a rule without explanation is counter-productive, for without the students being convinced of the rules of brackets, they will often make the mistake $9(x+y)=9x+y$ when it should be $9(x+y)=9x+9y$.

EXERCISE 14A

1 a $4c+12$ b $15-3p$ c $6+6y$ d $8a+2$
e $3h-27$ f $21f+49$ g $27y-18$ h $24-16m$
i $144+12e$ j $4n-24$ k $6m-6n$ l $ar-2a$

2 a $2m+4n$ b $3an-3a$ c $6b-2c$ d $8x-12y$
e $6pq-6q$ f $7jk+7j$

• Common factors

Emphasise the point that finding factors in algebra is very similar to finding factors in arithmetic. In algebra brackets are used. In most cases separate the factors to avoid confusion. Some of the students may have problems with the use of brackets.

EXERCISE 14B

1	$4(x+3y)$	2	$3(p-2q)$	3	$5(2b-1)$
4	$7(2m-3n)$	5	$4(3s+5t)$	6	$x(y+z)$
7	$y(y-z)$	8	$2y\ (y-z)$	9	$2(a+4b-2c)$
10	$7(p-2q+r)$	11	$xy(x+z+y)$	12	$4pq(r-3p)$

• Highest Common Factor and Lowest Common Multiple

In this section, students learn how to find the Highest Common Factor (HCF) and Lowest Common Multiple (LCM) of pairs of terms. The process is similar to the process that students have used in arithmetic.

• Rearranging formulas

Formulas are used to express one quantity in terms of other quantities. The subject of a formula is the letter that is left on its own on one side of the equality sign with all the other letters and numbers on the other side of the sign. A formula can be rearranged to change the subject. The procedure for changing the subject is very similar to the procedure for solving equations.

EXERCISE 14C

1 $B=\frac{V}{LW}$ 2 $h=\frac{A}{2\pi r}$ 3 $a=\frac{V-u}{t}$

4 $h=\frac{2A}{a+b}$ 5 $R=\frac{100(A-P)}{PT}$ 6 $h=\frac{A}{2\pi r}-r$

• Multiplication and division with fractions

Multiplying and dividing algebraic fractions is very similar to multiplying and dividing numerical fractions.

EXERCISE 14D

1 $\frac{b}{c}$ 2 $\frac{ae}{df}$ 3 $\frac{bd^2}{a}$ 4 $\frac{ad}{bc}$ 5 ae

6 $\frac{1}{ab}$ 7 $\frac{3b^2}{2a}$ 8 $\frac{5}{4}$ 9 $\frac{2}{3}$ 10 $\frac{(a+2b)^2}{ab}$

• Fractions in algebraic expressions

Emphasise the point that we can add and subtract fractions in algebraic expressions in exactly the same way as we add and subtract ordinary fractions. When the fractions have the same denominator we can add directly. When the fractions do not have the same denominator we need to find a common denominator.

The first exercise is an exercise on adding algebraic fractions.

EXERCISE 14E

1 $\frac{1}{6}(a+5)$ 2 $\frac{1}{9}(a+4)$ 3 $\frac{1}{7}(b+2)$ 4 $\frac{1}{12}(4a+9)$

5 $\frac{1}{9}(x+6)$ 6 $\frac{1}{6}(3e+5)$ 7 $\frac{1}{42}(6c+35)$ 8 $\frac{9a}{20}$

9 $\frac{1}{a}(c+d)$ 10 $\frac{1}{6}(a+8)$ 11 $\frac{1}{4}(b+1)$ 12 $\frac{1}{12}(20+7d)$

13 $\frac{2+ac+c}{2a+2}$ 14 $\frac{10-a}{6}$ 15 $\frac{1}{9c}(ac-4c+9b)$

The next exercise is an exercise on subtracting algebraic fractions.

EXERCISE 14F

1 a $\frac{1}{4}(a-1)$ b $\frac{1}{5}(3c-4)$ c $\frac{1}{7}(3-4d)$

d $\frac{1}{10}(25m-8)$ e $\frac{1}{9}(12q-2)$ f $\frac{1}{12}(9x-16y)$

g $\frac{1}{bc}(2c-3b)$ h $\frac{1}{3xy}(21y-2x)$

2 a $\frac{1}{4}(x-2)$ b $\frac{-1}{45}(22+9a)$ c $\frac{1}{56}(6-7a)$

d $\frac{3a-13}{12}$ e $\frac{2x-9}{6}$ f 1

3 a $\frac{1}{x(x+1)}$ b $\frac{-a-2b}{a\,(a-b)}$ c $\frac{p-4}{p(p-1)}$

d $\frac{12-17c}{3c\,(c+3)}$ e $\frac{25-4a}{10a}$ f $\frac{5z-18}{z(z-3)}$

• Algebraic equations

This important section gives practice in translating statements in English into mathematical language. Students learning in a second language can find this topic especially difficult, but it is important for them to master this because they will have to become proficient if they are to solve mathematical problems set in words.

EXERCISE 14G

1 $m+6=25$, 19 marbles

2 $\frac{1}{2}x=300$, K600

3 $\frac{1}{2}g=7$, 14 goats

4 $\frac{1}{4}p=32$, 128 pineapples (If she sold $\frac{3}{4}$, she has $\frac{1}{4}$ left.)

5 $b+(b-10)=48$, Ben has 29 sheep and Tom has 19 sheep

• Substituting in equations

A letter can have many values in an expression. In this section the students replace letters with particular numbers and evaluate expressions. In many cases they are given the value of one letter and are asked to find the other letter in the expression. They are in effect being asked to solve an equation.

EXERCISE 14H

1	a 31	b 19	c 3	
2	a 20	b 28	c 32	d 60
3	a 5	b 8	c 15	d 19
4	a 21	b 17	c 1	d 0
5	a 6	b 4	c 2	d 0
6	a 11	b 15	c 18	d 29
7	a 30	b 18	c 12	d 6
8	a 14	b 28	c 42	
9	a 32	b 25	c 60	
10	a 10	b 105	c 32	d 336

• The meaning of an inequality

This section introduces students to the four inequality signs, $>$(is greater than), $<$ (is less than), $\geqslant$ (is greater than or equal to) and $\leqslant$ (is less than or equal to).

$>$ and $<$ are quite straight-forward symbols. If $x>6$, for example, we know than x can be any number greater than 6. Students do have some difficulty with statements like $-100<2$, because they think that 100 is larger than 2. The point is that $>$ and $<$ tell us about the order of numbers on the number line.

There is some difficulty with $\leqslant$ 'is less than or equal to'. Some students think a statement like $6\leqslant6$ must be false. But $6\leqslant6$ is true. For an 'or' statement to be true only one part of the statement needs to be true. '$6\leqslant6$' is short for '6 is less than or equal to 6'. This is true because $6=6$. In the same way, the statement '$4 \leqslant 6$' (which is short for '4 is less than or equal to 6') is true because $4<6$.

Inequalities can be combined quite naturally. If $x<8$ and $x>4$, that means x is between 4 and 8. Write $4< x<8$ with x between the two numbers.

EXERCISE 14I

1 a $t<6$ b $t>9$ c $y>7$ d $a \leqslant 5$ e $p \geqslant 8$

2 a y is less than 7 b t is less than or equal to 4
c y is greater than 8 d t is greater than or equal to 3
e y is greater than 2 and less than 6
f y is greater than or equal to 3 and less than 9
g t is greater than or equal to 6 and less than or equal to 9

3 a $l<20$ b $h \leqslant 20$ c $8<d<12$ d $V \leqslant 5$

• Representing inequalities on the number line

When showing inequalities involving integers we put a dot for each number. When showing inequalities involving real numbers we show them with continuous lines. The end points are shown with small circles. There is a simple convention for distinguishing between $\geqslant$ and $>$.

If $x>5$ then 5 is not included, so a small open circle is used, but if $x \geqslant 5$, then 5 is included so a solid small circle is used.

EXERCISE 14J

1 a $x<5$

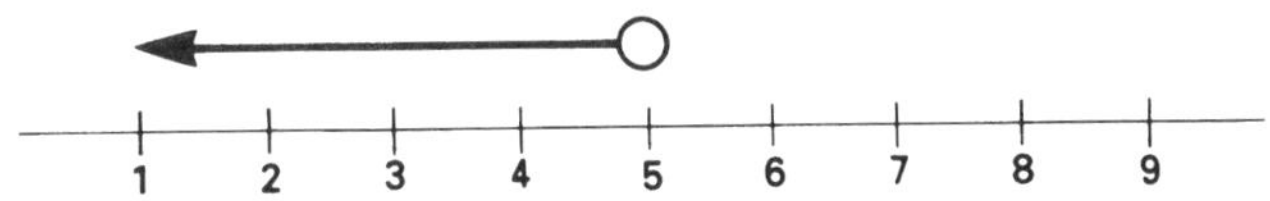

b $y>8$

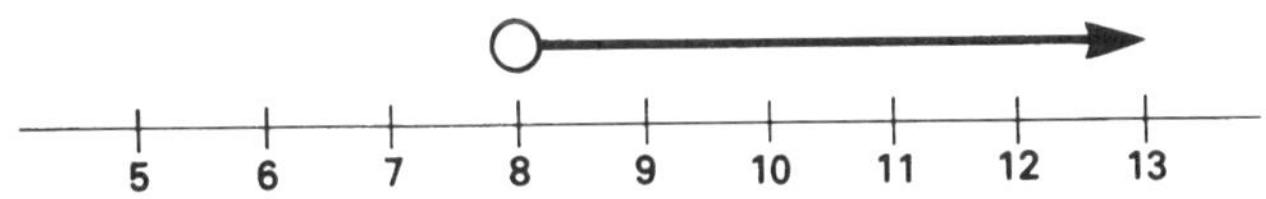

c $t \geq 9$

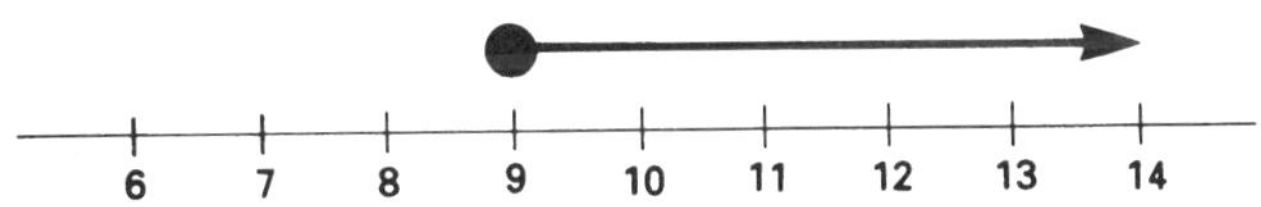

d $y \leq 2$

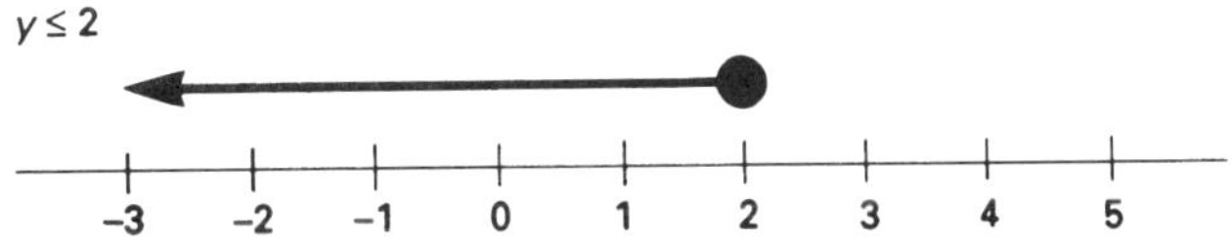

e $4>x>7$ (Note: harder question than for $4<x<7$)

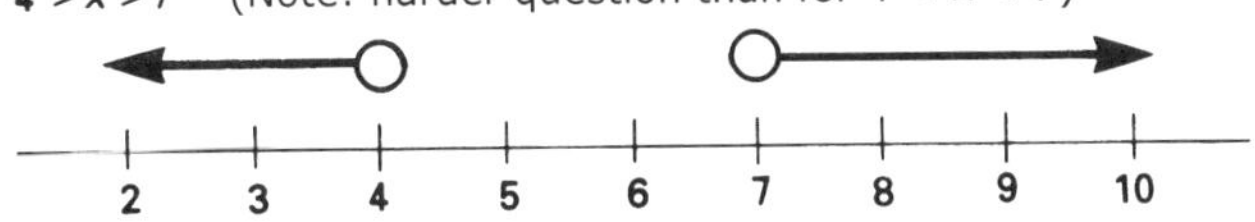

2 a

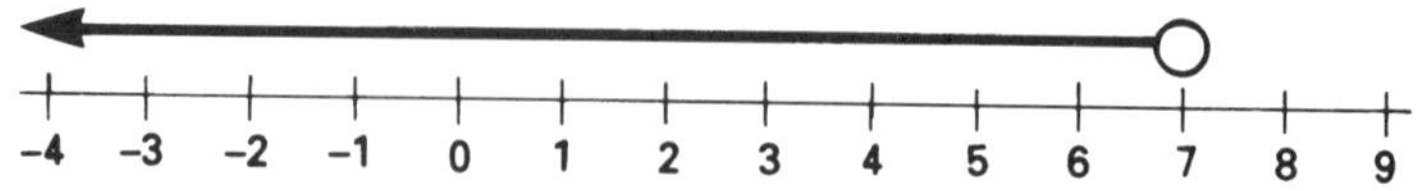

b

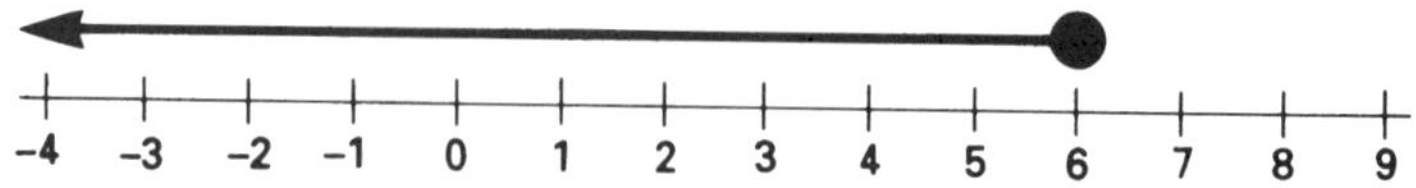

c

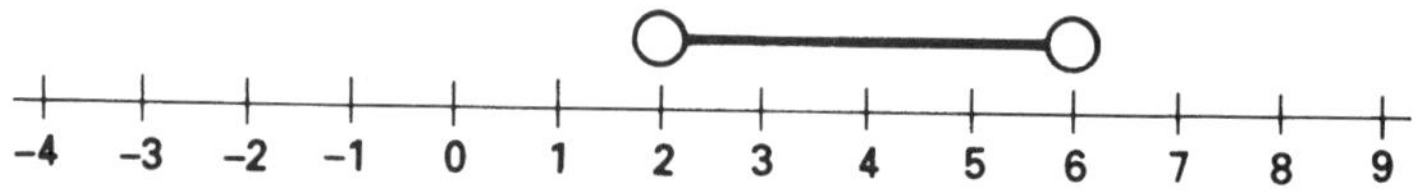

d

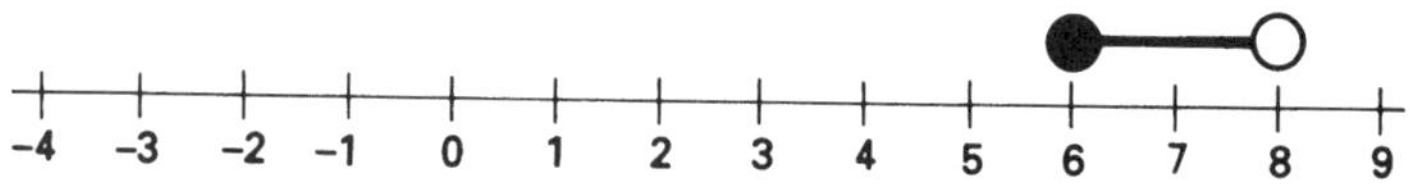

e

f

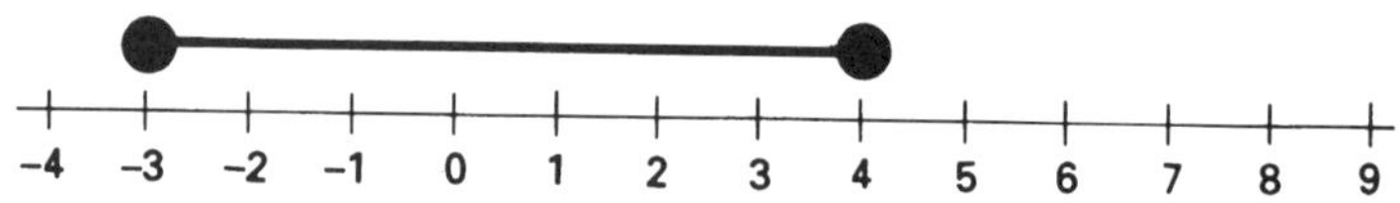

3 a

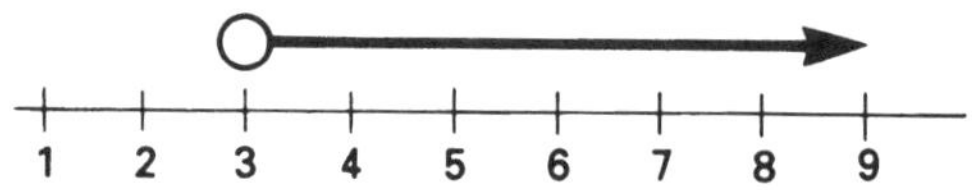

b

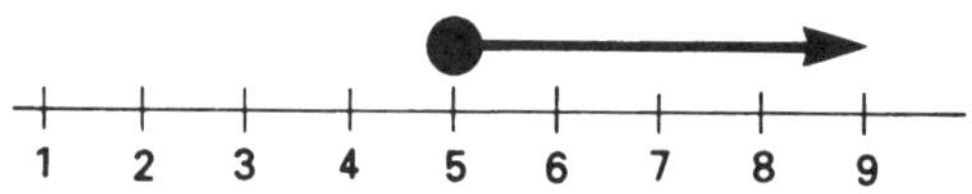

c

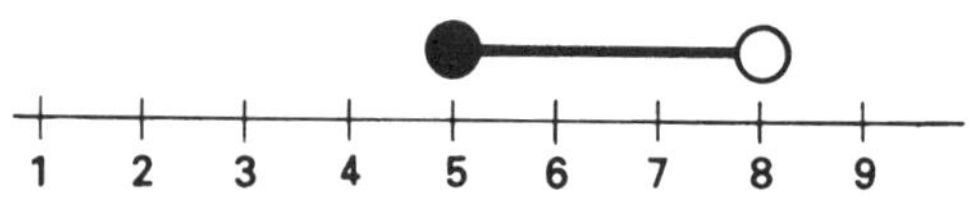

d

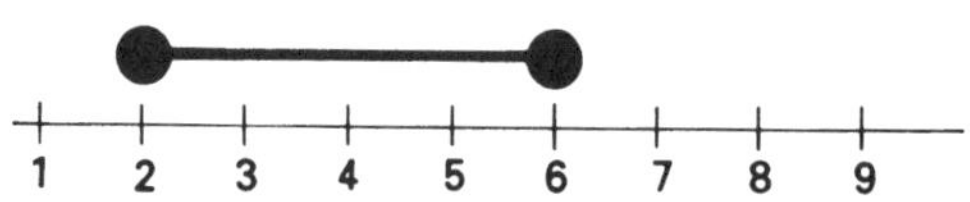

4 a $4 \leq x < 7$

b $b \leq 1$

c $-1 < y \leq 1$

d $x < 6$

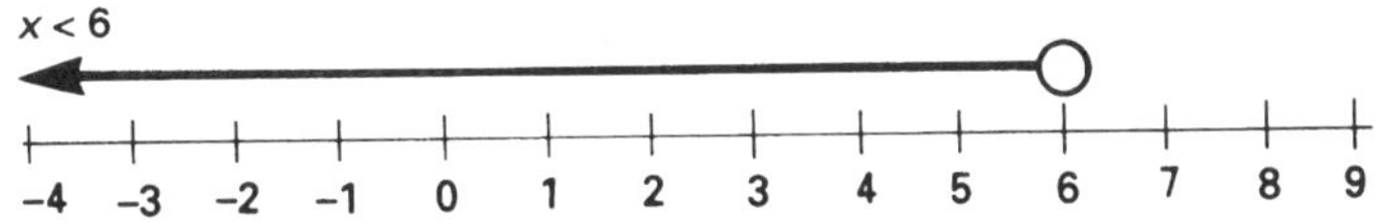

e $y \geq 0$

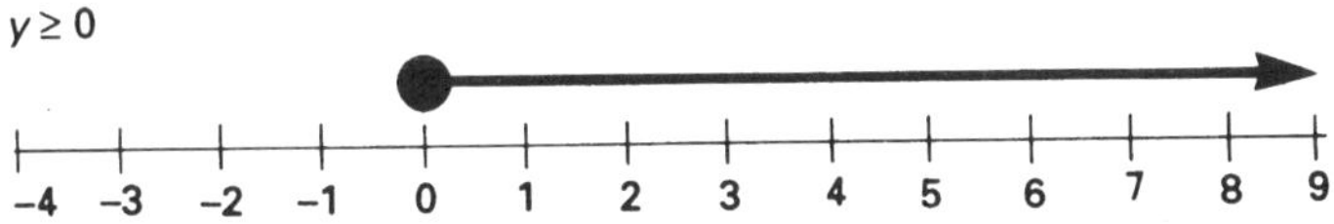

f $a \geq 2$

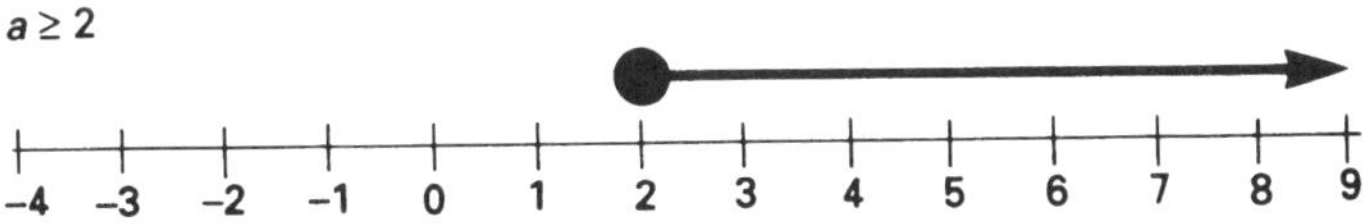

g $0 < p < 4$

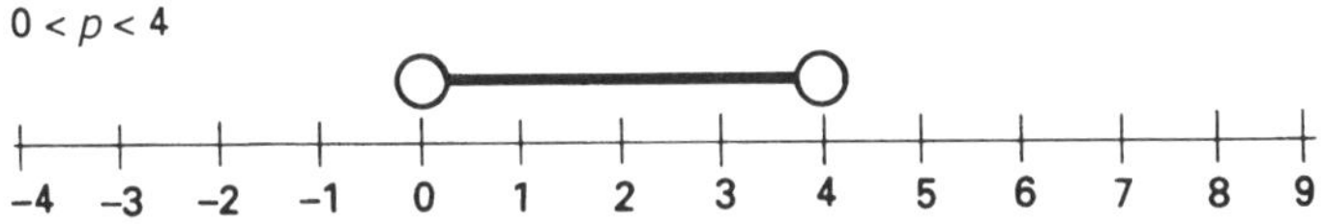

h $5 \leq q \leq 7$

• Solving inequalities

Inequalities are solved in the same way as equations, with one important exception. When we divide by a negative number we have to reverse the inequality.

EXERCISE 14K

1 a $r \geq 11$

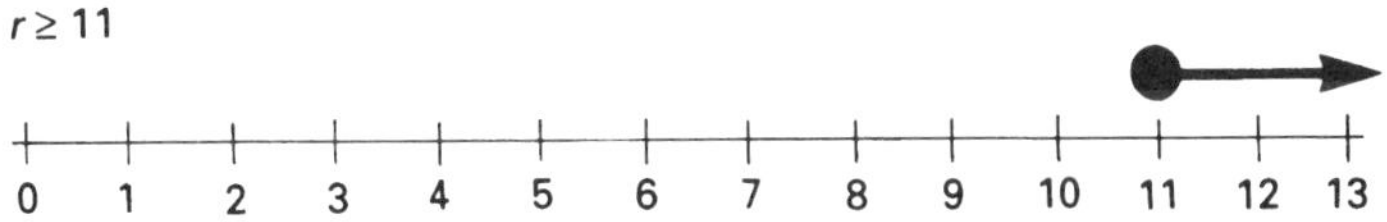

b $a < 1$

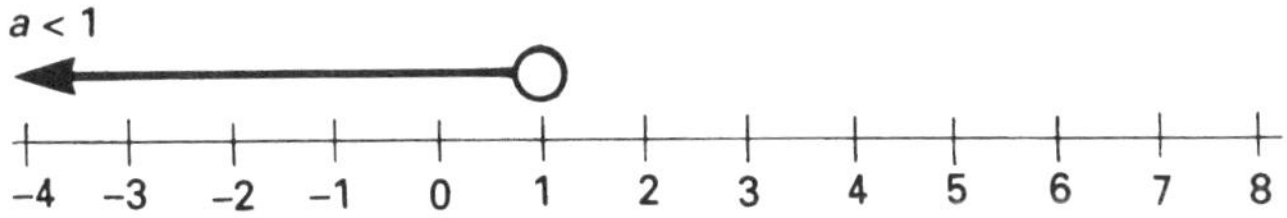

c $x \geq 2$

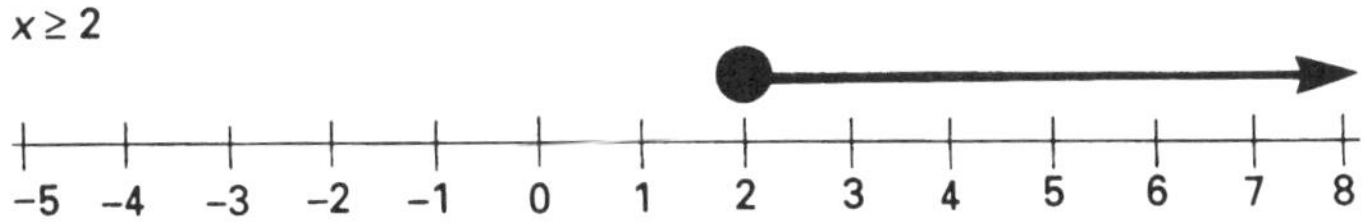

d $y > 4$

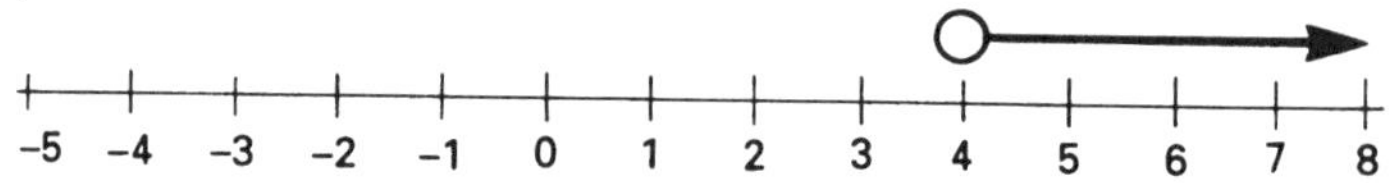

e $r < 16$

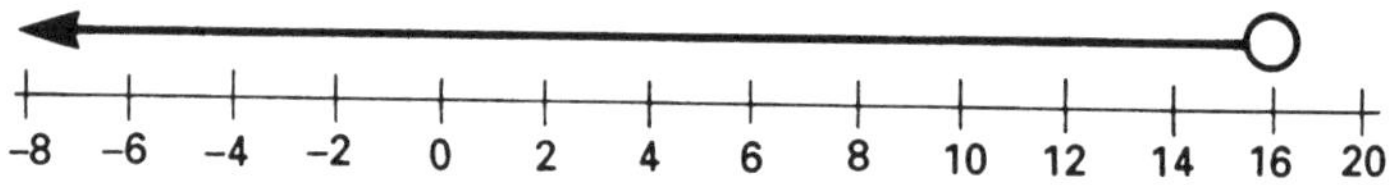

f $x \leq 2$

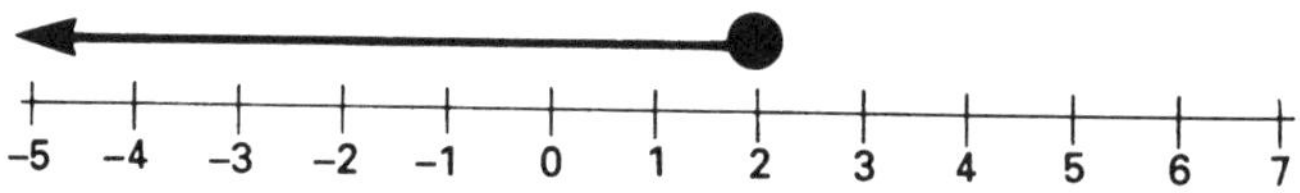

g $x < -2$

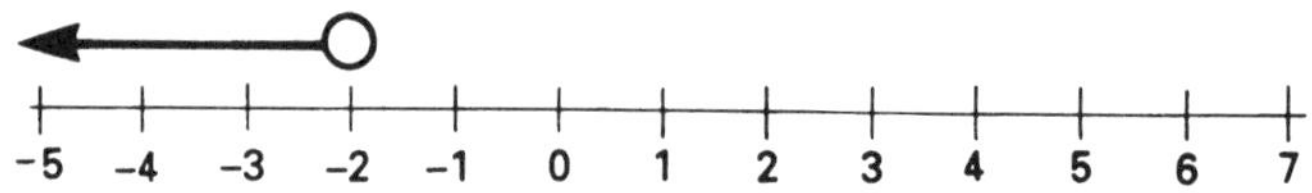

h $p > -4$

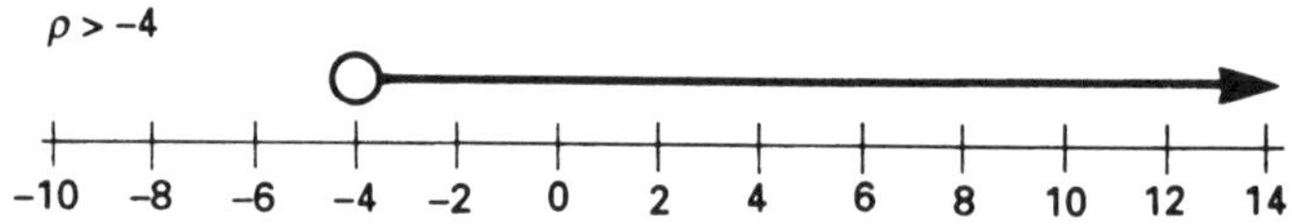

2 a $4 < r < 11$

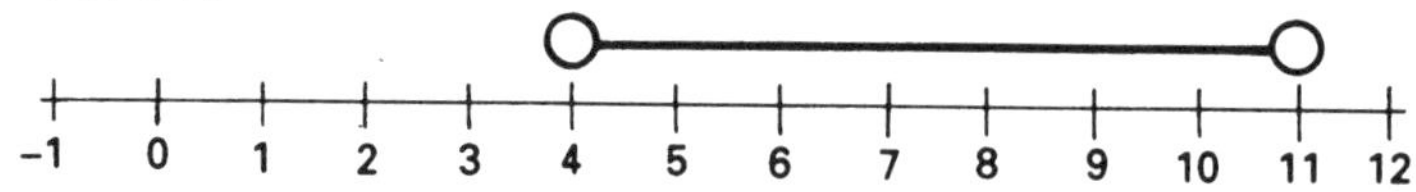

b $1 < a < 5$

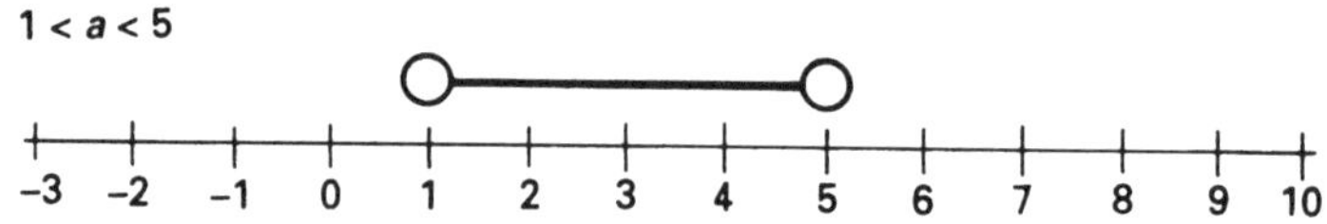

c $2 \leq x \leq 7$

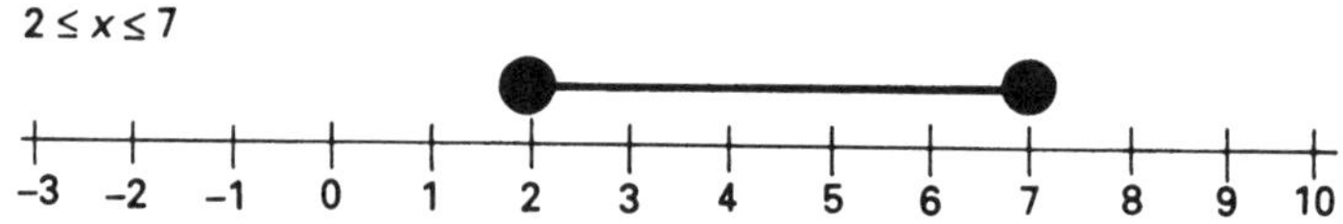

d $0 < y < 4$

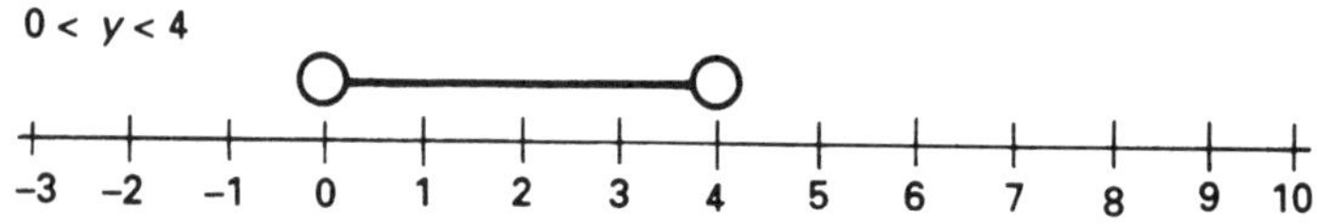

e $-3 \leq x < 2$

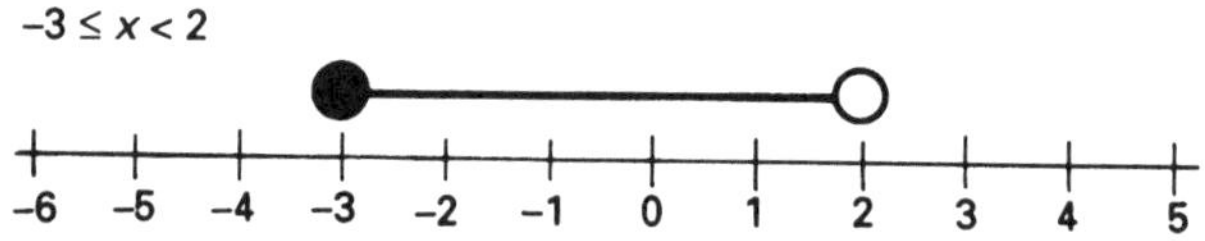

f $-2 < x \le 2$

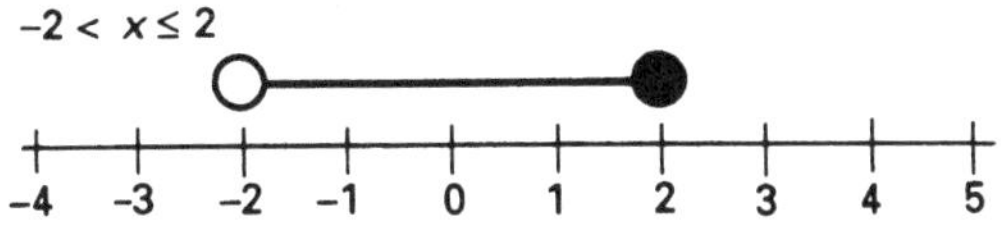

g $-2 \le x < 4$

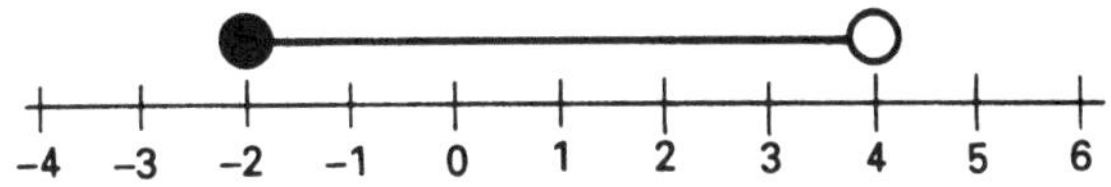

h $-3 < p < 2$

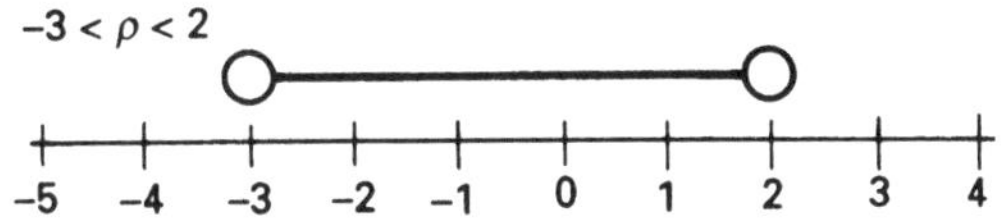

15 Geometric figures

• Aim of chapter The aim of the chapter is to teach the angle and length properties of quadrilaterals, including the special quadrilaterals: the square, the kite, the trapezium and the parallelogram, and the angle properties of parallel lines.

• Objectives By the end of the chapter the students will be able to:

1. Show the angle sum of any quadrilateral is 360°
2. Find and use the angle and length properties of squares
3. Find and use the angle and length properties of rectangles
4. Find and use the angle and length properties of kites
5. Find and use the angle and length properties of trapezia
6. Use the properties of alternate, corresponding and co-interior angles when a transversal cuts parallel lines
7. Find and use the angle and length properties of parallelograms.

• Quadrilateral This section consists of a practical exercise in which the pupils find out that the angle sum of any quadrilateral is 360°.

EXERCISE 15A The students should all draw different sizes and shapes of quadrilaterals. Discourage them from drawing rectangles. Question 5 shows how a quadrilateral can be divided into two triangles. From this we can see that the angle sum of a quadrilateral must be twice that of a triangle.

• Special quadrilaterals The square is the regular four-sided figure. In the exercise the properties are discovered by drawing. This work is most simply done on squared paper. If their exercise books do not have

• Squares

squares in them, try to give the students squared paper for this work. Squared paper exercise books are very useful in many topics: graphs, geometry and arithmetic.

The students should be allowed to do the work on their own in their exercise books and discover the results for themselves. The results can then be discussed towards the end of the lesson by the class as a whole for consolidation. It is important that the students have a correct summary of the properties of a square in their exercise books when they have finished the exercise.

EXERCISE 15B

1 Students should each draw a square in their exercise book and label it ABCD. These squares should not all be the same size so that the result can be seen to be true for different sizes of square.

2 The angles are all equal to 90°, $a=b=c=d=90°$
Angle ABC = angle BCD = angle CDA = angle DAC = 90°

3 The sides are all the same length.
AB = BC = CD = DA

4 Students may have forgotten what the word 'diagonal' means.

5 The two diagonals are the same length.
AC = BD

6 The diagonals bisect each other. The distance between a corner and the point where the diagonals meet is the same for all corners. The distance is half the length of a diagonal.
If we label the point where they meet O,

$OA = OB = OC = OD = \frac{1}{2}AC$

7 The diagonals bisect each other at right angles.
Angle AOB = angle BOC = angle COD = angle DOA = 90°

8 They are all 45°. The diagonals bisect the angles of the square.

• Rectangles

The approach used is very similar to that used for the square: the students draw the shape and find out its properties by measurement. It is worth pointing out to the students that a square is a special type of rectangle: it is a rectangle with all four sides equal.

As before, the students should discover the properties for themselves and the results should be discussed and summarised at the end of the lesson.

EXERCISE 15C

1 Students should draw different size rectangles in their exercise books. They should label them ABCD.

2 The angles are all equal to 90°, $a=b=c=d=90°$
Angle ABC = angle BCD = angle CDA = angle DAC

3 Opposite sides are the same length.
AB = CD and BC = DA

4 Students should now know what the word 'diagonal' means.

5 The two diagonals are the same length.
AC = BD

6 The diagonals bisect each other. The distance between a corner and the point where the diagonals meet is the same for all corners. The distance is half the length of a diagonal. If we label the point where they meet O,

$OA = OB = OC = OD = \frac{1}{2}AC$

7 Where the diagonals meet, opposite angles are equal.
Angle AOB = angle COD and angle BOC = angle DOA

8 The diagonals do not bisect the angles of a rectangle.

• Kites

Drawing a kite on squared paper can be simplified by using the properties of its diagonals. Draw a vertical line, bisect it and draw a horizontal line through the mid-point. If you draw the horizontal line so that it is not bisected by the vertical line, you have drawn a kite. If the vertical line bisects the horizontal line, then you have drawn a rhombus.

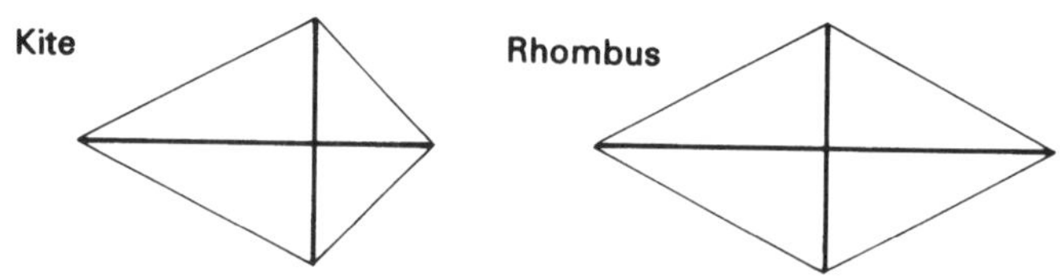

The drawing of the rhombus can be made much easier if it is done on squared paper.

The properties of a kite are discovered by practical activity, following the same procedure as for the square and rectangle.

EXERCISE 15D

1 Students should draw different size kites in their exercise books. They should label them ABCD.

2 $b = d$
Angle ABC = angle CDA

3 a is not equal to c.
Angle BCD does not equal angle DAC. Only one pair of opposite angles are equal. The angles between the pairs of unequal sides are equal, but the angles between the pairs of equal sides are not equal.

4

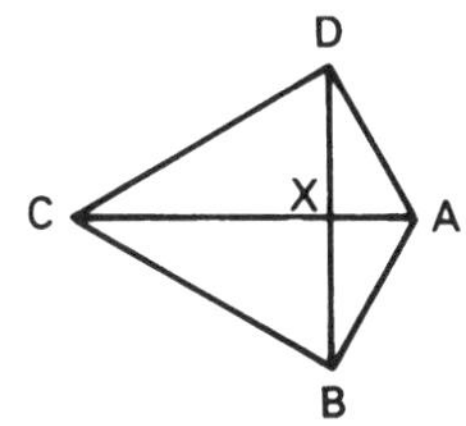

BX = XD
AX and CX are not equal.
One diagonal bisects the other.

5 Angle BAX = angle DAX
Angle BCX = angle DCX

6 Angle ABX does not equal angle ADX.
Angle CBX does not equal angle ABX.
Only one diagonal bisects the angles of the kite. This is the diagonal between the unequal angles.

7 They are all 90°.

Angle AXB = angle BXC = angle CXD = angle DXA = 90°
The diagonals meet at right angles.

• Trapeziums

Students will need to discover the angle properties of the trapezium before doing the exercise. They should draw a trapezium by drawing two parallel lines that are different lengths and joining them up to make a quadrilateral:

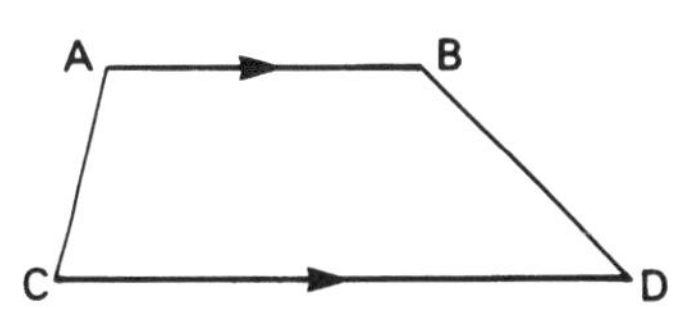

They then measure the angles. They will find that
angle DAB + angle ADC = 180° and
angle ABC + angle BCD = 180°

Before doing Exercise 15E, a class example would be useful:

Find the values of the letters in these diagrams:

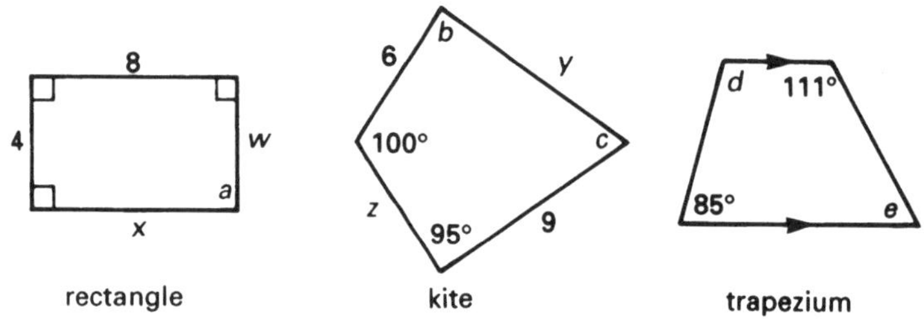

Answers:

$w = 4$, $x = 8$	$y = 9$, $z = 6$	$d = 95°$
$a = 90°$	$b = 95°$, $c = 70°$	$e = 69°$

EXERCISE 15E

1 a 105° b 100° c 80° d 270°

2 a AD = 3 cm b EH = 2.5 cm EF = 4.8 cm
c RN = 12 cm PQ = 24 cm d KL = 8 cm

• Transversals

Students have difficulty remembering which pairs of angles are equal when parallel lines are cut by transversals.
Corresponding angles go together quite easily:

They can be thought of as sliding up and down into each other:

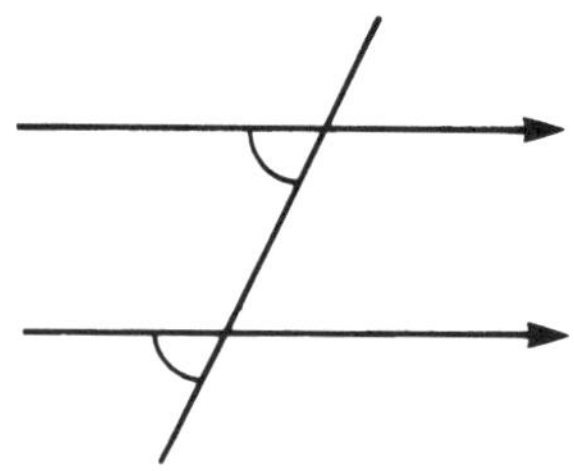

Alternate angles make a Z shape:

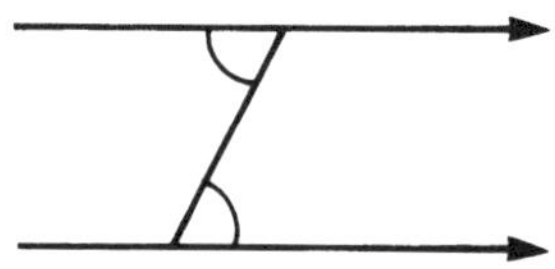

Co-interior angles are 'inside' the parallel lines and add up to 180°.

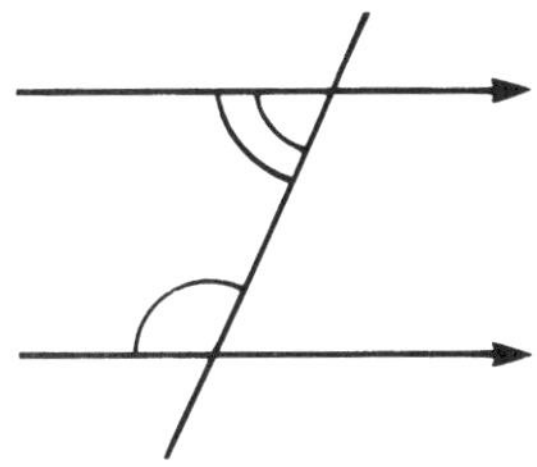

The exercise is a practical discovery exercise similar to the ones earlier in the chapter. The students should find out the angle properties of parallel lines for themselves by doing this exercise. It is important to review and sum up at the end, to make sure that they have discovered all that you want them to.

EXERCISE 15F

1 $a=b=49°$ $c=23°$ $d=72°$

2 $x=20°$ $y=120°$ $z=90°$

3 $p=q=115°$ $r=s=65°$

• Parallelograms

Now that the properties of parallel lines have been discussed, we can look at the properties of parallelograms. In the example, students are shown how to construct a parallelogram. In the exercise, a parallelogram is drawn and its properties found by measurement, as in the earlier sections of this chapter.

EXERCISE 15G

1 A quick way to draw a parallelogram is to draw two equal horizontal lines that are not lined up vertically and then join their ends:

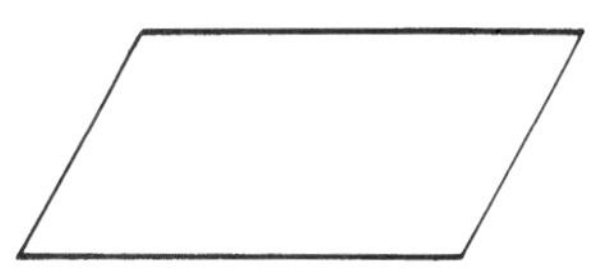

Using the squares in a squared exercise book, students can quite easily draw two lines the same length in the same direction and not under each other.

2 Yes, AB = CD

3 Yes, AD = BC

4 Angle ABC = angle ADC

5 Angle BCD = angle BAD

6 Angle ABC + angle BCD = 180°

7 The angles at X will make two pairs of equal, vertically opposite angles.

8 Angle XAB = angle XCD and angle XBA = angle XDC

9 AX = XD and BX = XD

10 There are 4 pairs of congruent triangles:

a On diagonal BD, triangles ABD and CDB are congruent.
b On diagonal AC, triangles ADC and CBA are congruent.
c With both diagonals drawn, triangles ABX and CDX are congruent.
d With both diagonals drawn, triangles ADX and CBX are congruent.

Notice the deliberate order in which the vertices of the congruent pairs of triangles are given. In **a**, triangles ABD and CDB are stated to be congruent. This means angle ABD = angle CDB, side AB = side CD and so on.

11 Yes

12 The properties are listed in the text-book.

• Properties of parallelograms

The answer to question **12** of the previous exercise, a list of the properties of a parallelogram, is given here. Before doing questions **6**, **7** and **8**, tell the students about the right angle, hypotenuse, side (RHS) condition for triangles to be congruent.

EXERCISE 15H

1 a AP = PC and DP = PB (diagonals bisect each other)
Angle APB = angle CPD (vertically opposite angles)
So triangle APB is congruent to triangle CPD. (SAS)
b AB = CD; AD = BC
c There are 8 pairs of equal angles:
ABC and CDA, BCA and DAC, CAB and ACD, ADB and CBD, DBA and BDC, BAD and DCB, DPC and BPA, DPA and BPC.

2 a Angle SRP = angle QPR (We are told they are both 80°.)
Angle SPR = angle QRP (We are told they are both 60°.)
PR is common to both triangles.
So triangle PSR is congruent to triangle RQP. (AAS)
b Corresponding equal sides are: PS = RQ, SR = QP
Equal corresponding angles are: SRP and QPR, SPR and QRP, PSR and RQP

3 AB is parallel to DC
so angle ABD = angle CDB (alternate angles)
AB = DC (given)
BD is common to both triangles.
So triangle ABD is congruent to triangle CDB. (SAS)

4 **a** K is the mid-point of AC (given) so AK = KC
Angle AKH = angle CKM (vertically opposite)
Angle HAK = angle MCK (alternate angles) since AB is parallel to MC (given)
Therefore triangles AHK and CMK are congruent. (AAS)

b CM = AH (corresponding sides of congruent triangles AHK and CMK)

c MK = HK (corresponding sides of congruent triangles AHK and CMK)

d We are told H is the mid-point of BA, so BH = AH
but AH = CM (proved in **b**), so BH = CM.
We are told that BH is parallel to CM
so BCMH is a parallelogram, as opposite sides BH and CM are parallel and equal.

e We have proved HK = KM
HKM is a straight line, so HK + KM = HM
So HGK + HK = KM and HK = $\frac{1}{2}$HM

f HM = BC (opposite sides of parallelogram BCMH)
HK = $\frac{1}{2}$HM = $\frac{1}{2}$BC

5 AB = DC and AD = BC (given)
BD is common, so triangles ABD and CDB are congruent. (SSS)

6 **a** AC is common to both triangles
AB = AD (given)
Angle ABC = angle ADC = 90° (given)
So triangles ABC and ADC are congruent. (RHS)

b BC = CD, as they are corresponding sides of congruent triangles ABC and ADC

7 **a** PR is common to both triangles.
QR = PS (given)
Angle PQR = angle PSR = 90° (given)
So triangles PQR and RSP are congruent. (RHS)

b PQ = RS, as they are corresponding sides of congruent triangles PQR and RSP.

8 **a** We are told QR is bisected at K, so QK = KR
PK is common to both triangles.
Angle PKQ = angle PKR = 90°(given)
So triangles PQK and PRK are congruent (RHS)

b Angle QPK = angle RPK as they are corresponding angles of congruent triangles PQK and PRK.

16 Symmetry

• Aim of chapter The aim of the chapter is to introduce students to basic ideas of reflection.

• Objectives By the end of the chapter the students will be able to:

1. Reflect a geometric shape in a line
2. Reflect a geometric shape in the x and y axes
3. Find the coordinates of the image of a point after reflection in the axes
4. Rotate a geometric shape and find its order of rotational symmetry.

This chapter is important because it introduces ideas that are going to become important later on. It is a practical chapter and there should be lots of activity for the students.

• Line symmetry Many shapes have line symmetry. A line of symmetry cuts a shape exactly in two equal parts. Here are some examples of shapes with lines of symmetry:

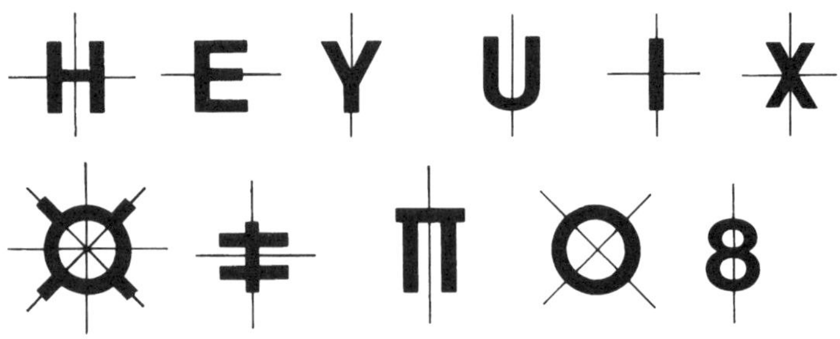

There are endless possibilities for shapes with 1, 2, 3, 4 and so on lines of symmetry. The remaining letters of the alphabet can be investigated, patterns can be made with circles, and so on.

Students should be able to draw all sorts of nice shapes with several lines of symmetry. They can make them with scissors: fold up a piece of paper and while it is folded cut holes out of the paper. When the paper is unfolded a symmetrical pattern will be revealed.

• Reflective symmetry

Many of the properties of reflection are effectively illustrated by examples using reflection in coordinate axes. The example shows that a shape and its image under a reflection are congruent.

EXERCISE 16A

1 a 1 b 1 c 6

2

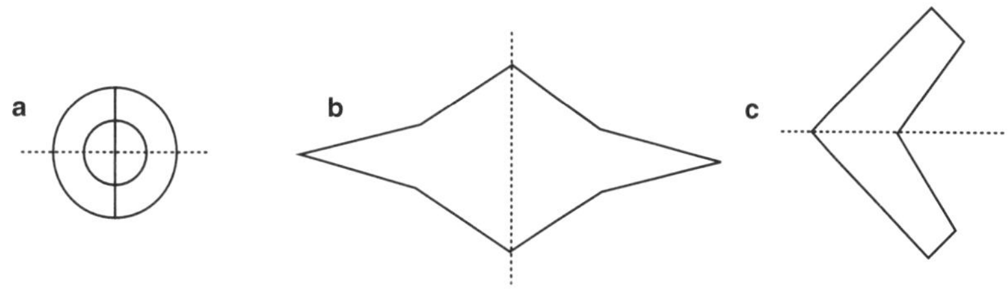

3 a is a reflection in the x axis.
c is a reflection in the line $y=x$.
d is a reflection in the y axis.
e is a reflection in the line $x=-\frac{1}{2}$.
f is a reflection in the line $y=-x$.

4 a A′(0, 2), B′(2, 2), C′(2, 5), D′(0, 4)
b A″(0, −2), B″(−2, −2), C″(−2, −5), D″(0, −4)

5 b The line $x=0$ is the y axis.
The images are A′(1, 0), B′(2, 4), C(6, 4), D′(6, 1).
c The angles and their images are equal.
$\phi=\phi'=48°$ $\theta=\theta'=65°$

6 b When we reflect in the line $y=x$, the x and y coordinates are swapped over. The image points are:
A′(4, −2), B′(1, −4), C′(1, −8), D′(4, −7), E(4, 3.5), F(6, 3)
c The image and the polygon are the same shape. The image has been turned over.

7 10 m

• Rotational symmetry

The properties of rotational symmetry are effectively illustrated by using examples such as those in the text-book. Rotation can also be illustrated by making the students pretend to be soldiers and making left and right turns (90°) and 'about turns' (180°) as if they were on a parade ground.

The order of rotational symmetry of a shape is the number of ways that it can fit into its own outline. The order of rotational symmetry of all shapes is at least one. No shape has order 0, because every shape fits its outline in one way, at least. A shape which has rotational symmetry fits its outline in more than one way during a rotation of one full turn. The teacher should use as many practical, familiar examples as possible.

EXERCISE 16B

1 a 3 b 1 c Infinite
2 a 3 b 1 c 4 d 1

• Line and rotational symmetry

In this section the teacher should discuss with the students which shapes have both line (reflective) and rotational symmetry. The teacher should use many different examples. Letters and computers are a good source of all kinds of interesting shapes which have a variety of lines and orders of symmetry.

EXERCISE 16C

1 a Both b Both c Both

2 a

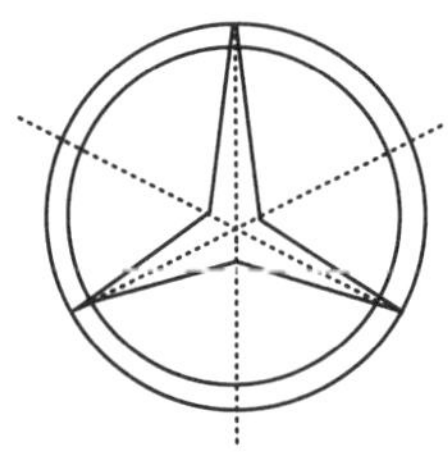

b 3

3

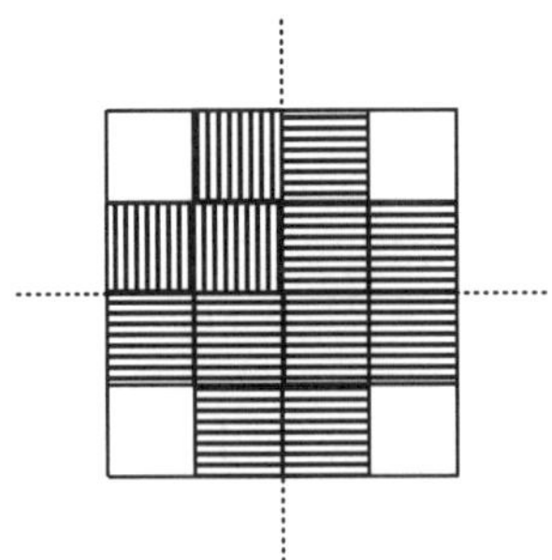

4

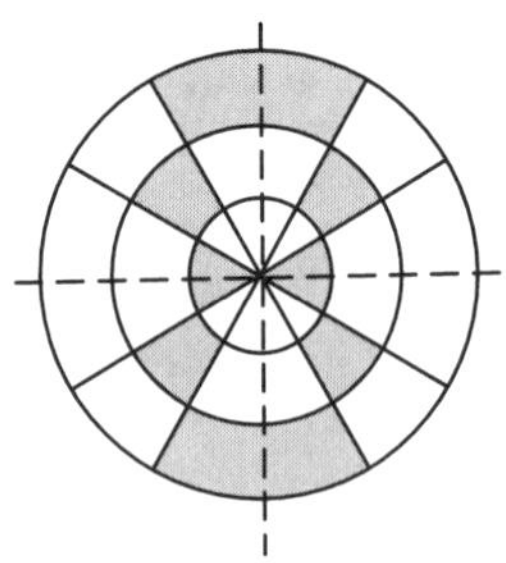

5

Letter	S	T	U	V	Y
Lines of symmetry	0	1	1	1	1
Order of rotational symmetry	2	1	1	1	1

1 Algebra – equations and formulas

• Aim of chapter

The aim of the chapter is to teach the students to use and rearrange formulas, including formulas that involve squares and square roots.

• Objectives

By the end of the chapter the students will be able to:

1. Form algebraic expressions and equations to describe problems
2. Simplify algebraic expressions
3. Substitute in formulas to evaluate unknowns
4. Rearrange formulas
5. Use and rearrange formulas involving squares and square roots
6. Solve simple vector equations.

• Do you remember? Use of symbols: algebraic expressions

The first section is a review of previous work.

• Algebraic equations

EXERCISE 1A

1 a $n+3$ b $(y-7)$ kg c $(b+8)$ cm d $\frac{f}{2}$

2 a $9p-5$ b $21-7q$ c $2x+2$
d $22-x$ e $5ab-3$ f $6xy-1$
g xyz h $ab+2bc-3ac+1$

3 a $m+n=25$ b $x+6=18$
c $10-t$ d $3m=12+n$

• Formulas and substitution

In this section there is plenty of practice at substituting in formulas.

EXERCISE 1B

1	a 9	b 15	c −2
2	a 89	b 110	c 310
3	a 3	b 3	c 3.5
4	a 18	b 37	c 500
5	a 8	b 5	c 7
6	a 45	b 10	
7	a 36	b 242	
8	a 650	b 1425	
9	a 18	b −6	c −12
10	a −13	b −1	c 13
11	a 10	b −4	c 0
12	a 16	b 12	c 5

• Rearranging formulas – finding in terms of

The solution of an equation will remain unchanged as long as you do exactly the same thing to both sides of the equation. If you add the same quantity to both sides or if you subtract the same quantity from both sides the solution of the equation will be the same as before.

When using formulas encourage students to identify their applications. Rearranging formulas is done in exactly the same way as solving equations. You can think of solving an equation in x as making x the subject of the equation.

For example, consider these two problems side by side:

a Solve the equation $7x+3=31$ and

b make x the subject of $y=mx+c$

We solve them thus:

a
$$\begin{aligned} 7x+3&=31 \\ 7x&=31-3 \\ &=28 \\ x&=28\div 7 \\ &=4 \end{aligned}$$

b
$$\begin{aligned} mx+c&=y \\ mx&=y-c \\ x&=(y-c)\div m \\ &=\frac{y-c}{m} \end{aligned}$$

The procedure is the same in both cases. Students find the equation easier to solve because they can simplify the arithmetic at each stage, whereas in **b** the algebra has to be carried all the way through.

• Arithmetic relations in symbols – some formulas

Some important formulas are listed in this section. They should all be very familiar to the students.

EXERCISE 1C

1 $r=\dfrac{C}{2\pi}$ 2 $b=\dfrac{r}{lh}$

3 $u=\dfrac{mr-e}{m}$ 4 $x=\dfrac{y-5}{3}$

5 $c=140-a$ 6 $b=\dfrac{13-c}{2}$

7 $h=\dfrac{1}{2\pi r}(A-2\pi r^2)$ 8 $a=\dfrac{2}{t^2}(S-ut)$

9 $V=\dfrac{RT}{P}$ 10 $h=\dfrac{2a}{a+b}$

11 $x=\dfrac{R}{2}-y$

• Formulas involving squares and square roots

When changing the subject of a formula with a square root in it, it is usually wise to remove the square root by squaring the whole formula at the beginning.

EXERCISE 1D

1 $r=\sqrt{\left(\dfrac{A}{\pi}\right)}$ 2 $r=\sqrt{\left(\dfrac{3V}{\pi h}\right)}$

3 $r=\sqrt{\left(\dfrac{Gmh}{F}\right)}$ 4 $x=\sqrt{\left(\dfrac{y}{4a}\right)}$

5 $g=\dfrac{4l\pi^2}{T^2}$ 6 $x=1/w\sqrt{(a^2w^2-r^2)}$

7 $M=\dfrac{4J\pi^2}{HT^2}$ 8 $2m$

9 25 10 197

11 **a** 40 **b** −104 **c** −300
d 288 **e** 93 **f** 92

12 56 13 165.321

14 21.2 **15** 30

16 **a** $\frac{4}{5}$ **b** $-1\frac{4}{5}$ **c** $\frac{12}{13}$

d $-\frac{16}{40}$ **e** 5 **f** $-\frac{2}{9}$

17 $\frac{12}{89}$ **18** 40

19 44 **20** 3

2 Number patterns

• Aim of chapter

The aim of the chapter is to extend previous work on number patterns and sequences.

• Objectives

By the end of the chapter, the students will be able to:

1. Find the value of a term in a sequence given the rule for finding the nth term
2. Generate a sequence from the pattern of the first few terms
3. Find a number's position in a sequence given the expression for the nth term of the sequence
4. Find an expression for the nth term of a sequence when there is a constant difference between terms
5. Find an expression for the nth term of a sequence when second differences are constant.

• Patterns in order

This section is a review of last year's work on sequences. Sequences can be generated by using rules. The constant difference rule is the simplest way to generate a sequence. For example, in this sequence the constant difference between a term and its successor is $+5$:

3 → +5 → 8 → +5 → 13 → +5 → 18 → +5 → 23

If the constant difference is negative, then each term is less than its predecessor. For example, the sequence 41, 37, 33, 29, ... has a constant difference of -4.

• Sequences with constant difference

Whilst constant difference rules are easy to use, it is tedious to find a large number of terms. For example, what is the 600th term of the above sequence? Finding a general term simplifies the answer to this problem. The method in the text-book uses the difference between terms.

A sequence such as 4, 8, 12, 16, 20, 24, ... has n^{th} term $4n$. The difference between a term and its successor is 4. When n increases by 1, then $4n$ increases by 4.
The sequence 5, 9, 13, 17, 21, ... also has a constant difference of 4.
Its terms are 1 more than the previous sequence, so its nth term is $4n+1$.

In general, the nth term of such sequences is $kn+c$ where k is the difference between terms and c is a constant.
For example, the above sequence 3, 8, 13, 18, 23, ... has constant difference 5, so $k=5$ and the nth term is $5n+c$.
When $n=1$, the nth term is 3
therefore, $3=5\times 1+c$ and $c=-2$.
The nth term is $5n-2$. We can check this is true by looking at later terms.

It can be argued that mathematically speaking it is wrong to ask questions like 'What is the next term of the sequence 5, 8, 11, 14, ... ?' It is possible to construct a formula which gives 5, 8, 11, 14 and then any number we like.

For example, the sequence 5, 8, 11, 14, 29, ... has general formula

$$(3n+2)+\frac{12}{24}(n-1)(n-2)(n-3)(n-4)$$

The sequence 5, 8, 11, 14, 74.5, ... has general formula

$$(3n+2)+\frac{57.5}{24}(n-1)(n-2)(n-3)(n-4)$$

The purist will say that the formula has to be stated before we can find the next term. However finding patterns is an important activity of school mathematics and so questions like this are valuable.

• Fractions in sequences

Fractional sequences can be difficult for students. The numerator and denominator should be treated separately and the result combined to find the answer. In some cases, the fractions have been simplified by the use of equivalent fractions which make it more difficult to observe the pattern. The working for the nth term for the numerator and denominator is the same as in the previous section.

EXERCISE 2A

1 a 2, 3, 4, 5, 6 101 b 0, 1, 2, 3, 4 99
c 7, 9, 11, 13, 15 205 d 2, 5, 8, 11, 14 299
e −1, 4, 9, 14, 19 494

f $1, -1, -3, -5, -7$ $\quad -197$
g $2, 1, 0, -1, -2$ $\quad 97$
h $8, 6, 4, 2, 0$ $\quad -190$

2 a $6n$ $\quad 240$ $\qquad$ b $8n+1$ $\quad 321$
c $5n+2$ $\quad 202$ $\qquad$ d $3n+5$ $\quad 125$
e $10n-3$ $\quad 397$ $\qquad$ f $10-2n$ $\quad -70$
g $6-3n$ $\quad -114$ $\qquad$ h $2.5+0.5n$ $\quad 22.5$

3 a $3n-1$ $\quad$ b 200

4 a $\frac{1}{7}, \frac{1}{8}$ $\quad \frac{1}{n}$ $\qquad$ b $\frac{9}{13}, \frac{11}{15}$ $\quad \frac{2n-1}{2n+3}$
c $\frac{7}{9}, \frac{8}{10}$ $\quad \frac{n+2}{n+4}$ $\qquad$ d $\frac{9}{35}, \frac{11}{42}$ $\quad \frac{2n-1}{7n}$

• Looking at second differences

In this section we look at sequences whose first differences are not constant. For example:

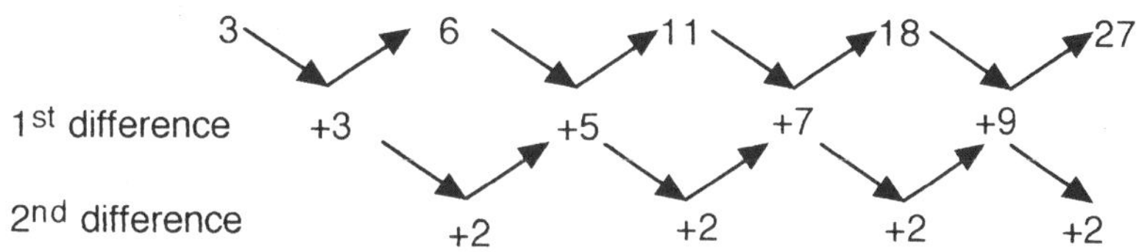

The second difference is constant. These sequences are usually quadratic. It could be of the form ax^2+bx+c. In this section, all the formulas are of the form kx^2+c. The formulas are found by comparing the sequence with the squares 1, 4, 9, 16, 25, ...

• Other patterns

Some sequences have patterns which cannot be found using the methods of the previous sections. Students need to use common sense to work out the pattern in each case. The teacher should discuss these examples with the students.
For example: 1, 6, 7, 12, 13, 18, 19, ...
1, 1, 3, 3, 5, 5, 7, 7, 9, 9, ...

• Problem solving and investigations

This section gives students the opportunity to find sequences from patterns. The teacher can generate his/her own patterns which students can investigate to find sequences that describe them.

EXERCISE 2B

1 a 35, 48 $\quad n^2-1$ $\qquad$ b 41, 54 $\quad n^2+5$
c 144, 196 $\quad 4n^2$ $\qquad$ d 14, 20 $\quad \frac{1}{2}(n-2)(n+1)$
e 111, 150 $\quad 3n^2+3$ $\qquad$ f 146, 198 $\quad (2n)^2+2$

2 **a** 7, 8, 9, 10; 11, 12, 13, 14, 15.
b 8
c 28

3 **a** (i)

```
        +
        +
        +
        +
+ + + + + + + + +
```

(ii) $3n+1$; 31

b (i)

```
+ + + + + + + + +
        +
        +
        +
        +
+ + + + + + + + +
```

(ii) $5n+2$; 52

4 **a** 120, 108, 96, 84, 72
b $132-12n$

5 **a** (i) 20 (ii) 64
b $29^2=841$

6 **a** (i) 20 m (ii) $4(n-1)+20$ (iii) 96 m
b 23rd tree

7 **a** (i) K91 000 (ii) K123 000 (iii) K75 000 + 8000
b 13th year

3 Numerical concepts

• Aim of chapter

The aim of the chapter is to reinforce the students' basic skills in arithmetic and the use and interpretation of recurring decimals.

• Objectives

By the end of the chapter the students will be able to:

1 Identify even, odd, prime, square and cube numbers, multiples and factors
2 Find the lowest common multiple and highest common factor of groups of numbers
3 Carry out operations on and with fractions
4 Carry out operations on and with decimals
5 Change fractions to decimals, including recurring decimals
6 Change decimals, including recurring decimals, to fractions.

• Do you remember?

This section is a review of what should be familiar material so it may not be necessary to spend too long on it. A few examples will soon tell you whether the students have remembered the topic.

EXERCISE 3A

1 a composite, even
b prime
c composite, even
d odd, composite
e composite, even
f even, composite, square
g even, composite, square
h even, composite, square

2 a 36 b 30 c 63
d 110 e 48 f 156

3 a 5 b 4 c 9
d 12 e 3 f 15

4 a 49 b 144 c 225
d 400 e 1296 f 3249

5 a 8 b 10 c 16
d 32 e 13 f 14

6 a 216 b 2744 c 9261
d 2700 e 91 125 f 729 000

7 a 4 b 6 c 10
d 12 e 20 f 25

• Relating HCF and LCM

The LCM of two numbers which are coprime is the product of the two numbers.

EXERCISE 3B

1 a 6 b 35 c 90 d 84 e 55 f 156

2 Yes

3 a (i) $238 = 2 \times 7 \times 17$ (ii) $672 = 2^5 \times 3 \times 7$
(iii) $1785 = 3 \times 5 \times 7 \times 17$ (iv) $6840 = 2^3 \times 3^2 \times 5 \times 19$
b (i) $14 = 2 \times 7$, 17 (ii) $21 = 3 \times 7$, $32 = 2^5$
(iii) $35 = 5 \times 7$, $51 = 3 \times 17$
(iv) $72 = 2^3 \times 3^2$, $95 = 5 \times 19$
c The LCM of each pair of numbers is the product of the prime factors of the numbers.
d The LCM of two coprime numbers is the product of the numbers.

4 a 315 b 110 c 84 d 715

5 The LCM of three coprime numbers is the product of the three numbers.

6 LCM = product of all the coprime numbers in the group.

EXERCISE 3C

1 a $15 = 3 \times 5$
LCM of 5 and 15 = 15
b $12 = 2^2 \times 3$, $15 = 3 \times 5$
LCM of 12 and $15 = 2^2 \times 3 \times 5 = 60$
c $18 = 2 \times 3^2$, $24 = 2^3 \times 3$
$\text{LCM} = 2^3 \times 3^2 = 72$
d $25 = 5^2$, $35 = 5 \times 7$
$\text{LCM} = 5^2 \times 7 = 175$

2 a (i) 5 (ii) 75 (iii) 15 (iv) LCM = 15
(v) LCM = product of numbers ÷ HCF
b (i) 3 (ii) 180 (iii) 60 (iv) LCM = 60
(v) LCM = product ÷ HCF

c (i) 6 (ii) 432 (iii) 72 (iv) LCM = 72
(v) LCM = product ÷ HCF
d (i) 5 (ii) 875 (iii) 175 (iv) LCM = 175
(v) LCM = product ÷ HCF

3 For each pair of numbers the results the students get should be the same as in question **2**.

4 The LCM of two numbers = the product of the numbers divided by their HCF.

5 Yes.

6 This question involves a quite sophisticated investigation that only the more able students should attempt.

If the three numbers are such that each is coprime to the other two (for example 5, 8 and 9), then the product equals the LCM, the HCF is 1 and product ÷ LCM = 1, the HCF.

If two of the numbers have a common factor, the rule no longer works. For example consider 5, 10 and 12. They have product 480, LCM 120 and HCF 1.
Product ÷ LCM = 4 ≠ HCF.

Some more examples:
8, 10 and 12 have product 960, LCM 120 and HCF 2.

Product ÷ LCM = 8 ≠ HCF.
6, 9 and 12 have product 648, LCM 36 and HCF 3.
Product ÷ LCM = 18 ≠ HCF.

In each case the LCM is a multiple of the HCF, as you would expect, but there is no simple rule for connecting product, LCM and HCF.

(There is a more complicated rule:
Consider $4 = 2^2$, $30 = 2 \times 3 \times 5$ and $70 = 2 \times 5 \times 7$. They have product 8400, $\text{LCM} = 2^2 \times 3 \times 5 \times 7 = 420$ and HCF 2.
$\text{Product} \div \text{LCM} = 20 = \text{HCF} \times 2 \times 5$. The numbers appearing here do not include the prime numbers that each appear in the prime factors of only one of the numbers, 3 and 7.
2 and 5 each appear more than once.
The numbers $8 = 2^3$, $12 = 2^2 \times 3$ and $18 = 2 \times 3^2$ have HCF 2, LCM $2^3 \times 3^2 = 72$ and product 1728.
The $\text{product} \div \text{LCM} = 24 = \text{HCF} \times 2^2 \times 3$. The two terms 2^2 and 3 appear more than once in the prime factors.)

If one number A is a factor of B, then the LCM of the three numbers A, B and C is the same as the LCM of the two numbers B and C. (Any multiple of B is also a multiple of A.) We can apply the rule of question **4** to B and C. For example 6, 8 and 12 have LCM 24. 8 and 12 also have LCM 24.

If the largest number is a multiple of the other two numbers then that largest number is the LCM of them all.

• Fractions – a review

The following sections review previous work with fractions.

• Rational numbers

Rational numbers is the sophisticated term for fractions. Any number that can be written as $\frac{p}{q}$, where p and q are integers, is called a **rational number.**

{Rational numbers}, $Q = \{\frac{p}{q}: p, q \text{ integers}, q \neq 0\}$

It is important to realise that q cannot be 0 as no number can be divided by 0, but that 0 is a rational number (in which case $p=0$).

• Adding and subtracting fractions

As this is a revision topic, addition and subtraction of fractions have been combined into one exercise. If your students have problems they may well benefit from more practice.

EXERCISE 3D

1	a $\frac{1}{2}$	b $\frac{11}{12}$	c $1\frac{1}{6}$	
	d $1\frac{7}{20}$	e $\frac{43}{51}$	f $1\frac{32}{45}$	
2	a $\frac{1}{12}$	b $\frac{1}{2}$	c $\frac{3}{8}$	
	d $-\frac{1}{24}$	e $\frac{3}{14}$	f $\frac{1}{18}$	
3	a $\frac{7}{2}$	b $\frac{23}{5}$	c $\frac{44}{7}$	
	d $\frac{49}{9}$	e $\frac{35}{12}$	f $\frac{93}{10}$	
4	a $2\frac{1}{3}$	b $2\frac{2}{5}$	c $2\frac{3}{4}$	
	d $4\frac{1}{6}$	e $9\frac{1}{4}$	f $9\frac{1}{4}$	
5	a $8\frac{11}{12}$	b $5\frac{1}{6}$	c $11\frac{7}{10}$	
	d $10\frac{5}{12}$	e $7\frac{13}{35}$	f $6\frac{8}{9}$	
6	a $2\frac{1}{4}$	b $2\frac{5}{12}$	c $3\frac{1}{10}$	
	d $\frac{11}{12}$	e $2\frac{23}{24}$	f $7\frac{11}{14}$	
7	a $11\frac{1}{8}$	b $12\frac{11}{24}$	c $4\frac{1}{2}$	
	d	$20\frac{13}{16}$	e $7\frac{23}{24}$	f $4\frac{38}{45}$

• Multiplying and dividing fractions

This section revises multiplication and division by a fraction, and reciprocals.

EXERCISE 3E

1 a $\frac{1}{2}$ b $\frac{2}{15}$ c $\frac{3}{10}$

d $\frac{1}{2}$ e $\frac{4}{9}$ f $\frac{1}{3}$

g $\frac{1}{2}$ h $\frac{7}{12}$ i $\frac{8}{11}$

2 a 7 b $9\frac{3}{8}$ c $9\frac{3}{7}$

d $14\frac{1}{2}$ e $\frac{5}{8}$ f 28

g 70 h 20 i $16\frac{1}{2}$

3 a $\frac{1}{7}$ b $\frac{1}{11}$ c $\frac{1}{6}$ d $\frac{1}{25}$

e 4 f 9 g 15 h 40

4 a $\frac{4}{3}$ b $\frac{9}{2}$ c $\frac{8}{5}$ d $\frac{11}{6}$

e $\frac{13}{2}$ f $\frac{27}{5}$ g $\frac{22}{7}$ h $\frac{19}{9}$

5 a $\frac{2}{3}$ b $\frac{4}{11}$ c $\frac{5}{8}$ d $\frac{3}{10}$

e $\frac{3}{17}$ f $\frac{5}{33}$ g $\frac{3}{35}$ h $\frac{8}{101}$

6 a $\frac{1}{2}$ b $\frac{3}{4}$ c $1\frac{1}{5}$

d 2 e $\frac{9}{10}$ f $2\frac{2}{7}$

g $1\frac{1}{3}$ h $\frac{10}{21}$ i 2

• Decimals – a reminder

This section reviews the work of last year on decimals. It also includes examples of recurring decimals. Calculators can reduce the tedium of the divisions most effectively.

EXERCISE 3F

1 a 0.6 b 0.875 c 0.25
d 0.375 e 0.5625 f 0.8

2 a 0.142 857 b 1 c 0.4
d 0.45 e 0.583 f 0.73

3 a 3.5 b 4.75 c 7.625
d 8.25 e 6.8 f 10.7

4 a 3.571 428 b 5.2 c 8.27
d 2.83 e 1.6 f 3.7

Students are now reminded how to change decimals to fractions. Harder examples where recurring decimals are changed into fractions are included.

Notice in Exercise 3G number **3b** that $0.\dot{9}=1$. This is because we have the infinite series $0.9+0.09+0.009+0.000\,9$ which is a geometric progression with first term 0.9 and common ratio 0.1. It has sum 1.

Changing a recurring decimal to a fraction can be done using algebra.

For example, question **3a** in the exercise below can be solved thus:

$$x=0.555\,555 \quad \text{(i)}$$
$$10x=5.555\,55 \quad \text{(ii)}$$

Subtracting (ii) − (i), $9x=5$ and $x=\frac{5}{9}$

Question **3i** in the exercise below can be solved thus:

$$x=0.123\,123\,123 \quad \text{(i)}$$
$$1000x=123.123\,123 \quad \text{(ii)}$$

Subtracting (ii) − (i), $999x=123$ and $x=\frac{123}{999}=\frac{41}{333}$

Question **4a** in the exercise below can be solved thus:

$$x=0.133\,333\,333 \quad \text{(i)}$$
$$100x=13.333\,333 \quad \text{(ii)}$$

Subtracting (ii) − (i), $99x=13.2$ and $x=\frac{13.2}{99}=\frac{132}{990}=\frac{22}{165}$

EXERCISE 3G

1 a $\frac{1}{2}$ b $\frac{7}{20}$ c $\frac{3}{10}$ d $\frac{13}{20}$

e $\frac{3}{20}$ f $\frac{1}{8}$ g $\frac{17}{40}$ h $\frac{51}{200}$

i $\frac{29}{40}$ j $\frac{39}{40}$

2 a $1\frac{1}{2}$ b $2\frac{4}{5}$ c $3\frac{3}{5}$ d $8\frac{4}{5}$
e $7\frac{3}{4}$ f $8\frac{3}{20}$ g $7\frac{6}{25}$ h $16\frac{17}{20}$

3 a $\frac{5}{9}$ b 1 c $\frac{1}{9}$ d $\frac{2}{3}$
e $1\frac{13}{99}$ f $\frac{25}{99}$ g $\frac{64}{99}$ h $\frac{8}{11}$
i $\frac{41}{333}$ j $\frac{302}{999}$ k $\frac{239}{999}$ l $\frac{115}{333}$

4 a $\frac{22}{165}$ b $\frac{289}{330}$ c $\frac{611}{4950}$ d $\frac{752}{2475}$

• Irrational numbers

This section contains a brief discussion of irrational numbers. The standard proof that $\sqrt{2}$ is an irrational number is too advanced at this stage. This section looks at finding simple estimates of the values of square roots. Later on the students will learn how to find them more accurately using tables.

• Real numbers

The set of all rational and irrational numbers on the number line make up the set of real numbers, R. Real numbers include -8, $-\sqrt{2}$, -3π, 0, $\frac{3}{4}$, $\sqrt{2}$, π, π^2, $\sqrt{15}$.

EXERCISE 3H

1 a 2.8 b 3.7 c 4.6 d 5.7
e 6.7 f 7.7 g 8.8 h 9.6

2

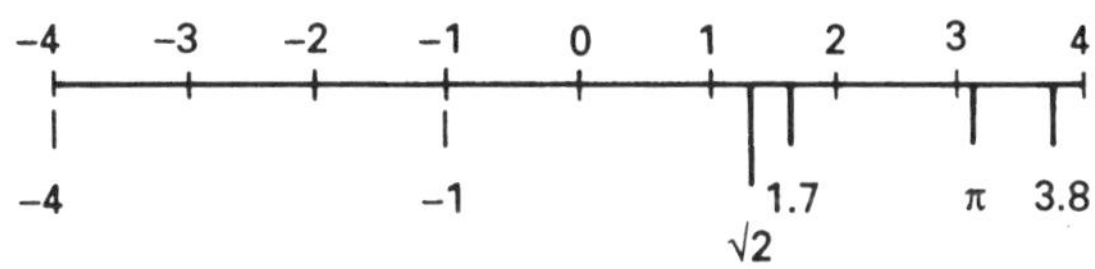

3

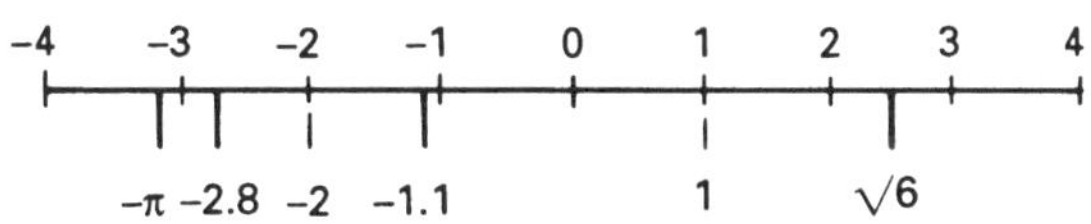

4 Vectors

• Aim of chapter

The aim of the chapter is to introduce the students to the basic concepts, skills and notation of translations and vectors.

• Objectives

By the end of the chapter the students will be able to:

1 Describe the translation of a shape across a plane and find its image using displacement vectors
2 Interpret negative vectors and the zero vector
3 Use column vectors to describe and find the images of a translation
4 Add and subtract displacement and column vectors
5 Multiply vectors by a scalar
6 Solve simple vector equations.

• Images and vector translations in two dimensions

Under a translation all points move the same distance in the same direction. Encourage the students through practical examples to see a translation as a shift in a straight line. A translation is defined by the distance moved between a point in the object and the corresponding point in the image, and by the direction. A translation is completely described if the distance moved and the direction of motion are known.

EXERCISE 4A

1 **a** 4 cm **b** horizontal **c** 2 cm **d** 3 cm
e Use thin paper which can be seen through for the tracing.
f 2, 12, 16, 19 **g** B, C, D, E
h 6 to 7 to 8 to 12 to 16 6 to 7 to 11 to 12 to 16
6 to 7 to 11 to 15 to 16 6 to 7 to 8 to 12 to 16
6 to 10 to 11 to 12 to 16 6 to 10 to 14 to 15 to 16

2 **a** PK, QM and RN are parallel
PQ and KM are parallel
PR and KN are parallel
PQ and KM are parallel
b PK = QM = RN

3 **a**, **c** and **e** are true
4 **a** 3 down, 2 right
b 2 down
c 2 left, 2 up
d 4 left, 1 up

• Vectors

The students have to learn to use the correct notation. In a text-book, the translation or displacement vector from A to image point A′ is shown as **AA′** in **bold** type. Students writing on paper and teachers using a chalk-board cannot easily copy this, so they underline $\underline{AA'}$ or put an arrow above it, $\overrightarrow{AA'}$.

• Column vectors

Column vectors are an easy way of describing a translation in terms of the number of squares along and up/down. To distinguish the ordered pair used to describe a translation from a coordinate pair, the two numbers are written vertically in a column. For this reason the vector is called a column vector.

EXERCISE 4B

1 $\overrightarrow{AB}=\begin{pmatrix}2\\2\end{pmatrix}$ $\overrightarrow{CD}=\begin{pmatrix}5\\0\end{pmatrix}$ $\overrightarrow{EF}=\begin{pmatrix}4\\1\end{pmatrix}$ $\overrightarrow{GH}=\begin{pmatrix}4\\-4\end{pmatrix}$

$\overrightarrow{IJ}=\begin{pmatrix}-4\\0\end{pmatrix}$ $\overrightarrow{KL}=\begin{pmatrix}0\\-3\end{pmatrix}$ $\overrightarrow{MN}=\begin{pmatrix}-4\\4\end{pmatrix}$ $\overrightarrow{PQ}=\begin{pmatrix}-1\\-4\end{pmatrix}$

$\overrightarrow{RS}=\begin{pmatrix}4\\0\end{pmatrix}$

2

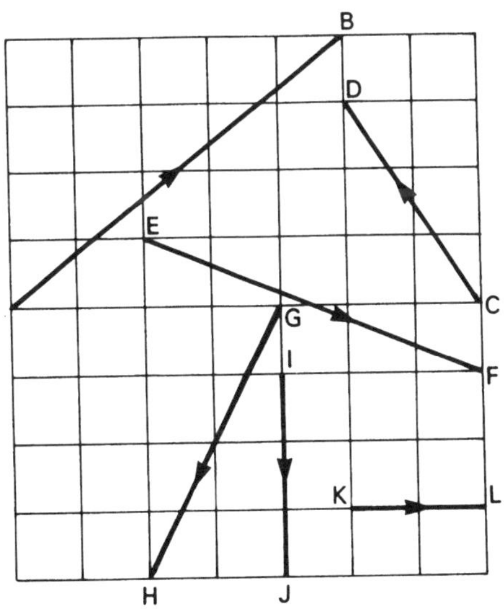

3 The images of A, B, C and D are:

a (4, 5)	(1, 6)	(3, −3)	(16, −3)
b (3, 7)	(0, 8)	(−4, −1)	(15, −1)
c (2, 4)	(−1, 5)	(−5, −4)	(14, −4)
d (2, 3)	(−1, 4)	(−5, −5)	(14, −5)

4 a $T^2 = \begin{pmatrix} -2 \\ 3 \end{pmatrix} + \begin{pmatrix} -2 \\ 3 \end{pmatrix} = \begin{pmatrix} -4 \\ 6 \end{pmatrix}$

b $T^3 = \begin{pmatrix} -4 \\ 6 \end{pmatrix} + \begin{pmatrix} -2 \\ 3 \end{pmatrix} = \begin{pmatrix} -6 \\ 9 \end{pmatrix}$

c $T^4 = \begin{pmatrix} -6 \\ 9 \end{pmatrix} + \begin{pmatrix} -2 \\ 3 \end{pmatrix} = \begin{pmatrix} -8 \\ 12 \end{pmatrix}$

d $T^5 = \begin{pmatrix} -8 \\ 12 \end{pmatrix} + \begin{pmatrix} -2 \\ 3 \end{pmatrix} = \begin{pmatrix} -10 \\ 15 \end{pmatrix}$

5 a (3, 4) b (4, 6) c (8, 9) d (1, 7)

6 The image of A is (4, 4). The image of B is (1, 5).
The image of C is (6, 7). The image of D is (2, −2).

7

a $\overrightarrow{AB} = \begin{pmatrix} 5 \\ 2 \end{pmatrix}$ $\overrightarrow{DC} = \begin{pmatrix} 5 \\ 2 \end{pmatrix}$

b $\overrightarrow{AD} = \begin{pmatrix} 1 \\ 3 \end{pmatrix}$ $\overrightarrow{BC} = \begin{pmatrix} 1 \\ 3 \end{pmatrix}$

8

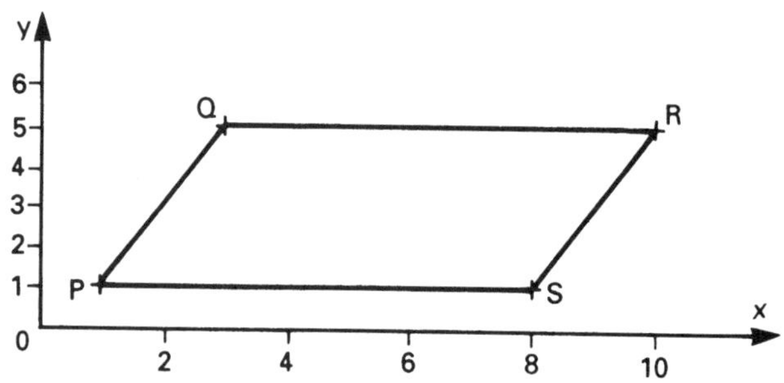

PQRS is a parallelogram.

9 a $\overrightarrow{PQ} = \begin{pmatrix} 2 \\ 2 \end{pmatrix}$ and $\overrightarrow{QP} = \begin{pmatrix} -2 \\ 2 \end{pmatrix}$

b $\overrightarrow{RS} = \begin{pmatrix} 3 \\ -6 \end{pmatrix}$ and $\overrightarrow{SR} = \begin{pmatrix} -3 \\ 6 \end{pmatrix}$

c $\overrightarrow{PQ} = -\overrightarrow{QP}$ and $\overrightarrow{RS} = -\overrightarrow{SR}$

10 a Q = (8, 1) b R = (0, 3) c S = (1, −2)

11 a $\overrightarrow{AB} = \begin{pmatrix} 1 \\ 6 \end{pmatrix}$

b A′ = (2, 0) and B′ = (3, −6) $\overrightarrow{A'B'} = \begin{pmatrix} 1 \\ -6 \end{pmatrix}$

c A″ = (−2, 0) and B″ = (−3, 6) $\overrightarrow{A''B''} = \begin{pmatrix} -1 \\ 6 \end{pmatrix}$

• Equal vectors

For two vectors to be equal they do not have to be in the same place. All that is required is that they should be the same length and that they should be in the same direction (parallel). The opposite sides of a parallelogram have the same vector (because they are equal and parallel), but they are not the same line. Two column vectors are equal if they have the same x number and they have the same y number.

• Adding vectors

Students may find it a little strange that a journey from Zomba to Blantyre and then from Blantyre to Balaka is regarded as being the same as a journey directly from Zomba to Balaka. The direct journey is obviously shorter and quicker. But with vectors we are concerned with the starting and finishing points only. The two journeys are the same in so far as they start at the same point and finish at the same point. A vector describes the change in position in a journey, and is measured by the distance away from the starting point at the end of the trip and by the direction the finishing point is from the starting point. The vector representing a 100 m race is longer than that representing a 400 m race, as the latter race is around a running track and the finish is at the same place as the starting point.

Vector addition is commonly carried out using column vectors, as these are the easiest to use. The examples and the exercise explore several different situations using column vectors.

• Subtracting vectors

Vectors are subtracted by subtracting the corresponding x and y coordinates.

EXERCISE 4C

1 a $\begin{pmatrix} 12 \\ 7 \end{pmatrix}$ b $\begin{pmatrix} 13 \\ 15 \end{pmatrix}$ c $\begin{pmatrix} -1 \\ 3 \end{pmatrix}$

d $\begin{pmatrix} -4 \\ -5 \end{pmatrix}$ e $\begin{pmatrix} 0 \\ 0 \end{pmatrix}$ f $\begin{pmatrix} 1 \\ -2 \end{pmatrix}$

2 a $\overrightarrow{XY} = \begin{pmatrix} 1 \\ 2 \end{pmatrix}$ $\overrightarrow{YZ} = \begin{pmatrix} 3 \\ 1 \end{pmatrix}$ $\overrightarrow{ZX} = \begin{pmatrix} -4 \\ -3 \end{pmatrix}$

b $\overrightarrow{XY}=\begin{pmatrix}3\\2\end{pmatrix}$ $\overrightarrow{YZ}=\begin{pmatrix}-2\\2\end{pmatrix}$ $\overrightarrow{ZX}=\begin{pmatrix}-1\\-4\end{pmatrix}$

c $\overrightarrow{XY}=\begin{pmatrix}0\\4\end{pmatrix}$ $\overrightarrow{YZ}=\begin{pmatrix}4\\-2\end{pmatrix}$ $\overrightarrow{ZX}=\begin{pmatrix}-4\\-2\end{pmatrix}$

d $\overrightarrow{XY}=\begin{pmatrix}1\\-3\end{pmatrix}$ $\overrightarrow{YZ}=\begin{pmatrix}-3\\0\end{pmatrix}$ $\overrightarrow{ZX}=\begin{pmatrix}2\\3\end{pmatrix}$

e $\overrightarrow{XY}=\begin{pmatrix}5\\3\end{pmatrix}$ $\overrightarrow{YZ}=\begin{pmatrix}0\\-3\end{pmatrix}$ $\overrightarrow{ZX}=\begin{pmatrix}-5\\0\end{pmatrix}$

f $\overrightarrow{XY}=\begin{pmatrix}-3\\0\end{pmatrix}$ $\overrightarrow{YZ}=\begin{pmatrix}0\\3\end{pmatrix}$ $\overrightarrow{ZX}=\begin{pmatrix}3\\-3\end{pmatrix}$

3 a $x=-3$ $y=7$ b $x=1$ $y=0$
c $x=4$ $y=6$ d $x=-1$ $y=-2$
e $x=0$ $y=-1$ f $x=2$ $y=-6$

4 a $\overrightarrow{AB}=\begin{pmatrix}1\\-1\end{pmatrix}$ $\overrightarrow{BC}=\begin{pmatrix}-6\\-3\end{pmatrix}$ $\overrightarrow{CD}=\begin{pmatrix}0\\5\end{pmatrix}$

b $\begin{pmatrix}1\\4\end{pmatrix}$ c $\begin{pmatrix}-5\\1\end{pmatrix}$

5 a, b

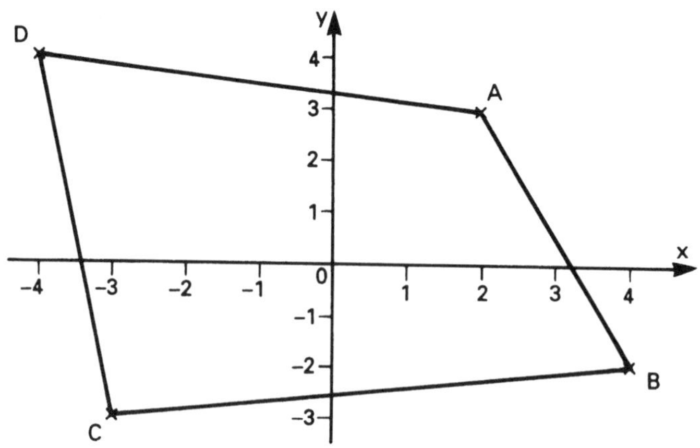

c B=(4, −2), C=(−3, −3) and D=(−4, 4)

d $\overrightarrow{AD}=\begin{pmatrix}-6\\1\end{pmatrix}$ e $\begin{pmatrix}0\\0\end{pmatrix}=0$

6 a, b

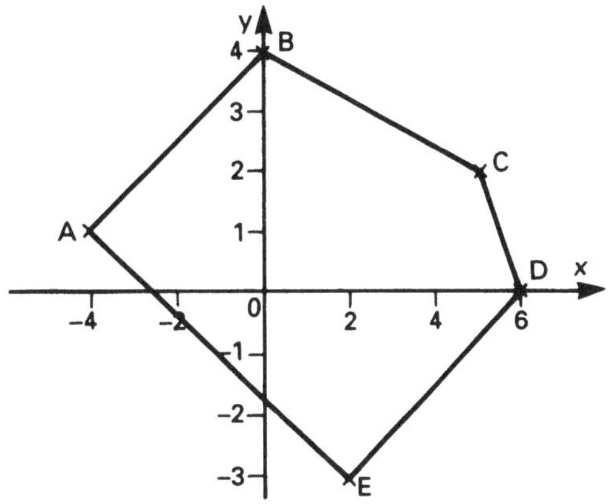

c B = (0, 4)   C = (5, 2)   D = (6, 0)

$d = \begin{pmatrix} 6 \\ -4 \end{pmatrix}$ e $\begin{pmatrix} 0 \\ 0 \end{pmatrix} = 0$

• Negative and zero vectors

Two important results are discussed here. Firstly $\overrightarrow{BA} = -\overrightarrow{AB}$. Secondly, the sum of the vectors round the sides of a polygon is the zero vector, for by going round the polygon we have come back to where we started from and have, in effect, gone nowhere. For a quadrilateral, we have $\overrightarrow{AB} + \overrightarrow{BC} + \overrightarrow{CD} + \overrightarrow{DA} = 0$

• Multiplication of vectors by a real number

Vectors are not numbers, for they have direction as well as length. Consequently, they cannot be multiplied together in the same sort of way as numbers can. Later on, the students who continue with mathematics will learn how to multiply two vectors together, using the vector product and the scalar product. At this level, multiplication of two vectors is not considered. This section looks at the multiplication of a vector by a number.

The vector $2\underline{a}$ is the same direction as $\underline{a}$ (that is to say it is parallel to $\underline{a}$) but it is twice as long.

EXERCISE 4D

1 a (i) IJON (ii) BCHG (iii) CDIH (iv) NOTS
b (i) $2\underline{a}$ (ii) $3\underline{b}$ (iii) $3\underline{a} + 2\underline{b}$ (iv) $4\underline{a} + 3\underline{b}$
c (i) True (ii) True (iii) False

2 a $\begin{pmatrix} 9 \\ 12 \end{pmatrix}$ b $\begin{pmatrix} -4 \\ 13 \end{pmatrix}$ c $\begin{pmatrix} 10 \\ 6 \end{pmatrix}$ d $\begin{pmatrix} 14 \\ 20 \end{pmatrix}$

e $\begin{pmatrix} -5 \\ 11 \end{pmatrix}$ f $\begin{pmatrix} 16 \\ 24 \end{pmatrix}$ g $\begin{pmatrix} 2 \\ 3 \end{pmatrix}$

3 a $\begin{pmatrix} 8 \\ 1 \end{pmatrix}$ b $\begin{pmatrix} 1 \\ -2 \end{pmatrix}$ c $\begin{pmatrix} 2 \\ 5 \end{pmatrix}$

e $\underline{x} = \frac{1}{2}(\underline{p} - 2\underline{q}) = \begin{pmatrix} 4 \\ \frac{1}{2} \end{pmatrix}$ f $\underline{x} = \frac{1}{2}(\underline{p} + \underline{q}) = \begin{pmatrix} -\frac{1}{2} \\ 2 \end{pmatrix}$

g $\underline{x} = 2\underline{r} = \begin{pmatrix} -4 \\ -2 \end{pmatrix}$

4 a $\overrightarrow{AB} + \overrightarrow{BC} + \overrightarrow{CD} = \underline{\overrightarrow{AD}}$ b $\overrightarrow{AG} + \overrightarrow{GH} + \underline{\overrightarrow{HR}} = \overrightarrow{AR}$

c $\overrightarrow{QR} + \overrightarrow{RS} + \underline{\overrightarrow{ST}} = \overrightarrow{QT}$ d $\overrightarrow{AB} + \underline{\overrightarrow{BR}} + \overrightarrow{RS} = \overrightarrow{AS}$

5 a $\begin{pmatrix} 12 \\ -8 \end{pmatrix}$ b $\begin{pmatrix} 8 \\ -4 \end{pmatrix}$

6 a (5, 3) b (7, 2)

7 The translation is $\begin{pmatrix} 1 \\ -3 \end{pmatrix}$, E = (4, −4), F = (−1, −6)

8 (−1, 3)

9 a (7, 5) b (0, 13) c (9, 12) d (5, 6)

10 P = (3, −1), Q = (7, 0 − 1), R = (9, 1) and S = (5, 1)
T = (−3, 2)

a $\begin{pmatrix} -6 \\ 3 \end{pmatrix}$ Find the vector *a* of the translation.

b U = (−3, 2), V = (3, 4), W = (2, 3)

c The coordinates of the images of the vertices of PQRS are (−7, 9), (−3, 9), (−1, 11) and (−5, 11).

5 Geometry: plane figures and Pythagoras

• Aim of chapter The aim of the chapter is to introduce the students to the basic concept of area and to Pythagoras' rule.

• Objectives By the end of the chapter the students will be able to:

1 Identify the different quadrilaterals by their properties
2 Find the areas of rectangles and squares in square centimetres, metres and kilometres, and in hectares, from their dimensions
3 Find the areas of triangles from their dimensions
4 Find the areas of parallelograms, kites and trapezia from their dimensions
5 Find the areas of composite figures
6 Use tables to find the squares and square roots of numbers
7 Demonstrate Pythagoras' rule
8 Use Pythagoras' rule to find the lengths of the third side of a right-angled triangle when the other two sides are known
9 Find the length of any vector.

• Quadrilaterals This section reminds students of the meaning of a few words.

• Special quadrilaterals The text-book systematically goes through all the special quadrilaterals.

• Parallelograms The first special quadrilateral discussed is the parallelogram which is defined as a quadrilateral with opposite sides parallel. The properties are found by measurement and also by formal proof. Less able students will find the proofs difficult and measurement should suffice. More able students should be encouraged to want to have these results proved.

• Rhombuses A rhombus is a quadrilateral with all four sides equal. The proofs of the properties that are stated in the text-book are left as an exercise for the students. Special mention is made of the fact that the diagonals of a rhombus bisect each other at right angles. This property makes it easy to draw rhombuses.

• Rectangles A rectangle is a quadrilateral with opposite sides equal and all angles right-angled. The proofs of the properties that are stated in the text-book are left as an exercise for the students.

• Squares A square has all sides equal and all angles right-angles. The proofs of the properties that are stated in the text-book are left as an exercise for the students.

• Kites A kite has two pairs of adjacent sides equal. The proofs of the properties that are stated in the text-book are left as an exercise for the students.

• Trapeziums The isosceles trapezium is mentioned in the text.

EXERCISE 5A

1 AEFK – rectangle DNYP – rhombus
DLYP – kite HMSO – square
JUWZ – trapezium TRXV – parallelogram
(Some students may also write down TRZV – isosceles trapezium.)

2 **b** Parallelogram

3

Property	Kite	Rectangle	Parallelogram	Rhombus	Square
Only one pair of opposite sides parallel	x	x	x	x	x
Both pairs of opposite sides parallel	x	√	√	√	√
Two pairs of adjacent sides equal	√	x	x	√	√
Both pairs of opposite sides equal	x	√	√	√	√
All sides equal	x	x	x	√	√

Property	Kite	Rectangle	Parallelogram	Rhombus	Square
Only one pair of opposite angles equal	√	x	x	x	x
Both pairs of opposite angles equal	x	√	√	√	√
All angles equal (to 90 degrees)	x	√	x	x	√
Only one diagonal bisected by the other	√	x	x	x	x
Diagonals bisect each other	x	√	√	√	√
Diagonals equal in length	x	√	x	x	√
Diagonals cross at right angles	√	x	x	√	√
Only one pair of opposite angles bisected by a diagonal	√	x	x	x	x
Both pairs of opposite angles bisected by a diagonal	x	x	x	x	√

4 $x=131°$, $y=49°$, $z=82°$

5 (i) a $x=60°$, $y=30°$, $z=120°$
(ii) a $p=60°$, $q=60°$, $r=35°$, $s=30°$, $z=35°$
(iii) a $x=62°$, $y=62°$, $z=42°$
(iv) a $m=140°$, $x=20°$, $y=20°$, $z=20°$

• Area

The section is a short review of work done in primary school. The basic building block of area is the 1 cm square. When we ask for the area of a shape we are in effect asking how many 1 cm squares we can cover it with.

• Rectangles

The formula for the area of a rectangle is the basic formula from which the areas of all the other shapes follow.

A square is merely a special rectangle with equal length and breadth.

EXERCISE 5B

1 a $44\,cm^2$ b $3400\,cm^2$ c $0.6\,m^2$
d 3 ha e $19.8\,km^2$ f 96 ha

2 a $144\,cm^2$ b $1600\,m^2$ c 1.44 ha
d $36\,km^2$ e 6.25 ha

3 The square. It has area $144\,cm^2$; the rectangle has area $143\,cm^2$.

4 16 m

5 108 kg

6 a $80\,cm^2$ $(14 \times 4 + 6 \times 4)$
b $105\,cm^2$ $(15 \times 10 - 9 \times 6 + 3 \times 3)$
c $256\,cm^2$ $(20 \times 8 + 16 \times 6)$
d $78\,cm^2$ $(12 \times 10 - 6 \times 7)$
e $224\,cm^2$ $(16 \times 20 - 4 \times 8 - 8 \times 8)$
f $1024\,cm^2$ $(15 \times 20 - 11 \times 18)$

• Triangles

The formula for a triangle is derived from that for a rectangle. We start with the right-angled triangle, which is half a rectangle and so its area, $\frac{1}{2}$ base $\times$ height, follows naturally. Any scalene triangles can be thought of as being made from two right-angled triangles and so this formula is quite simply demonstrated to apply to all triangles.

EXERCISE 5C

1 a $60\,cm^2$ b $300\,cm^2$ c $2.4\,m^2$
d 3 hectares e $24\,cm^2$

2 a $54\,cm^2$ b $30\,cm^2$ c $180\,cm^2$ d $10\,cm^2$

3 a Base 4.2 cm, height 2.3 cm, area $4.83\,cm^2$
b Base 3.5 cm, height 2.4 cm, area $4.2\,cm^2$
c Base 3.4 cm, height 2.8 cm, area $4.76\,cm^2$
d Base 3.2 cm, height 2.3 cm, area $3.68\,cm^2$

4 a 20 b 12 c 8 d 54 e 45

5 a $80\,cm^2$ $(6 \times 8 + \frac{1}{2} \times 8 \times 8)$
b $188\,cm^2$ $(6 \times 8 + 2 \times \frac{1}{2} \times 6 \times 10 + 2 \times \frac{1}{2} \times 8 \times 10)$
c $150\,cm^2$ $(12 \times 20 - \frac{1}{2} \times 9 \times 20)$
d $70\,cm^2$ $(15 \times 2 - 2 \times \frac{1}{2} \times 10 \times 11)$

• Parallelograms

If a parallelogram is divided into two congruent triangles, the formula for its area, base $\times$ height, can be deduced.

• Kites

The area of a kite is also developed by dividing it into two congruent triangles along a diagonal. The simple formula for the area of a kite, half the product of its diagonals, then comes out quite simply.

• Trapeziums

In the same way, if a trapezium is seen as being made of two triangles of equal height, the formula for its area follows quite simply and is more easily remembered as a result. The area of a trapezium $= \frac{1}{2}(a+b) \times h$, where a and b are the lengths of the two parallel sides and h is their distance apart.

EXERCISE 5D

1 a $48\,\text{cm}^2$ b $135\,\text{cm}^2$ c $195\,\text{cm}^2$ d $102\,\text{cm}^2$
e $26\,\text{cm}^2$ f $432\,\text{cm}^2$

2 a $70\,\text{cm}^2$ b $300\,\text{cm}^2$ c $80\,\text{cm}^2$ d $100\,\text{cm}^2$

3 9 cm
Area = base × height, so $18 \times 5 = 10 \times h$.

4 10 cm
$\text{Area} = 120 = \frac{1}{2} \times 24 \times d$

5 7 cm
$91 = \frac{1}{2}(10+16) \times h$

• Tables of squares

At the back of the text-book there is a table of the squares of numbers between 1 and 100, correct to 3 significant figures. This table can be used to find the square of any number, no matter how big or how small. Calculators are of course much quicker, and more accurate, but this table is quite accurate enough and reasonably quick and easy to use.

EXERCISE 5E

1 a 23.3 b 49.7 c 88.9 d 41.0

2 a 339 b 1790 c 4870 d 7740

3 a 0.060 5 b 0.002 94 c 0.767 d 0.002 08

4 a 16 400 b 214 000 c 2030 d 123 000

• Square roots

This section looks at the size of square roots. It will be useful later on for estimating the size of a computation when square roots are involved. It is easy to find the square roots of numbers which are either perfect squares or where the numerator and denominator of their fractional equivalent are perfect squares.

The square roots of such numbers are included in this section.

EXERCISE 5F

1	a $\frac{2}{3}$	b $\frac{1}{5}$	c $\frac{1}{10}$	d $\frac{8}{9}$
2	a $2\frac{1}{4}$	b $2\frac{1}{2}$	c $1\frac{1}{2}$	d $1\frac{2}{3}$
3	a 2 and 3	b 5 and 6	c 12 and 13	d 9 and 10

• Square root tables

The easiest way for students to find square roots is to use a calculator. If they do not have one of these, square root tables will usually give a sufficiently accurate answer. In the back of the students' text-book there are two tables, one for numbers from 1 to 10 and one for numbers from 10 to 99, accurate to 3 significant figures. In the text the student is reminded that sometimes this is not sufficient to differentiate between the square roots of different numbers. For example, from the table we find that $\sqrt{7.43} = \sqrt{7.44} = 2.73$ to 3 significant figures.

The section looks at the square roots of numbers that are in the two tables before looking at larger and smaller numbers. To find these we express the number whose square root we want as a number in the table multiplied or divided by a power of 100. 100 is used because the square root of 100 is 10. We do not use 10, as the square root of 10 is 3.162, which is not as convenient.

EXERCISE 5G

1	a 2.38	b 3.12	c 2.53	d 2.83
2	a 8.23	b 8.68	c 8.00	d 9.49
3	a 24.1	b 29.4	c 23.2	d 26.5
4	a 0.737	b 0.869	c 0.860	d 0.775
5	a 0.260	b 0.274	c 0.184	d 0.283

• Pythagoras' rule

Pythagoras' theorem has probably more proofs than any other mathematical theorem – there are several different ones. This section starts by introducing the word 'hypotenuse'.

The rule is introduced by asking the students to look at some special cases on squared paper. The areas of the squares on the three sides are found. The square on the hypotenuse is divided up into four triangles and a small square in the middle. In each case we find that for a right-angled triangle, LMN, with right angle at M, $LM^2 + MN^2 = LN^2$.

The result is then proved using a rather nice algebraic proof. This may be unfamiliar to many teachers, but it is elegant, quite simple and rather short. It is satisfying to use algebra to prove a major geometrical result. In the old days, this proof would have been frowned upon, for it is not geometrical, but these days, it is considered quite legitimate. The students are not expected to reproduce it in an examination, so the teacher is quite free to choose any satisfactory proof.

• Is a triangle right-angled?

The converse of Pythagoras' theorem is useful when we want to determine whether a triangle is right-angled or not. This is done by investigating whether the lengths of the sides are connected by the Pythagoras relationship. The longest side will be the hypotenuse. In triangle ABC, with AC the longest side:
If $AB^2 + BC^2 > AC^2$ then triangle ABC is acute-angled.
If $AB^2 + BC^2 = AC^2$ then triangle ABC is right-angled.
If $AB^2 + BC^2 < AC^2$ then triangle ABC is obtuse-angled.

EXERCISE 5H

1 a Yes b No c Yes

2 a Obtuse b Right c Right d Acute

3 No, $6^2 + 2^2 < 6.5^2$

4 No, $20^2 + 25^2 \neq 32^2$

5 a 14 b 9.9 c 12
d 6.7 e 50 f 3.4

6 a 4.0 b 9.2 c 3.4
d 15.0 e 22.4 f 2.1

7 8.6 cm

8 a RT = 7.14 cm b QR = 14.28 cm

9 BD = 7.55 cm, BC = 7.81 cm

10 7.07 cm

11 a 4.47 cm b $57.9\,\text{cm}^2$

12 7.21 cm

13 2 m

• Vector length

This section teaches an important application of Pythagoras' theorem. Some students have difficulty finding the horizontal and vertical distances between two points on a graph. The key result is:

If vector $a = \begin{pmatrix} x \\ y \end{pmatrix}$ then the length of a is $\sqrt{(x^2 + y^2)}$

EXERCISE 5I

1 a 13 b 10 c 5.7 d 2.8

2 a 4.47 cm b 12.8 cm c 8.49 cm

3 BC = CA = 5 cm

4 AB = AC = 5; BC = $\sqrt{50}$, $AB^2 + AC^2 = BC^2$

6 Travel graphs

• Aim of chapter

The aim of the chapter is to teach students how to solve travel problems using the formula $D = S \times T$ and distance–time graphs.

• Objectives

By the end of the chapter, the students will be able to:

1 Calculate distance travelled when the time and speed are known
2 Calculate the speed of a journey when distance and time are known
3 Interpret distance–time graphs
4 Draw distance–time graphs.

• Finding speed

This section revises earlier work on travel at a constant speed. If we are travelling at a constant speed, the speed is calculated using Distance ÷ Time.
Calculations involving the distance, speed and time of a journey require one of three equivalent formulas:

$$\begin{aligned} \text{Distance} &= \text{Speed} \times \text{Time} \\ \text{Speed} &= \text{Distance} \div \text{Time} \\ \text{Time} &= \text{Distance} \div \text{Speed} \end{aligned}$$

In the text-book, all three formulas are used. The teacher may prefer to use only one of them, $D = S \times T$, and solve all problems using this. The advantage of this approach is that the students only have to remember one formula. Sometimes, with three formulas, they can get the formulas mixed up.

However, we do not normally travel at a constant speed. Sometimes we go faster, sometimes slower. The average speed is the Total distance covered ÷ time for journey.

• Finding distance

In the text-book, a variety of examples are given, using different forms of travel.

• Finding time

This section looks at a familiar problem. We want to travel to a place and we know how far we have to go. We know how fast we can travel and we need to work out how long the trip will take.

EXERCISE 6A

1 50 km/h

2 5 hours

3 4200 km

4

	Distance (km)	Speed (km/h)	Time (hours)
a	150	25	6
b	450	90	5
c	96	24	4
d	240	80	3
e	960	80	12
f	460	115	4
g	42	14	3
h	1700	850	2

• Distance –Time graphs

Journeys can be shown on graphs. The distance from a place is usually shown on the vertical axis. The time is usually shown on the horizontal axis. The journeys of more than one person can be shown on the same graph. Where their two lines meet we can read off the distance covered and the time at which they meet.

• Different directions

The direction of travel is shown on a distance–time graph, and the slope of the line shows the rate of travel.

EXERCISE 6B

1 a 80 minutes
b 7.5 km/h
c 4.3 km/h

2 a 1 hour b 80 km/h
c 20 km/h d 30 km/h

3

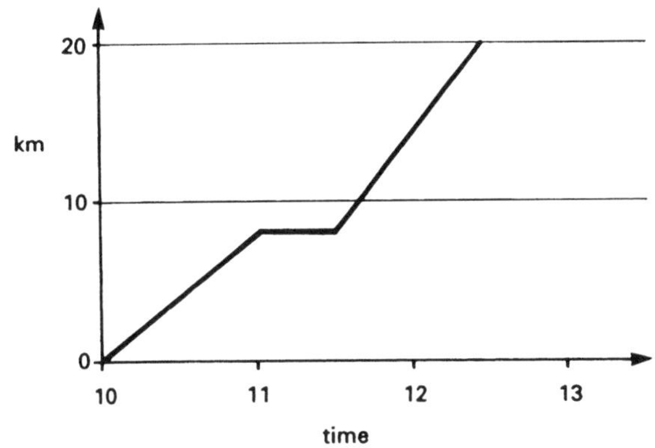

Average speed $= \frac{20}{2.5} = 8$ km/h

4

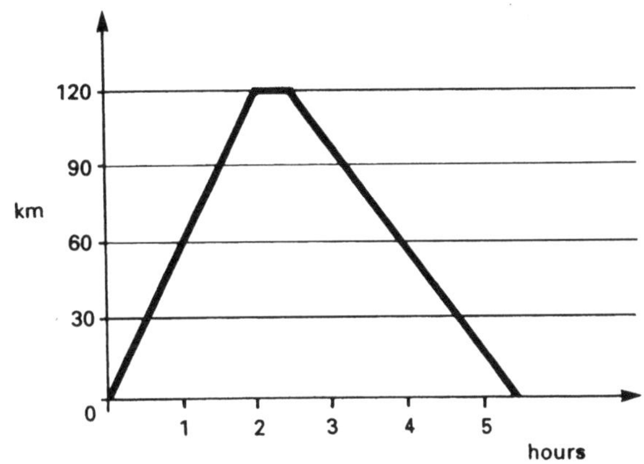

Average speed = 240 km ÷ 5 h = 48 km/h

5 **a** 30 minutes and 60 minutes **b** 40 km/h **c** 15 km/h

6

a

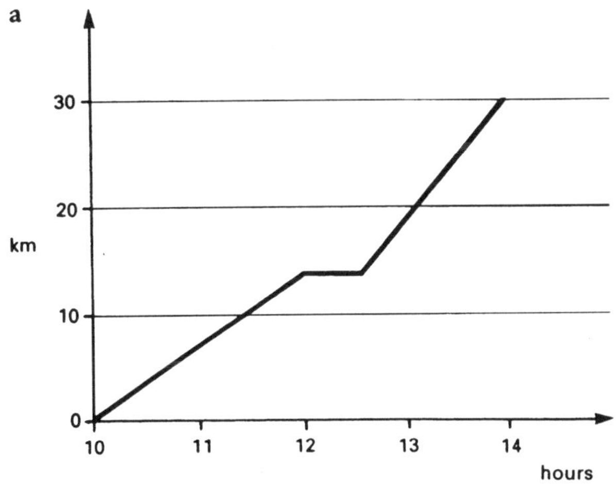

b 7.5 km/h

7 a 10.00 b 25 km/h c 1.5 hours

• Crossing points

The graphs in the previous section were all single journey graphs. In this section there is more than one journey on the same graph. From the point where the two graphs meet we can determine the time and the distance at which the meeting took place.

EXERCISE 6C

1 a 6.30 a.m. b 1 hour c 3 hours
d (i) The first part, from 6.00 to 6.30 (ii) $26\frac{2}{3}$ km/h
e 80 km/h f 8.15 a.m. g 60 km

2 a Bus 4 hours, Car 2 hours
b (i) 30 minutes (ii) 30 minutes
c 30 minutes
d (i) 75 km/h and 62.5 km/h (ii) $66\frac{2}{3}$ km/h
e (i) 100 km/h (ii) 100 km/h
f 80 km from Blantyre, at 11.48 a.m.

3 a 44 km ÷ 45 minutes = 58.7 km/h b 36 minutes
c 10.15 a.m. d 22 km/h

4

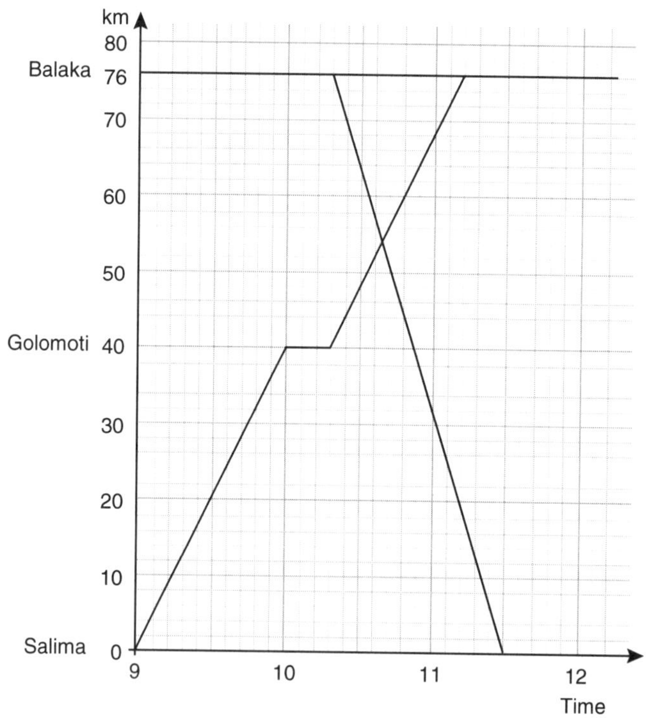

b 11.12 a.m
c 63.3 km/h
d About 10.39
e About 54 km
(These answers are only approximate, taken from the graph. Accept answers close to these.)

7 Indices and logarithms

• Aim of chapter

The aim of the chapter is to introduce the students to logarithms and their use to simplify arithmetical computations, and at the same time to consolidate earlier work on indices.

• Objectives

By the end of the chapter the students will be able to:

1 Apply the laws of indices
2 Find roots of indices
3 Interpret negative, zero and fractional indices
4 Simplify algebraic expressions using indices
5 Write large numbers in standard form
6 Find the logarithms of numbers greater than one
7 Use logarithms to facilitate multiplication of numbers greater than one
8 Use logarithms to facilitate division of numbers greater than one.

• Indices

This section quickly reminds students what 5^7, for example, means. In the following sections the rules for operating with indices are developed.

• Adding indices

Simple examples are used to enable students to discover that $a^m \times a^n = a^{m+n}$ for natural numbers.

• Subtracting indices

Simple examples are used to enable students to discover that $a^m \div a^n = a^{m-n}$ for natural numbers.

• Multiplying indices

Simple examples are used to enable students to discover that $(a^m)^n = a^{mn}$ for natural numbers.

• Roots of indices

This section reminds students what, for example, $\sqrt[3]{125}=5$ means. It is another way of writing $5^3=125$.
Students are reminded that the square root of a number is the most commonly used root and that $\sqrt[2]{15}$ is written as $\sqrt{15}$, with the 2 omitted.

• Dividing indices

Simple examples are used to enable students to discover that $\sqrt[n]{(a^m)}=a^{m \div n}$ for natural numbers.

• Rules for operations on indices

This section summarises the four important index rules that have been developed for the natural numbers:

$$a^m \times a^n = a^{m+n}$$

$$a^m \div a^n = a^{m-n}$$

$$(a^m)^n = a^{mn}$$

$$\sqrt[n]{(a^m)} = a^{m \div n}$$

EXERCISE 7A

1	a 4^7	b 6^7	c 9^{15}	d 12^{14}
	e 10^7	f 5^{12}	g 3^6	h 16^{10}
2	a 6^8	b 9^4	c 4^2	d 2^2
	e 5^3	f 3^1	g 6^5	h 5^0
3	a 7^{10}	b 6^{20}	c 8^{18}	d 8^{49}
	e 4^{15}	f 5^{24}	g 3^{15}	h 2^{36}
4	a 4^3	b 9^3	c 8^2	d 5^2
	e 6^4	f 3^3	g 2^2	h 7^5
5	a x^9	b y^9	c a^5	
	d $12a^7$	e $4p^3$	f $3q^5$	
6	a x^2	b x^7	c $x^1=x$	
	d $2b^2$	e $3r^5$	f $4p^1=4p$	
7	a x^4	b b^{10}	c a^6	
	d z^{12}	e r^{15}	f x^{24}	
8	a x^2	b y^2	c p^5	
	d a^2	e b^2	f c^4	

• Negative indices

The meaning of negative indices is developed by applying the index law $a^m \div a^n = a^{m-n}$ with n greater than m so the result is a negative index.

For example, $6^2 \div 6^4 = 6^{2-4} = 6^{-2}$. In other words, $\frac{1}{6 \times 6} = 6^{-2}$.
If the laws are to continue to operate for negative numbers, then a^{-m} must equal $\frac{1}{a^m}$.

• Index zero

Many students find it hard to accept that $a^0 = 1$, no matter what positive or negative number a is (0^0 is not defined.) But it follows from the law for dividing indices:
By the law $a^x \div a^x = a^{x-x} = a^0$
but $a^x \div a^x = 1$, since any number divided by itself is 1,
so $a^0 = 1$.

EXERCISE 7B

1	a 25	b 2.6	c 8
2	a 9	b 25	c 16
	d 33	e $\frac{1}{5}$	f 80
	g 12	h 32	i 64
3	a 7	b 65	c 16
	d 17	e −18	f 80
4	a m^2n^4	b $a^4b^4c^2$	c $20d^5e^3$
	d a^4b^{-2}	e $5g^2f^{-3}$	f $\frac{1}{3}ac^{-1}$
5	a 2×3^2	b $2^2 \times 3^2$	c $2^3 \times 3^2$
	d $2^5 \times 3$	e $3^2 \times 5^2$	f $2^6 \times 3$

• Fractional indices

The fractional indices have been kept simple. The justification of the meaning of fractional indices is developed using the rules already established for indices that are whole numbers. If the rules for indices are to continue to operate in the same way as they do for whole numbers then the meaning of a fractional index has to be as it is developed in this section.

EXERCISE 7C

1	9	2	5	3	2
4	27	5	32	6	16
7	2	8	125	9	11

• The standard form

Standard form is an important way of expressing very large and very small numbers. It is sometimes called **scientific notation.** Numbers in standard form are always written in the form $a \times 10^n$ where $1 \leqslant a < 10$. For large numbers, n will be a positive integer. For very small numbers, n will be a negative integer.

EXERCISE 7D

1 a one b two c three
d six e ten

2

$$64 = 6.4 \times 10^1$$
$$640 = 6.4 \times 10^2$$
$$6400 = 6.4 \times 10^3$$
$$64\,000 = 6.4 \times 10^4$$
$$640\,000 = 6.4 \times 10^5$$
$$64\,000\,000\,000 = 6.4 \times 10^{10} \text{ so } n = 10$$

3 a 5.6×10^3 b 2.84×10^3 c 1.54×10^4
d 4.63×10^5 e 4×10^6 f 4.96×10^7
g 2×10^9 h 5.8402×10^6 i 9.38×10^9

4 a 5000 b 460 c 850 000
d 5850 e 6 400 000 f 6241.5
g 64 000 000 h 580 000 i 244 000 000

5 a 6.67×10^3 b 1.496×10^8 c 2.9979×10^5
d 1×10^3 e 1.36×10^5

6 a 143 000 b 350 c 3120
d 31 500 e 86 400 f 31 536 000

7 a 8×10^7 b 9×10^{11}
c 2×10^9 d 2.1×10^6

• Logarithms

In many places logarithms are no longer on the mathematics syllabus. They have been superseded by calculators which are quicker and more accurate. They are now not much more expensive than a text-book of mathematical tables.

Logarithms are closely connected to indices. Another way of saying $10^2 = 100$ is to say that the **logarithm** of 100 **in base 10** is 2. Logarithms to base 10 are called **common logarithms**. The section looks at logarithms in bases other than 10. We use base 10 for calculations, but an understanding of other bases is important and helps with understanding of how base ten logarithm calculations work.

Students often find it quite hard to accept that $\log_a a$ is always 1 and $\log_a 1$ is always 0, no matter what positive whole number a is. This is because $a^1 = a$ and $a^0 = 1$.

EXERCISE 7E

1 2 2 2 3 5 4 4
5 7 6 1 7 0 8 0
9 6 10 1.5

In this section students use the table printed in the text-book. This table is sufficient for them. More accurate tables (able to find precisely the logarithm of numbers with 3 significant figures) will be introduced later. Two significant figures are sufficient for initial practice and understanding. The logarithm of a number with three significant figures is estimated by reducing the number to two significant figures first.

EXERCISE 7F

1 a 0.531 b 0.672 c 0.230
d 0.881 e 0.568 f 0.839

2 a 7.4 b 8.3 c 2.1
d 6.4 e 3.1 f 7.2

3 a 0.322 b 0.771 c 0.982
d 0.903 e 0.000 f 0.602

• Multiplication using logarithms

All the problems in this section have answers that are less than 10. This is because we do not introduce the logarithms of larger numbers until the next section. Here students learn to turn a complicated multiplication problem into a much simpler addition of logarithms.

• Antilogarithms

It is explained how these are needed in order to multiply using logarithm tables.

Students are encouraged to make a rough estimate (R.E.) of the final result to check that the answer is about the right size. This is a good habit, not just with logarithms but even when using a calculator or carrying out other numerical computations.

EXERCISE 7G

1 5.2 2 8.7 3 6.8
4 4.1 5 8.0 6 3.8

• Logarithms of numbers more than 10

Now that the students have learnt about logarithms which can be read straight off from the table, they can move on to logarithms where they need to know about the **characteristic** and the **mantissa**. The text-book explains how this is done.

EXERCISE 7H

In this exercise the table in the text-book has been used and numbers are rounded to 2 significant figures before writing down the answer or doing the calculation. The answers will differ if the students are using 3-figure tables or calculators.

1 a $\log 130 = 2.114$ b $\log 11 = 1.041$
c $\log 500 = 2.699$ d $\log 72\,000 = 4.857$

e log 2700 = 3.431 f log 34 000 = 4.531
g log 450 000 = 5.653 h log 820 = 2.914

2 a 24 b 1.2 c 9.5 d 800
e 55 000 f 440 000 g 10 000 000 h 3.6

3 a 8.7 b 8.9 c 8.1 d 73
e 6500 f 100 000 g 540 000

4 a $x = 0.447$ b $x = 3.531$ c $x = 4800$
d $x = 57$ e $x = 6.5$ f $x = 0.914$

5 a 340 000 b 23 000 000 c 3 500 000
b 1 200 000 e 6 800 000

• Division using logarithms

The section justifies how we change a division problem into a simpler problem requiring the subtraction of logarithms.

EXERCISE 7I

1 a 1.5 b 7.3 c 3.1 d 4.5
e 75 f 61 g 10 h 220

2 a 12 b 13 c 5.9 d 3.2

3 a 36 b 98

8 Algebraic variables – linear equations

• Aim of chapter

The aim of the chapter is to teach students to solve linear equations.

• Objectives

By the end of the chapter the students will be able to:

1 Distinguish between true, false and open statements
2 Solve linear equations algebraically
3 Write word problems as linear equations and solve them
4 Solve harder linear equations, with the unknown on both sides of the equals sign, algebraically.

• Open statements

The chapter starts by looking at open sentences. These are sentences that are neither true nor false. For example, the sentence $3x-4=14$ is neither true nor false. Replacing x by the number 6 will make it a true sentence. Replacing it by any other number will make it false.

Finding the correct number(s) to make an algebraic open sentence true is finding the solution of the equation.

• Meaning of variables

The value of x can vary. For that reason, x is called a variable. This is an important term, at the basis of much subsequent work on functions. Students often find it hard to appreciate that in an expression such as $y=3x+5$, the value of x is not one fixed number but that it can vary.

EXERCISE 8A

1 a True b False c False d Open
e True f Open g False h False

2 a She b x c He, me d a e a

3 a Any number less than 15
b Any of the class' teachers
c $y=3$
d Any number greater than 9
e Any prime number 2, 3, 5, 7, 11, 13, 17, 19, ...

4 a True b False c False
d True e False

• Linear equations

It is best to start by solving simple one operation equations. These can usually be solved by inspection.

EXERCISE 8B

1 a $x=8$ b $y=6$ c $d=10$ d $p=12$
e $x=7$ f $k=7$ g $y=40$ h $r=35$
i $x=13$ j $q=47$ k $g=100$ l $s=90$
m $x=4$ n $x=3$ o $x=6$

2 a Yes b No c No d Yes e No

• Solving equations

This section looks at the systematic solution of equations that are more complicated than the single operation equations in the previous section.

EXERCISE 8C

1 a $x=-2$ b $x=-4$ c $x=-2$ d $x=-8$

2 a $x=20$ b $x=18$ c $x=2$ d $x=-16$

3 a $x=5$ b $x=4$ c $x=-2$ d $x=4$

4 a $x=6$ b $x=14$ c $x=24$ d $x=16$

5 $5x+3=33$, the number is 6

6 $4x-7=13$, the number was 5

7 $\frac{x}{3}+4=19$, the number was 45

8 $\frac{x}{2}+5=12$, the number was 14

9 a $x=4$ b $x=14$ c $x=4$ d $x=7$

• Harder linear equations

We now look at some harder equations. These equations are sometimes harder because there are terms in x on both sides of the equation. Note that it is not necessary to get all the x terms on the left–hand side. In some cases, such as the example in the text-book, $10-x=4+2x$, it is simpler to get all the x terms on the right and thereby avoid having negative x.

As a general rule, if an equation has brackets in it, it is better to remove them first.

EXERCISE 8D

1 a $x=4$ b $a=8$ c $y=15$ d $a=7$
e $p=2$ f $a=8$ g $k=5$

2 a $y=3$ b $x=-2$ c $c=4\frac{2}{3}$ d $k=27$
e $b=-4$ f $x=13$ g $y=6$

3 a $x=-2$ b $x=15$ c $a=7$ d $y=-5$

4 a $x=4$ b $x=11$ c $a=8$ d $r=2$

5 a $x=5$ b $x=5$ c $x=5$ d $x=3$

6 $5(x+3)=40$, the number is 5

7 $\frac{(x-6)}{5}=4$, the number is 26

8 $9(x+5)=180$, I am 15 years old

9 $x-15=\frac{1}{4}x$, I have 20 beads

10 $7n=n+12$, I have 2 marbles

9 Simultaneous equations

• Aim of chapter

The aim of the chapter is to teach students how to understand and solve linear simultaneous equations algebraically and graphically.

• Objectives

By the end of the chapter the students will be able to:

1 Solve simultaneous equations algebraically using substitution and elimination
2 Solve simultaneous equations graphically
3 Use simultaneous equations to solve problems.

• Algebraic equations

Simultaneous equations are so called because the two open statements have to be true simultaneously, that is, at the same time. This will be at the point where their graphs cross. When the solution has been found it has to satisfy both equations.

• Solving simultaneous linear equations algebraically

There are two ways of solving simultaneous equations algebraically: by elimination or by substitution. Most equations are more easily solved by elimination. There are several examples in the text of how this is done. When the signs are different, we have to add. For a letter to be cancelled out the coefficients of that letter in both equations have to have been made the same. When eliminating, the student has to decide whether to add or subtract the equations. When the coefficients are both positive or both negative we have to subtract.

• Solving simultaneous equations using multiplication

This section summarises the procedure to be followed. The questions in the exercise have all been chosen to give straightforward answers. Never set questions with answers like $x = 8\frac{3}{11}$. Choose the numbers to work out more simply. We do not want students wasting a lot of time on tedious arithmetical computations when we are trying to teach algebra. The simplest way to make up suitable examples is to think of the answers you want and then make up the equations from the answer you have chosen.

• Steps for solving simultaneous equations

This section summarises the steps for solving simultaneous equations by the method of matching one of the unknowns in the two equations.

EXERCISE 9A

1 $x=4, y=-1$ 2 $x=4, y=2$ 3 $x=3, y=2$
4 $x=2, y=1$ 5 $x=2, y=-\frac{2}{3}$ 6 $x=2, y=2$
7 $x=4, y=1$ 8 $x=3, y=5$ 9 $x=-1, y=1$
10 $x=-2, y=3$ 11 $x=4, y=0$ 12 $x=4, y=-\frac{1}{2}$
13 $x=2.2, y=0.6$ 14 $x=4, y=3$

• Graphs of equations in two unknowns

This section gives practice in making tables of values and drawing graphs of equations in two unknowns.

EXERCISE 9B

1 $y=x-5$

x	0	3	5
$x-5$	-5	-2	0

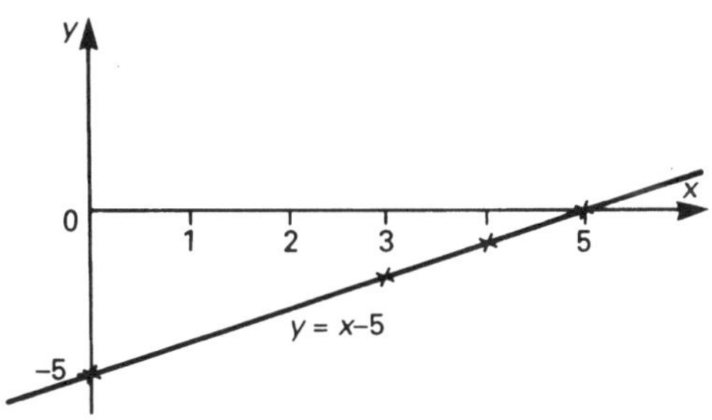

2 $y=2x-3$

x	0	2	4
$2x-3$	-3	1	5

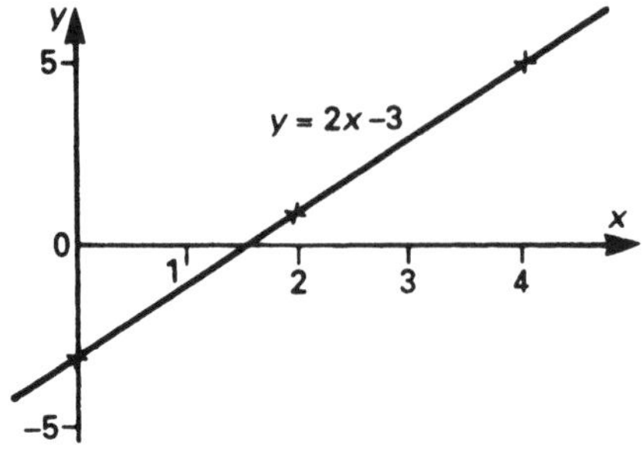

3 $y=\frac{2}{3}x+\frac{4}{3}$

x	-5	-2	1
$\frac{2}{3}x+\frac{4}{3}$	-2	0	2

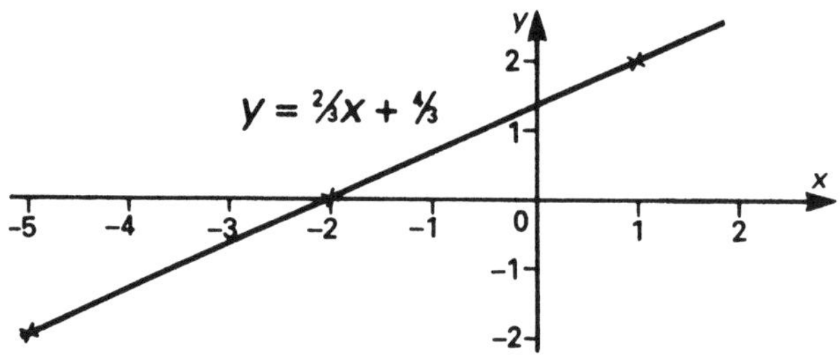

4 $y=x$

x	-3	0	3
y	-3	0	3

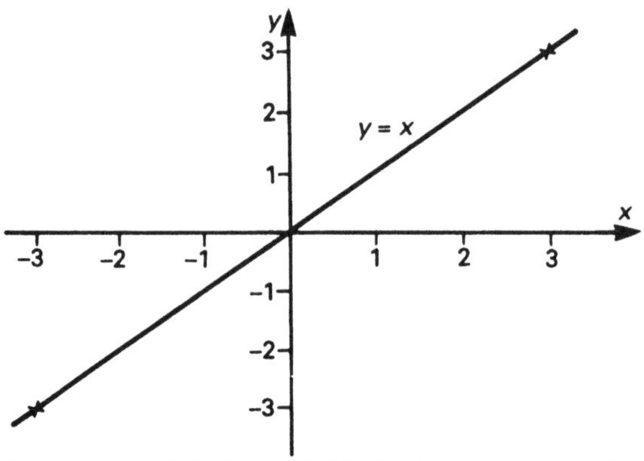

5 $y=5$

x	-3	0	3
y	5	5	5

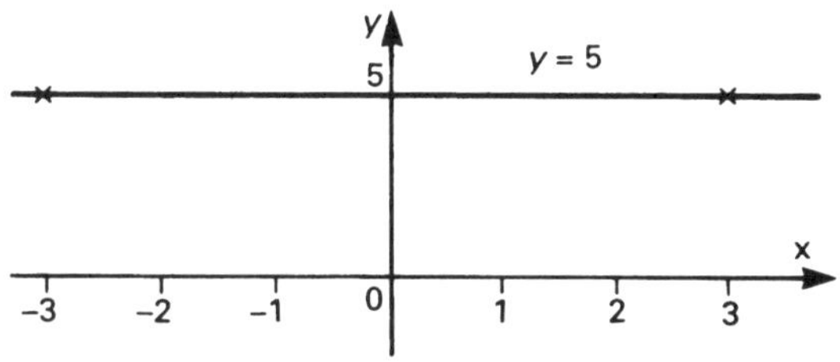

6 $x=4$

x	4	4	4
y	-2	0	2

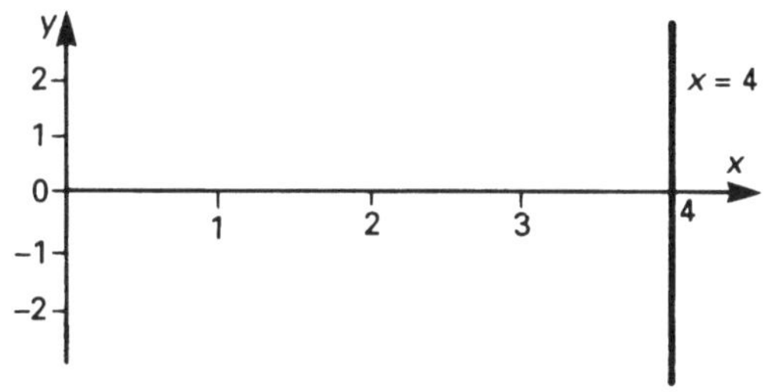

• The graphical method of solving simultaneous equations

The point of intersection of two straight lines gives the values of x and y that are the simultaneous solution of those two equations. When drawing the graphs it is necessary to plot only two points for each line, but it is prudent to plot three points to ensure that no careless mistake has been made in calculating the coordinates or plotting the points. If the three points are in a straight line, we can be confident that no careless mistake has been made.

• Simultaneous equations with no solution

When the graphs of two equations are parallel they never meet and so the two equations have no simultaneous solution.

• Simultaneous equations with an infinite number of solutions

When both equations are actually the same – one equation is a multiple of the other – there are an infinite number of simultaneous solutions.

EXERCISE 9C

It would take up too much space to include all the twelve diagrams asked for in this exercise. Consequently only the diagrams for the first three questions are shown. The solutions for all of the simultaneous equations are given below. As the solutions will be obtained graphically, when the solution is not an integer, the answer is given as a decimal, correct to 1 decimal place. As a small amount of error is inevitable when drawing graphs, accept as correct any answer which differs from the answer given by up to 0.1.

1 $x=\frac{1}{2}$, $y=-1\frac{1}{2}$ **2** $x=-12$, $y=-9$ **3** $x=2$, $y=-1$
4 $x=-3.3$, $y=-3.7$ **5** $x=2$, $y=-2$
6 $x=0.6$, $y=0.1$ **7** $x=1.2$, $y=-0.9$
8 $x=1$, $y=0$ **9** $x=-2$, $y=-6$
10 $x=0.5$, $y=3$ **11** $x=-0.75$, $y=1.25$ **12** $x=3$, $y=1$

Graphical solutions to questions **1–3**:

1 $y=-3x$ and $y=x-2$

x	0	1	2
$-3x$	0	-3	-6
$x-2$	-2	-1	0

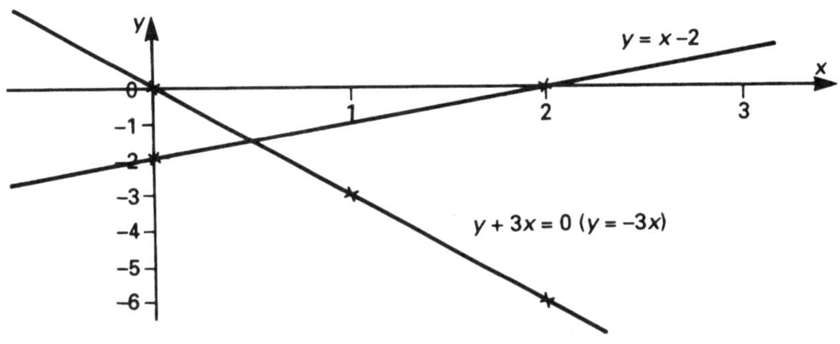

Solution: $x=0.5$, $y=-1.5$

2 $y=\frac{3}{4}x$ and $y=x+3$

x	-12	-4	0
$\frac{3}{4}x$	-9	-3	0
$x+3$	-9	-1	3

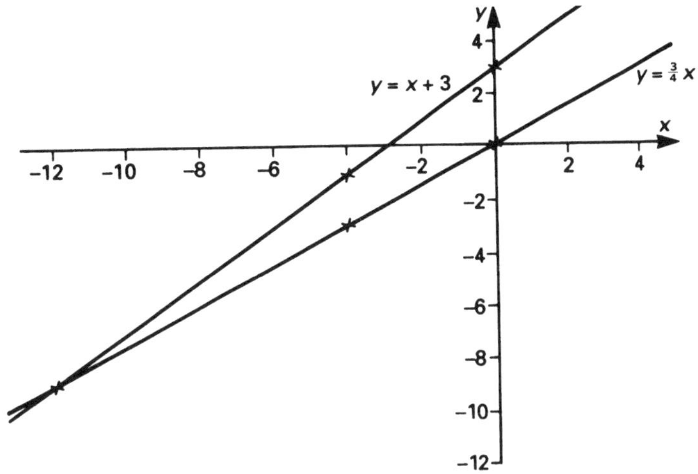

Solution: $x=-12$, $y=-9$

3 $y=1-x$ and $y=\frac{1}{2}x-2$

x	0	2	0
$1-x$	1	-1	-3
$\frac{1}{2}x-2$	-2	-1	0

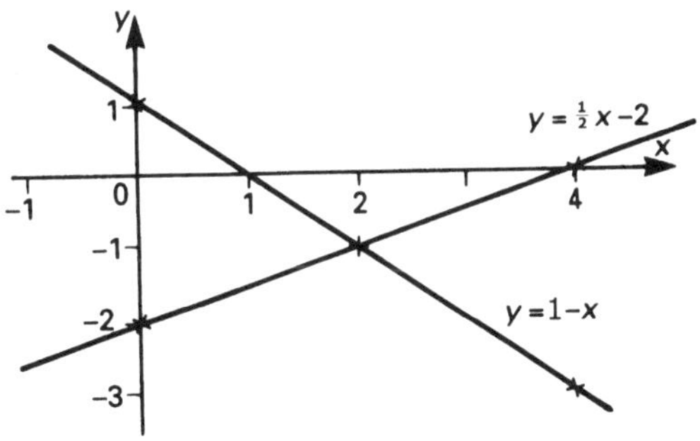

Solution: $x=2$, $y=-1$

EXERCISE 9D

When deciding which of these questions should be done graphically and which algebraically, look at the answers. Those with answers which are not whole numbers will probably be easier to do graphically.

1 $x=2$, $y=-1$ 2 $s=-4$, $t=7$ 3 $x=-2$, $y=-1$
4 $x=-6$, $y=3$ 5 $x=3$, $y=-2$ 6 $x=0$, $y=0$

7 $x=-1\frac{1}{2}$, $y=7$ 8 $x=5$, $y=2$ 9 $x=\frac{1}{3}$, $y=\frac{1}{6}$

10 $x=12$, $y=-7$ 11 $x=6$, $y=-1$ 12 $x=4$, $y=-\frac{1}{2}$

13 $x=2.2$, $y=0.6$ 14 $x=0$, $y=2$ 15 $x=-15$, $y=12$

16 $x=4$, $y=3$ 17 $x=2\frac{1}{2}$, $y=-1\frac{1}{3}$ 18 $x=2$, $y=-3$

19 $x=8\frac{1}{2}$, $y=2$ 20 $x=4$, $y=-2$ 21 $x=1.8$, $y=-1.4$

22 $x=-9$, $y=16$ 23 $x=1$, $y=0$

24 $x=\dfrac{c_2 - c_1}{m_1 - m_2}$, $y=\dfrac{m_1c_2 - m_2c_1}{m_1 - m_2}$

• Applications – problem solving

This is a most important section. Students must be able to translate problems from English into the language of mathematics, and this takes practice. It is usually more difficult to write down the equations than to solve them.

EXERCISE 9E

In this exercise the letters used for the two unknown numbers are x and y unless otherwise stated.

1 The numbers are 1 and 6.
The equations are $x+y=6$, $x - y=4$, $x=1$ and $y=5$.

2 The numbers are 4 and 2.
The equations are $x+y=6$, $2x=y+6$, $x=4$ and $y=2$.

3 There are 15 sheep and 5 goats.
If there are s sheep and g goats,
$s+g=20$ and $s=3g$, so $s=15$ and $g=5$.

4 $x=9$ and $y=4$
The equations are $\frac{x}{3}+\frac{y}{4}=y$, $3y+x=21$.

5 There are 8 blue balls and 10 red balls.
If there are b blue balls and r red balls,
$b+r=18$ and $b=r-2$.

6 There were 8 sets of type A pens and 4 sets of type B pens.
If a is the number of type A sets of pens and b is the number of type B sets of pens,
$b+r=12$ and $3a+2b=32$

7 There are 112 pupils and 8 teachers.
If p is the number of pupils and t is the number of teachers,
$p+t=120$ and $14t=p$
(This second equation is tricky; most pupils will write $14p=t$ but they must remember that there are 14 times as many pupils as teachers, so it should be written $14t=p$.)

8 Shirts cost K50 and pairs of trousers K100 each.
If one shirt costs s Kwachas and each pair of trousers costs t Kwachas,
$3t+4s=500$ and $t=2s$

9 There are 1 type I table and 8 type II tables.
If there are a type I tables and b type II tables,
$a+b=9$ and $6a+4b=38$

10 Eva is 16 years old and her brother is 12 years old.
If Eva is e years old and her brother is b years old,
$5e+3b=116$ and $2b+3e=72$

11 There are 24 men and 12 women.
If there are x men and y women,
$x=2y$ and $\frac{5}{6}x+\frac{1}{3}y$, so $x=24$ and $y=12$.

12 Alice is 12 years old and Nuwe is 4 years old.
Let Alice be a years old and Nuwe be n years old,
$a+n=16$ and $a+4=2(n+4)$, so $a=12$, $n=4$

13 $x=1\frac{1}{2}$, $y=3\frac{1}{2}$

14 $x=3$, $y=1$

15 $p=8$ and $q=\frac{18}{5}$
The equations are
$\frac{1}{2}(p-q)=\frac{1}{5}p+\frac{1}{6}q$, $\quad 3q=p+\frac{1}{2}(q+2)$

10 Successive translations

• Aim of chapter The aim of the chapter is to look at successive translations and vectors.

• Objectives By the end of the chapter the students will be able to:

1 Multiply a column or displacement vector by a whole number
2 Interpret successive translations using displacement vectors
3 Work out combinations of successive translations using column vectors.

• Translations This section reviews earlier work with vectors.

• Adding vectors The addition of vectors is revised. Displacement vectors are added by combining letters:

$\overrightarrow{AB} + \overrightarrow{BC} = \overrightarrow{AC}$

• Zero vector The zero vector **0** is the identity vector for vectors and represents a journey that ends up where it started:

$\overrightarrow{AB} + \overrightarrow{BC} + \overrightarrow{CD} + \overrightarrow{DA} = \mathbf{0}$

• Multiplication of vectors A vector can be multiplied by a whole number (a scalar). If the number is positive, the resulting vector is parallel to and in the same direction as the original vector. If the number is negative, the resulting vector is in the opposite direction.

• Successive translations Successive translations can be thought of as the successive stages of a journey. This section contains problems involving motion around geometric figures.

• More multiples of vectors This section continues the work of the earlier section on the multiplication of vectors. Multiplication expresses repeated addition and multiplication of a vector expresses successive identical translations.

EXERCISE 10A

1 a $\begin{pmatrix}-2\\6\end{pmatrix}$ b $\begin{pmatrix}12\\0\end{pmatrix}$ c $\begin{pmatrix}2\\12\end{pmatrix}$

d $\begin{pmatrix}4\\19\end{pmatrix}$ e $\begin{pmatrix}-10\\-4\end{pmatrix}$ f $\begin{pmatrix}10\\11\end{pmatrix}$

2 a $x=13$ and $y=-4$ b $x=-3$ and $y=-5$
c $x=0.5$ and $y=-1.5$ d $x=-5$ and $y=1$
e $x=0$ and $y=-3.5$

3 $6\underline{a}+4\underline{b}$ $24\underline{a}+16\underline{b}$
($9\underline{a}-6\underline{b}$ is parallel but in the opposite direction)

4 $\begin{pmatrix}3\\5\end{pmatrix}$, $\begin{pmatrix}6\\10\end{pmatrix}$ and $\begin{pmatrix}-24\\-40\end{pmatrix}$ are parallel.

5 $y=+6$ or -6
Let $2y\underline{a}+3\underline{b}=k(24\underline{a}+y\underline{b})$ where k is some number.
So $2y=24k$ and $3=ky$
$k=\frac{3}{y}$ and $2y=24\times\frac{3}{y}$
$2y^2=72$ and $y=\pm 6$

6 a $\underline{c}$ b $\underline{a}$ c 0

7 a $\underline{a}+\underline{b}$ b $\underline{a}+\frac{1}{2}\underline{b}$ c $\underline{a}-\underline{b}$ d $\underline{a}-\frac{1}{2}\underline{b}$

8 a $\underline{b}-\underline{a}$ b $\frac{2}{3}(\underline{b}-\underline{a})$ c $\frac{1}{3}(\underline{a}+2\underline{b})$

9 a $\underline{a}+\underline{b}$ b $\frac{1}{2}\underline{a}$ c $\frac{1}{2}(\underline{a}+\underline{b})$ d $\frac{1}{2}\underline{b}$

10 a $\underline{b}-\underline{a}$ b $\frac{1}{2}\underline{a}$ c $\frac{1}{2}\underline{b}$ d $\frac{1}{2}\underline{b}-\frac{1}{2}\underline{a}$

11 a (2, 3) (−1, 7) (8, 4) (2, 6)
b $\begin{pmatrix}4\\6\end{pmatrix}$
c (4, 6) (1, 10) (10, 7) (4, 9)
d (iv) 5 : 6.1 (v) 3.2 : 6.3

12 a (0, 3) (2, 3) (1, 5)
b (−4, −4) (−2, −4) (−3, 2)
c (2, −4) (4, −4) (3, −2)
d $\mathbf{M}=\begin{pmatrix}2\\-4\end{pmatrix}$

11 Inequalities and regions

• Aim of chapter

The aim of the chapter is to teach the students to solve inequalities and represent their solution on the number line and on coordinate diagrams.

• Objectives

By the end of the chapter the students will be able to:

1 Use the four inequality symbols $>$, $<$, $\geqslant$ and $\leqslant$ separately, as in $x>5$, and in pairs, such as in $4<x\leqslant 9$
2 Describe sets of numbers using inequality symbols
3 Represent inequalities on the number line
4 Solve inequalities
5 Use inequalities to solve problems
6 Show inequalities as regions on graphs.

• Comparing quantities

This section introduces the idea of comparison before applying it mathematically. The teacher should discuss with students everyday examples of the comparison of quantities. Emphasise that when the compared quantities are not equal, the statements are called inequalities. Children often think that the word 'more' in a problem is an instruction to add the numbers in the problem. Consider a problem such as '*I have 6 more bananas than my friend. If I have 14 bananas, how many does my friend have?*' The answer, $14-6$, shows that this idea is wrong.

• Inequality symbols

This section discusses the meaning of the four inequality symbols that the students have previously used. The two strict inequalities which are exemplified by $n>20$ and $s<70$ in the text cause few problems. The whole numbers greater than 20 start 21, 22, 23, and so on. The other two inequalities, which are exemplified by $r\geqslant 10$ and $d\leqslant 100$ in the text, cause more problems because the endpoint is included. The whole numbers such that $r\geqslant 10$ start with 10 and continue 11, 12, 13 and so on.

• Sets of numbers

Set language is a useful way of describing a group of sets. In this section students express the idea that x is between two numbers using inequality symbols. When listing the members of a set it is important to take note of the set of numbers being used. The choice of set should always be stated.

EXERCISE 11A

1 a The jeans are more expensive than the skirt.
b My typing is slower than my shorthand.
c The hall is cooler than our classroom.

2 a Joe is shorter than Sue *or* Sue is taller than Joe.
b Diana is heavier than Cohen
or Cohen is lighter than Diana.

3 This question gives students the opportunity to explore the comparison of quantities. Their answers will be varied.

4 a $t<4$ b $x \geqslant 7$
c $x>17$ d $y \geqslant -3$
e $p \leqslant 4$ f $m \leqslant -8$

5 a $6<x<10$ b $5 \leqslant x<9$
c $4<x \leqslant 7$ d $-3 \leqslant x \leqslant 10$
e $-5 \leqslant y<4$

6 a 7, 8, 9 b 5, 6, 7, 8
c 5, 6, 7 d $-3, -2, -1, \ldots 8, 9, 10$
e $-5, -4, -3, \ldots 2, 3$

7 a p is less than 6 b x is less than 13
c 5 is less than e d r is less than or equal to 11
e y is greater than or equal to -5 and less than 4
f m is greater than 5 and less than 21
g d is greater than -3 and less than or equal to 21
h y is greater than or equal to 2 and less than or equal to 14

8 a $w>12$
b $l \leqslant 6$
c $n<200$
d $b>2000$
e $10<a<20$

9 a {1, 2, 3, 4, 5, 6, 7} b 5, 7, 9
c 9, 10, 11 d 6, 9, 12, 15
e 4, 5, 6, 7 f 5, 7, 11, 13, 17

• Representing inequalities on the number line

Showing the end-points of sets of numbers is the main difficulty. When the endpoint is included (because the symbol $\leqslant$ or $\geqslant$ is being used) a solid dot is used. When the end-point is not included (because $<$ or $>$ is being used) an empty dot is used.

EXERCISE 11B

1

a $x < 5$

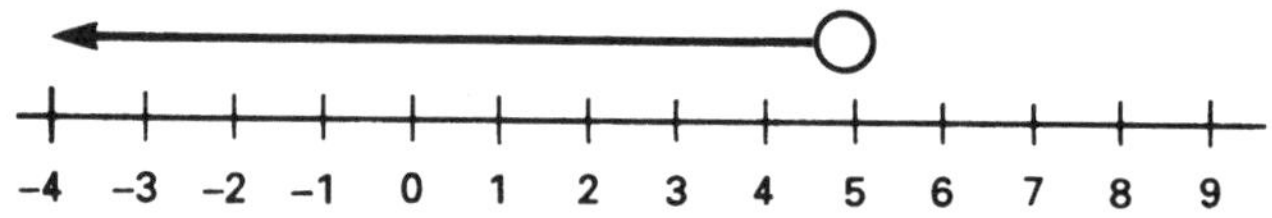

b $y \geqslant 4$

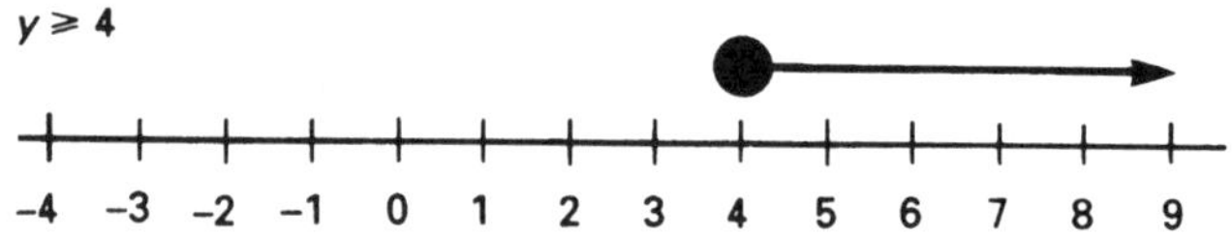

c $r > 5$

d $0 < q < 5$

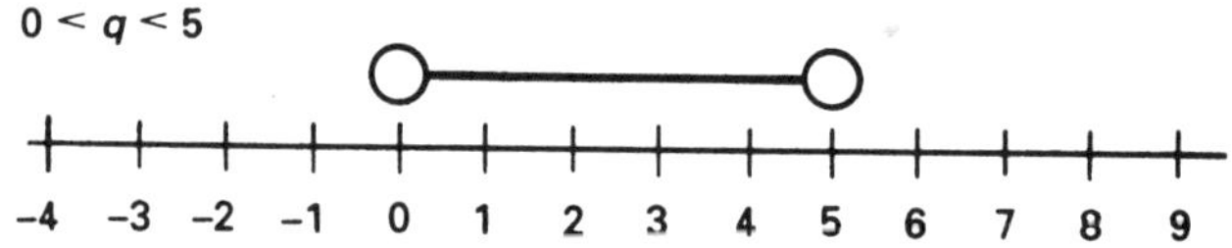

e $-2 \leqslant m \leqslant 3$

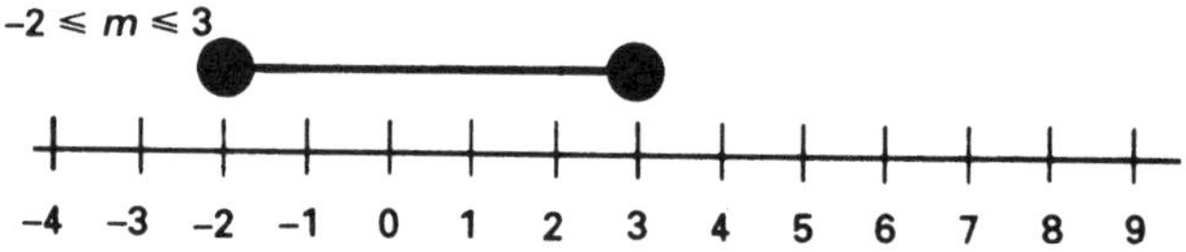

f

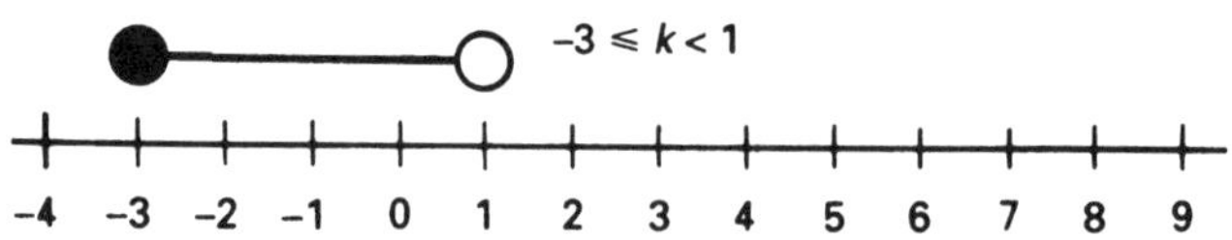

g $2 < h \leqslant 7$

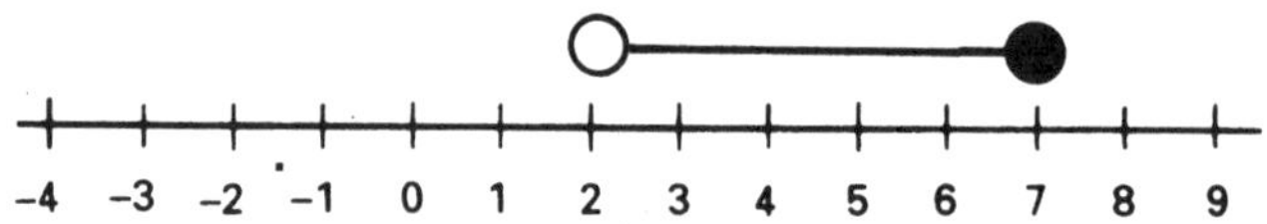

h

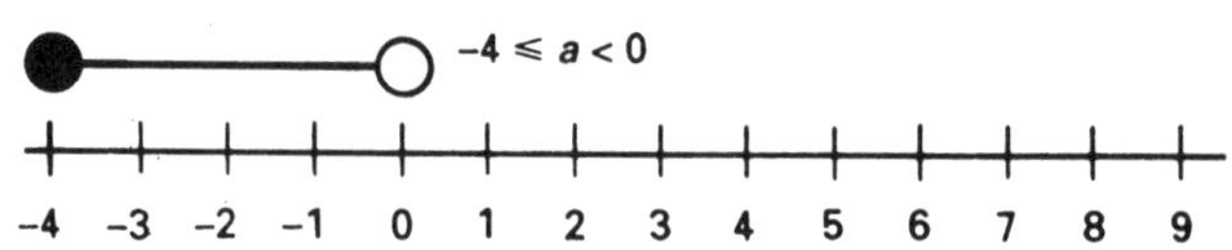

2 a $2 \leqslant x < 5$
b $x \leqslant -1$
c $-3 < y \leqslant -1$
d $x < 4$
e $x \geqslant -2$
f $x > 0$
g $-2 < x < 2$
h $3 \leqslant x \leqslant 5$

• Solving inequalities

Inequalities are solved in exactly the same way as we solve equations. We can add a number to both sides of an inequality without affecting it. The only problem arises when we multiply or divide an inequality by a negative number: $4 > 2$ but $-4 < -2$. The sign has been turned round. This point is stressed in the text-book.

EXERCISE 11C

1

a $r \geqslant 2$

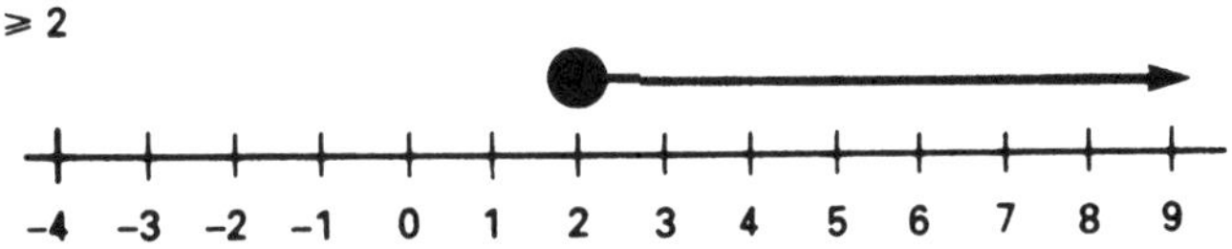

b $x < -8$

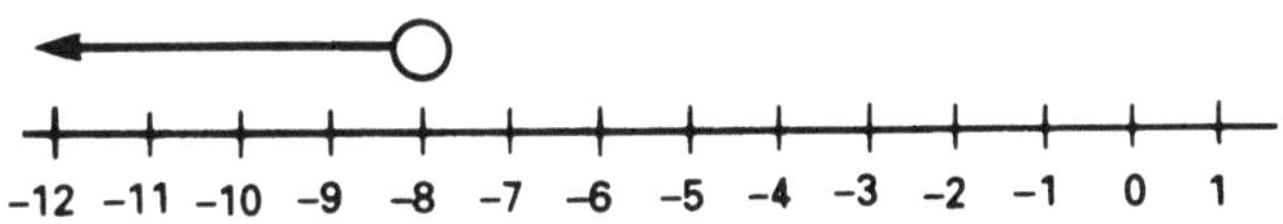

c $x \geqslant 0$

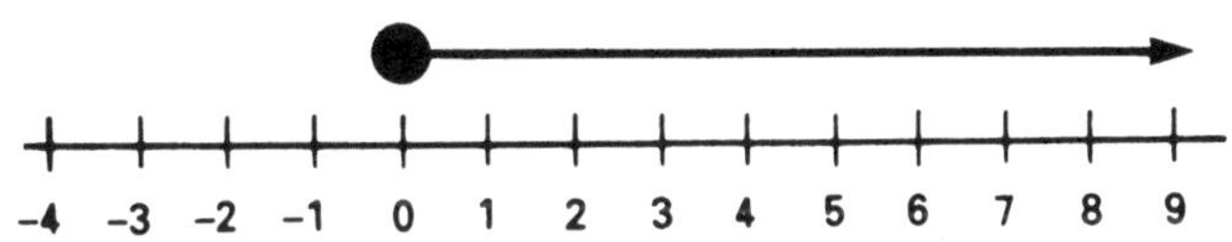

d $y > 15$

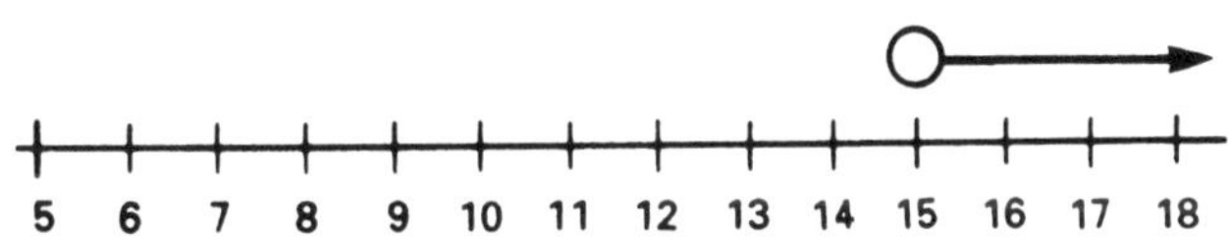

e $x < -3$

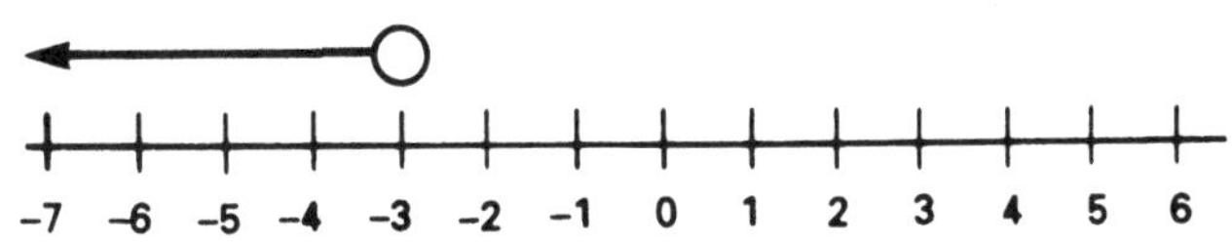

f $x > -3.5$

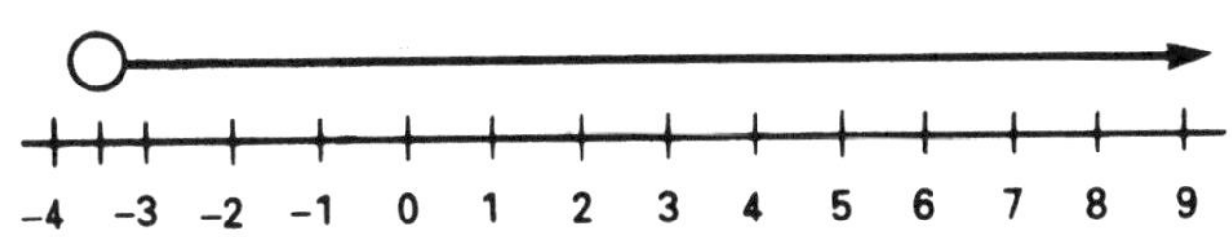

2

a $2 < a < 7$

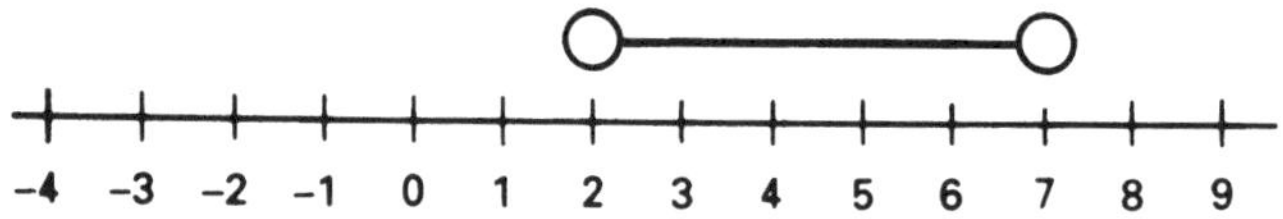

b $-6 < a < -4$

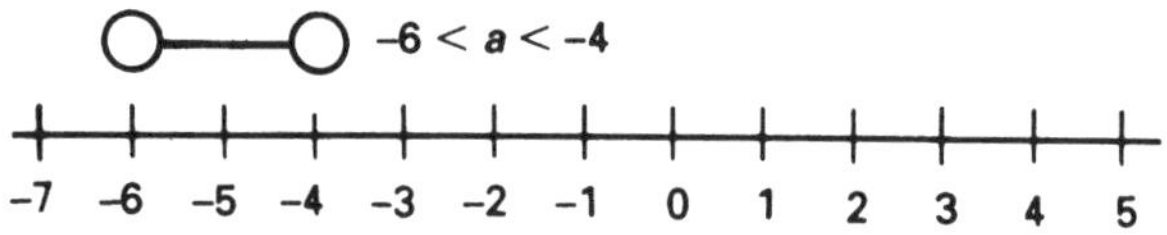

c $1 \leqslant x \leqslant 3.5$

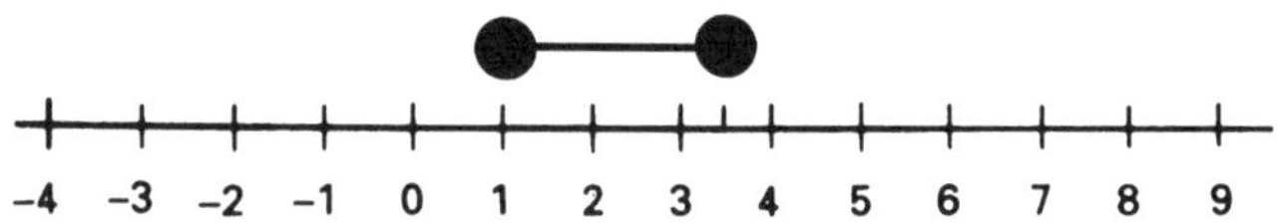

d $-4 < b < 0$

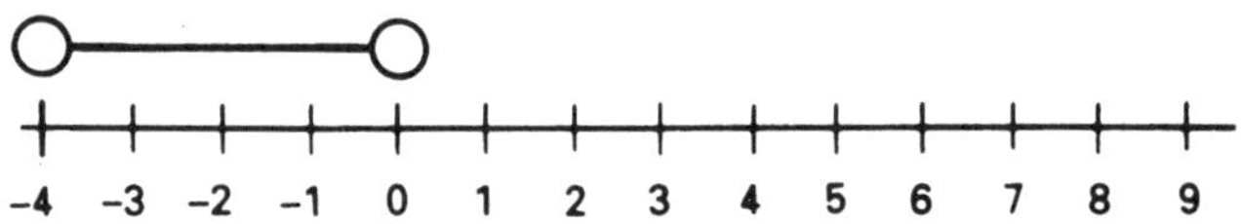

e $-2 \leqslant y < 3$

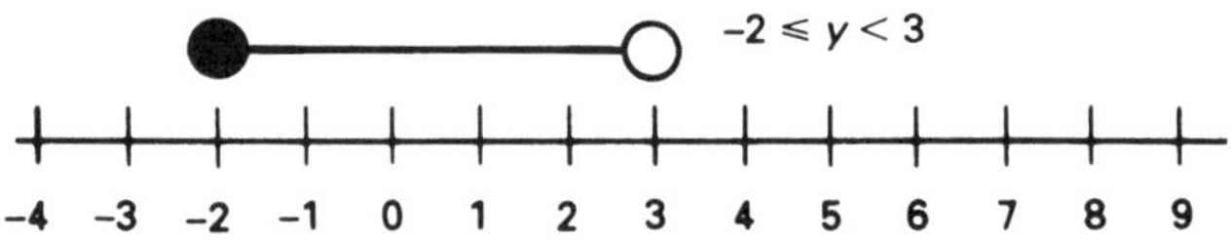

f $-6 < x \leqslant -1$

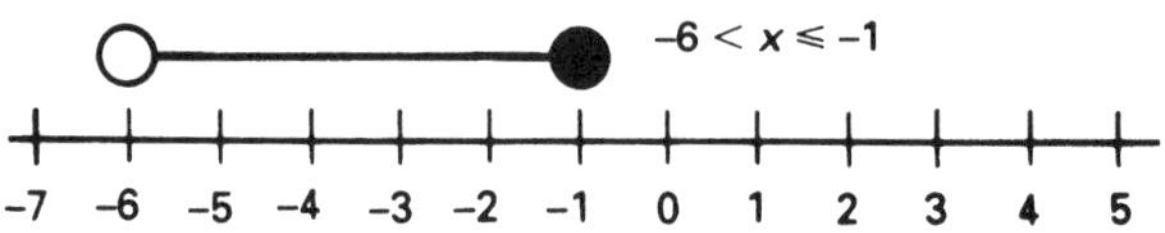

g $-2 \leqslant r < 4$

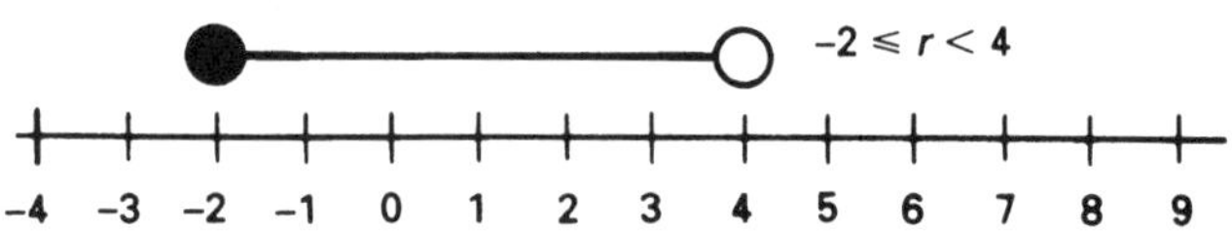

h $-2 < p < 2$

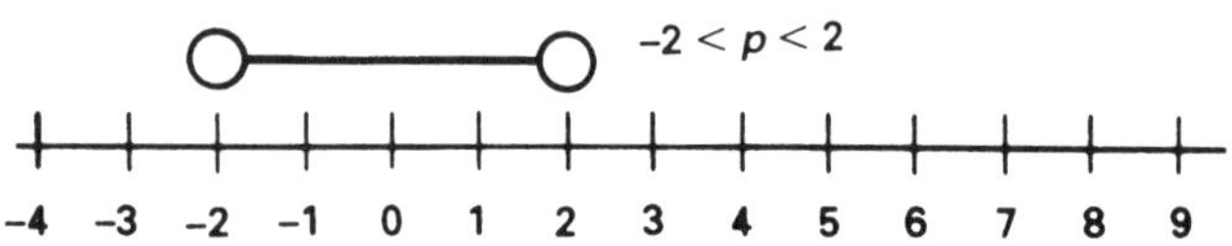

3 $x < 0$

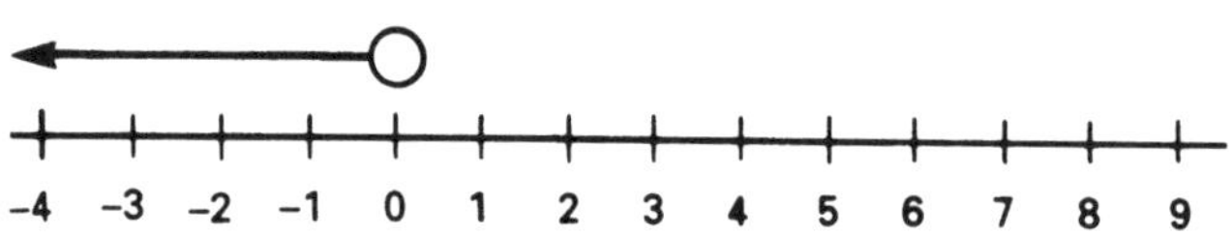

4 $x \geqslant 0$

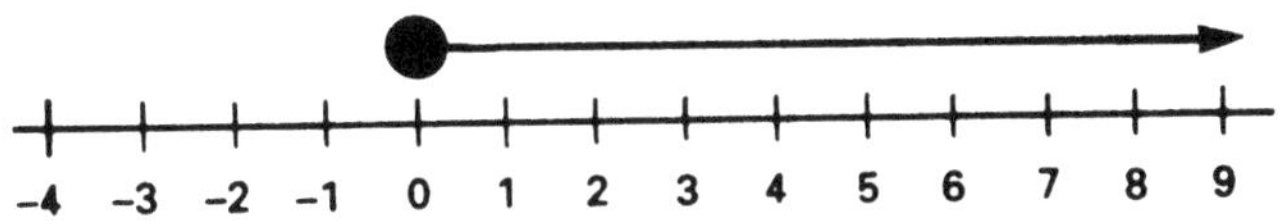

5 As the numbers in this question are only natural numbers and not the real numbers, they will be shown on the number line by individual points, and not with a continuous line.

a $\{x: x \text{ is a natural number}, x < 4\} = \{1,2,3\}$

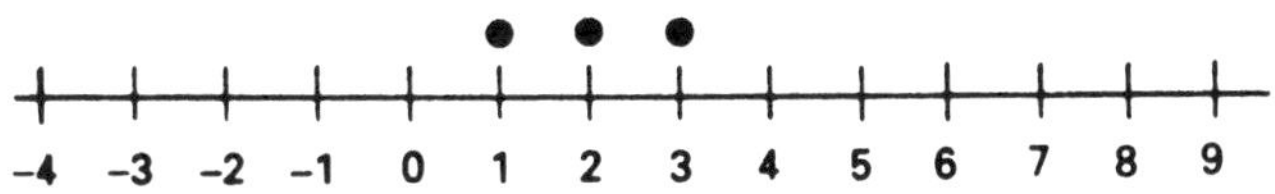

b $\{4,6,8,10\}$

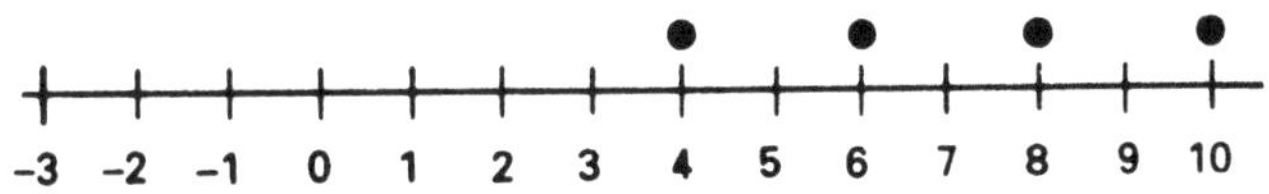

c $\{5,7,11,13\}$

• Using inequalities to solve problems

As with previous exercises of this type the difficulty for most students is to translate the English statements into mathematical ones.

EXERCISE 11D

1 The numbers are 4 and 12.
Let the smaller number be x: then the larger number is $3x$.
$x+3x=4x$, so $4x \geqslant 16$ and $x \geqslant 4$

2 The numbers are 6 and 18. Let the smaller number be x: then the larger number is $3x$. So $4x \geqslant 24$ and $x \geqslant 6$.

3 The numbers are 8 and 56.

Let the smaller number be x: then the larger number is $7x$.
$7x - x \leqslant 48$ and $x \leqslant 8$
The numbers are largest when x is largest, that is, when $x=8$.

4 The maximum dimensions are 10 metres by 40 metres.
If the width is x metres, then the length is $4x$ metres.
The perimeter $= 10x \leqslant 80$, so $x \leqslant 10$.
The maximum dimensions are when $x=10$.

5 The greatest possible ages are Ekanya 24 and Kapere 8 years old.
If Kapere is x years old, Ekanya is $3x$ years old.
$x+3x \leqslant 32$, so $x \leqslant 8$

6 Their least possible ages are Rose 16 and Alice 21 years old.
If Alice is x years old, Rose is $x-5$ years old.
$x+x-5 \geqslant 36$, so $x \geqslant 20.5$
Ages are stated as whole numbers, so x must be 21 or more.

7 100 km/hr
The first 30 km took $\frac{30}{40}=\frac{3}{4}$ hour.
To complete the journey in not more than $1\frac{1}{4}$ hours.
Ariyo has half an hour to cover 50 km.
The minimum average speed required $=50 \div \frac{1}{2}=100$ km/hr.

• Showing inequalities on a graph: regions

We now extend inequalities to graphs. The convention used is to shade the unwanted region. This is so that the region that we want is not covered with a lot of shading making it hard to see. For strict inequalities, $<$ or $>$, the area is bounded by a dotted line. For the inequalities, $\leqslant$ or $\geqslant$, the boundary is marked by a continuous line. When an area bounded by several lines is to be shown we draw the lines in turn and then shade the side of the line not covered by the inequality. The clear area which we are left with is the required region.

The examples at this stage are deliberately kept simple. The work here is the first stage towards the later development of linear programming.

EXERCISE 11E

1

a

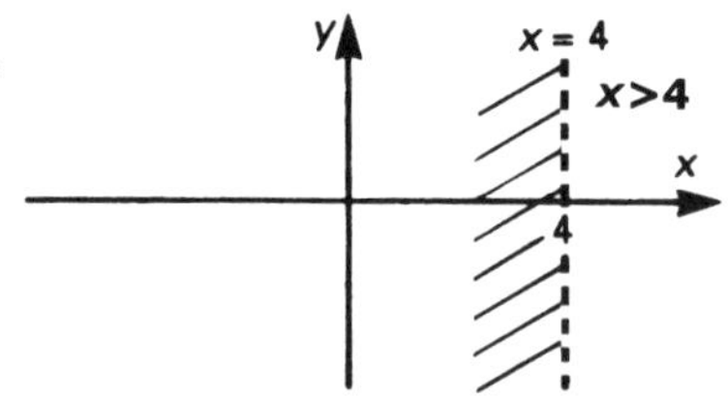

b

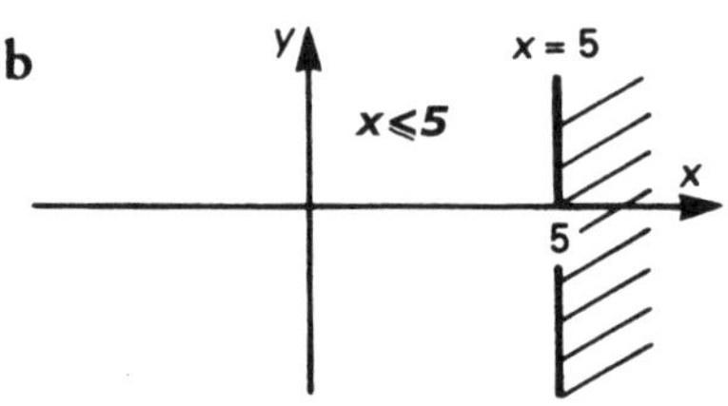

c

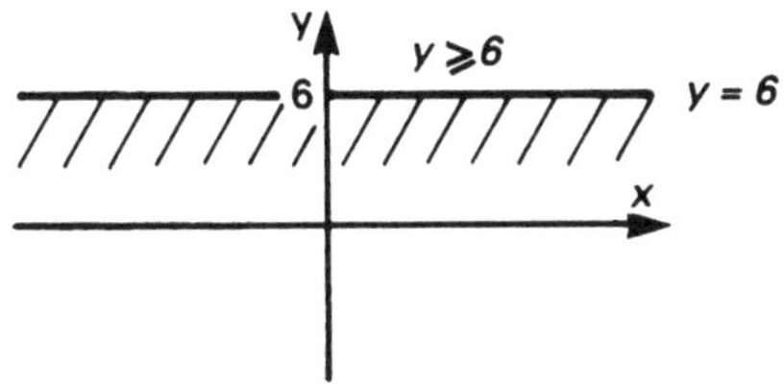

d

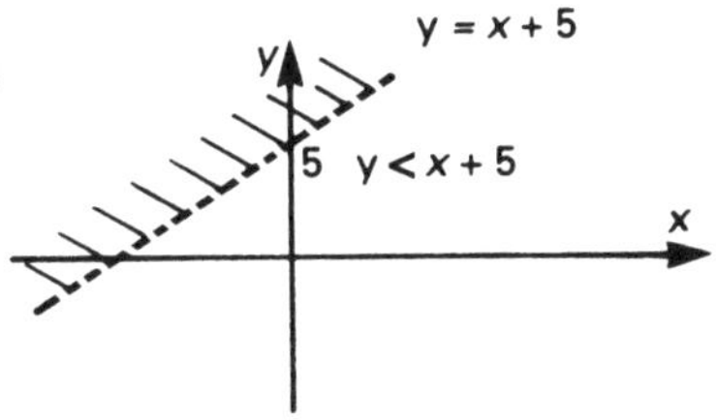

e

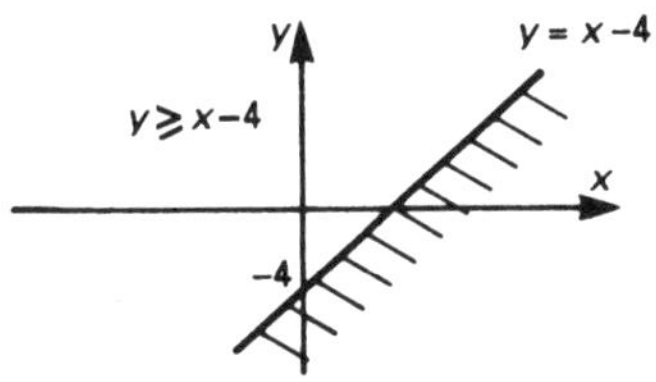

f

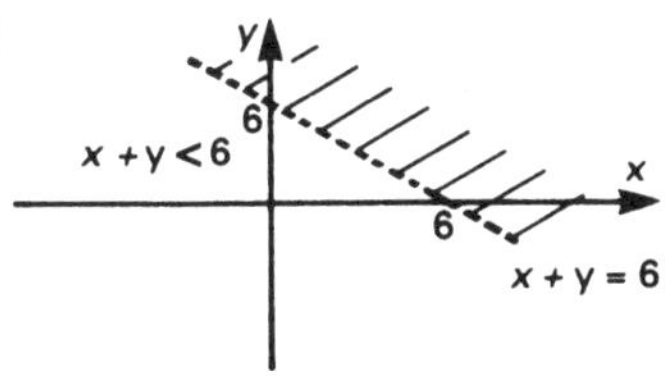

g

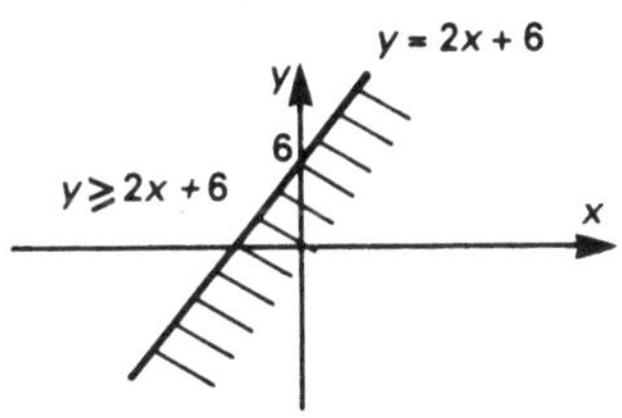

2 **a** $x > y$ and $x + y < 6$

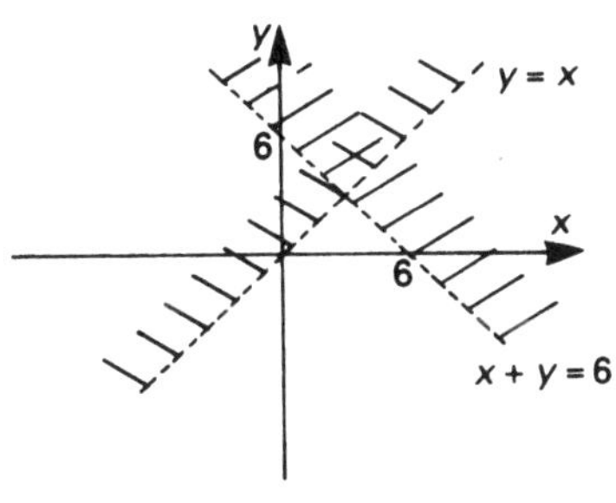

b x < y and x + y > 6

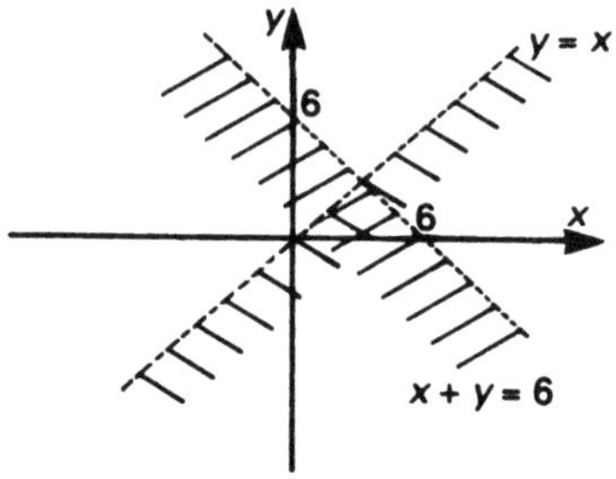

c x + y ⩽ 6 and x < y

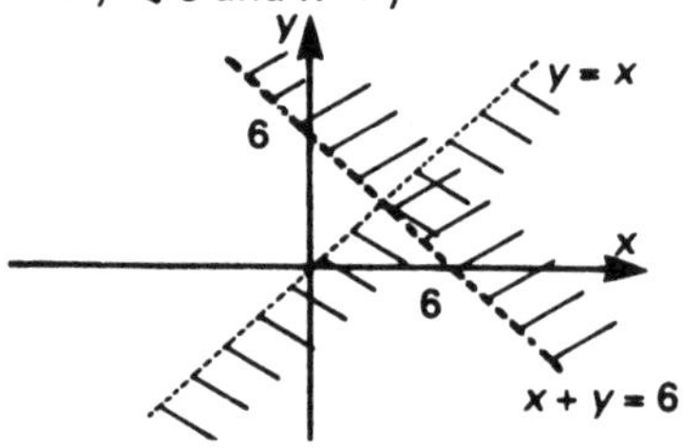

12 Geometrical constructions

- **Aim of chapter**

The aim of the chapter is to introduce students to the concept of a locus and how to construct loci.

- **Objectives**

By the end of the chapter, the students will be able to:

1 Sketch and describe the locus of a moving object
2 Construct perpendiculars, bisectors and parallel lines accurately with a ruler and a compass
3 Construct the inscribed and circumscribed circles of a triangle.

- **Paths of moving objects**

Moving objects travel along a path. In some cases we can predict what the path will look like, while in other cases we cannot. For example, the path traced by a moving snail cannot be predicted because the snail will move according to rules we do not know. When an object moves according to a rule, the path it moves along is called its locus. The locus can often be sketched. For example, the locus of the centre of a wheel moving on flat ground is a line parallel to the ground:

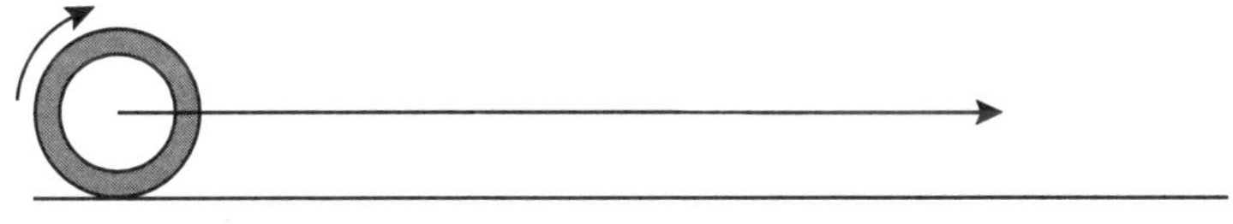

The locus of a point on the rim of the wheel is not so simple:

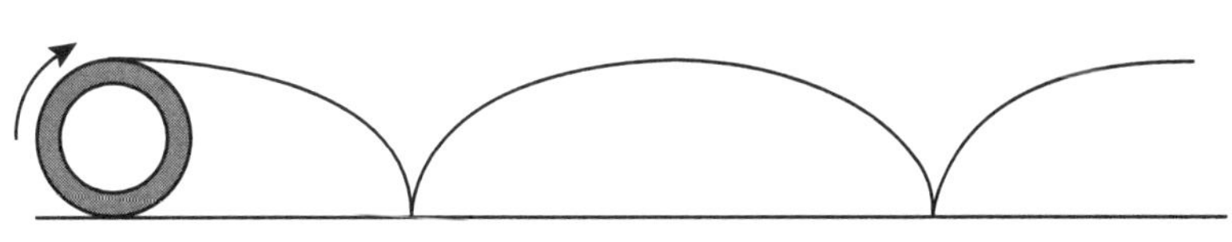

The teacher should use other similar examples.

EXERCISE 12A

1 a 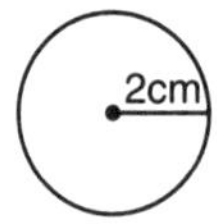

b 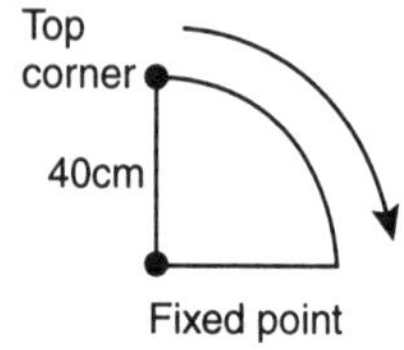

c 

2 Angle bisector of AB and AC

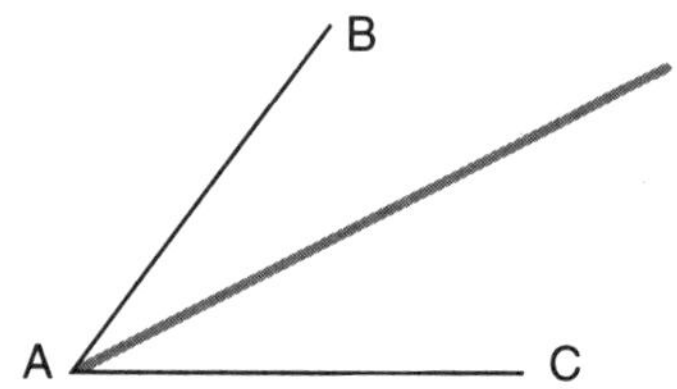

3 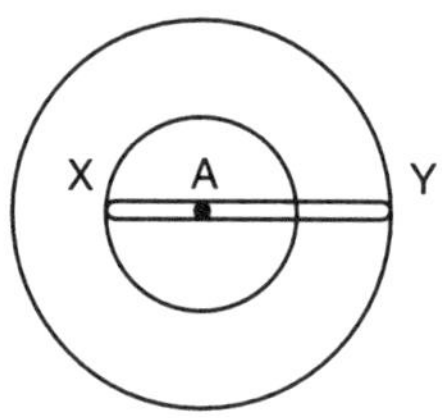

a X's locus is a circle centre A, radius XA.

b Y's locus is a circle centre A, radius YA.

4 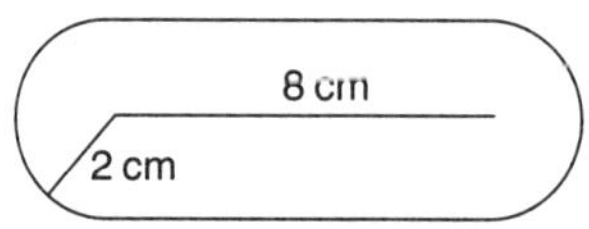

The locus is like a running track:

Two straights and semi-circles radius 2 cm at the ends.

5 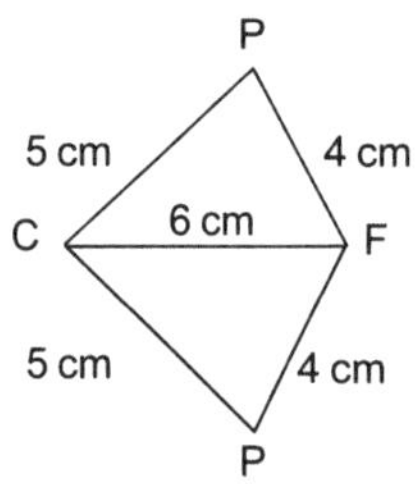

The locus is two points, 4 cm from F and 5 cm from C.

6 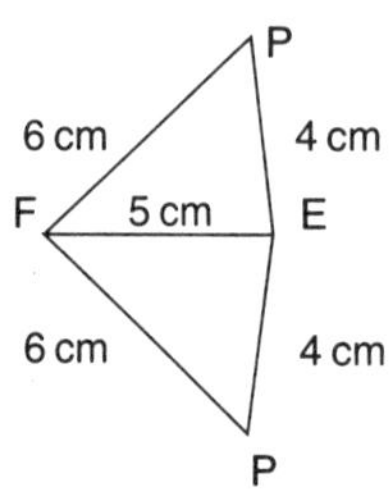

The locus is two points, 4 cm from E and 6 cm from F.

• Regions

Sometimes a moving object may trace out an area rather than a line. The locus in this case is the region that it covers.
If the boundary is part of the region, the locus boundary is shown as a solid line: ———— . If the boundary is not included, it is shown as a dotted line: ………… .

EXERCISE 12B

1 a Perpendicular bisector of CD
b No
c The shaded area

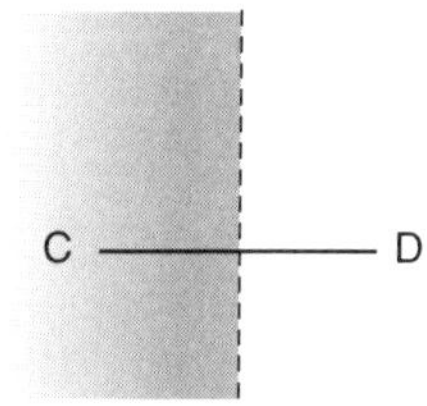

2 a Circle radius 3 m, centre the post
b Yes
c Area of circle radius 3 cm, centre the post.

3 a Like a running track: two straights 3 m long and semi-circles with radius 4 cm at the ends
b Yes
c Area inside the boundary

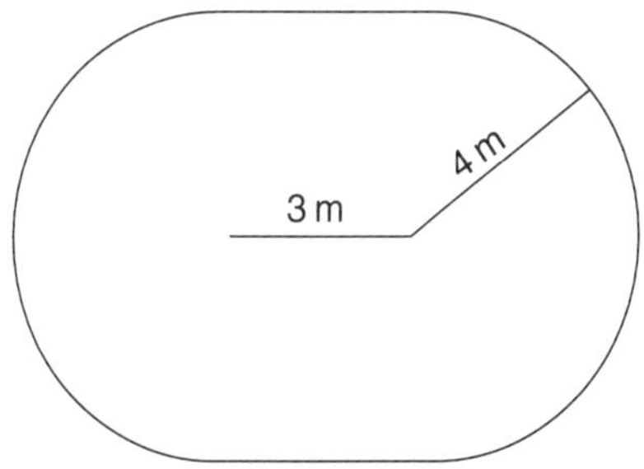

4 a Two arcs centres P and Q radius 3 m and lines parallel to and 1 m from the fences.
b Yes
c As shaded in the diagram, all points more than 3 metres from the trees and 1 m from the fences

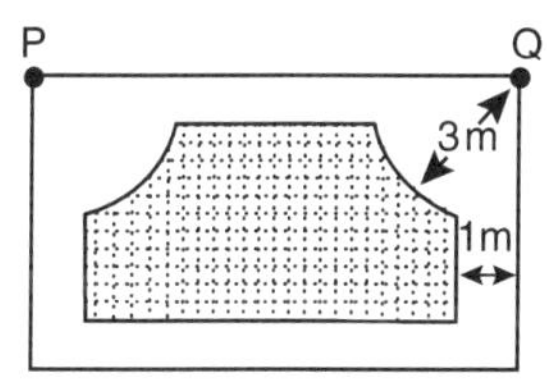

5 a Points 4 cm or 5 cm from A and 4 cm or 5 cm from B
b Yes 4 cm line, no 5 cm line.
c As shaded in the diagram, all points at least 4 cm and less than 5 cm from A and B.

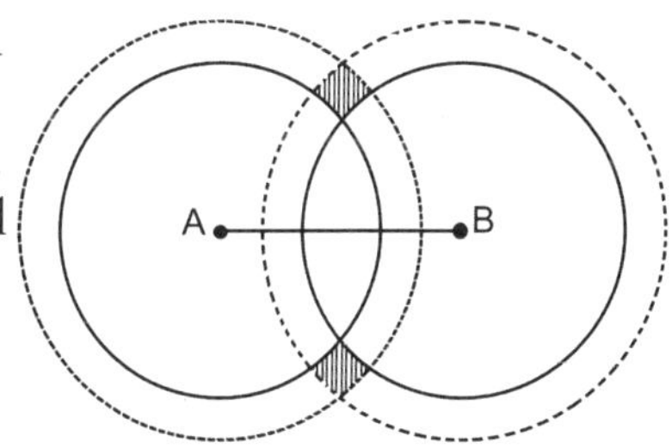

• Constructions

This section starts by reviewing basic constructions which students should be familiar with. Go quickly through the construction of perpendiculars, bisectors of lines and angles and triangles.

The textbook explains why the constructions work. If the constructions are understood, then they are very much easier to remember.

When constructing the perpendicular bisector of a line, we use the fact that the diagonals of a rhombus bisect each other at right angles.

When constructing the locus of points equidistant from two lines, we use the fact that the diagonals of a rhombus bisect its angles.

When solving problems requiring a construction, students should be encouraged to start by doing a rough sketch.

EXERCISE 12C

1 a A sketch:
b BC = 10.5 cm
Angle ABC = 40°
c CD = 6.9 cm
d BE = 10.5 cm

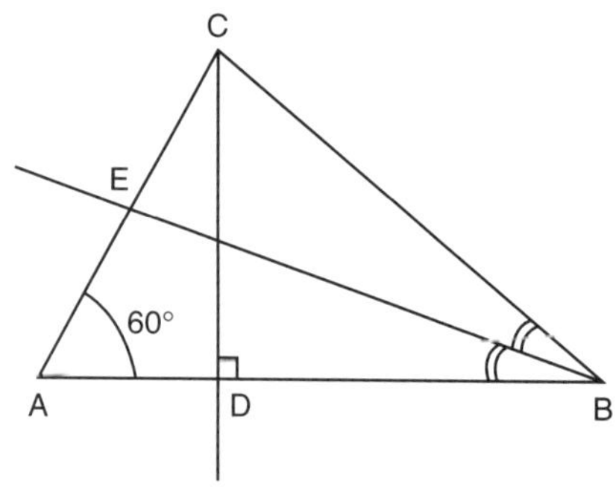

2 A sketch:

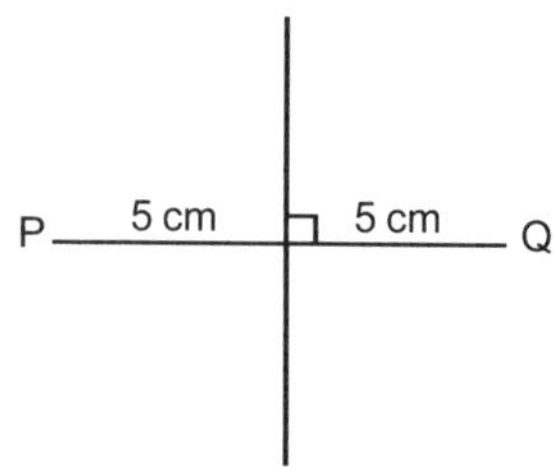

3 A sketch:

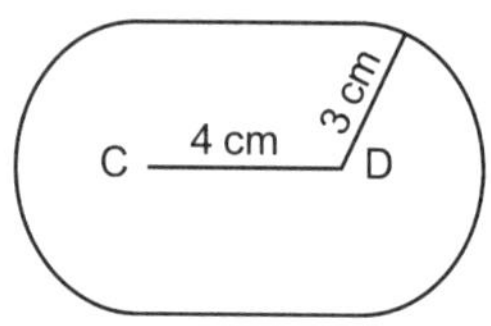

4 A sketch:

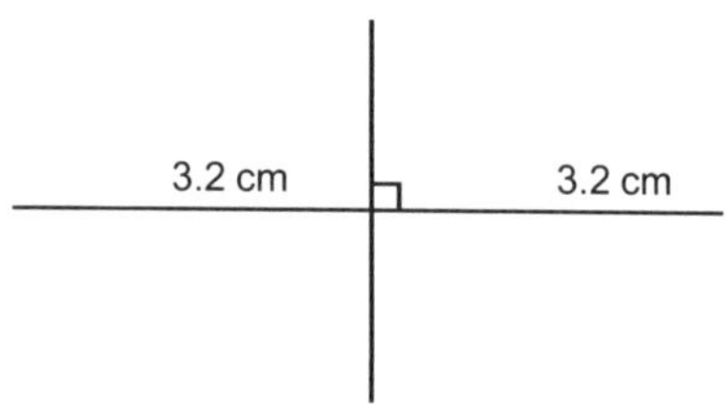

5 A sketch:

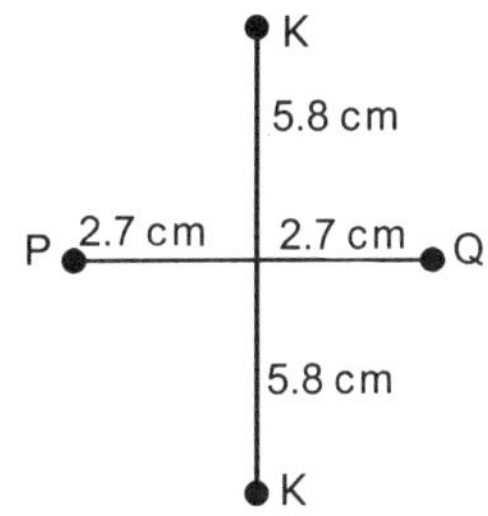

6 A sketch:
Yes CD is parallel to AB.

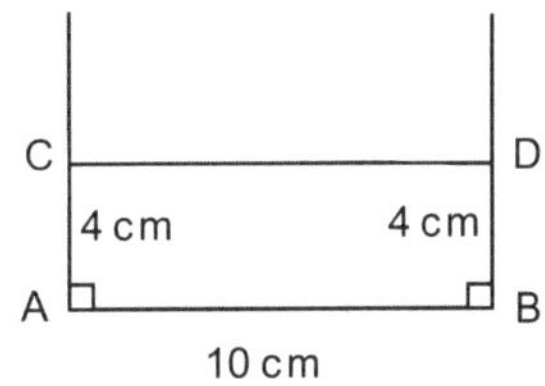

• Parallel lines

The construction in this section is of a line parallel to another line. This uses the method of the last question in the previous exercise. The procedure is set out step-by-step.

EXERCISE 12D

1 a A sketch:

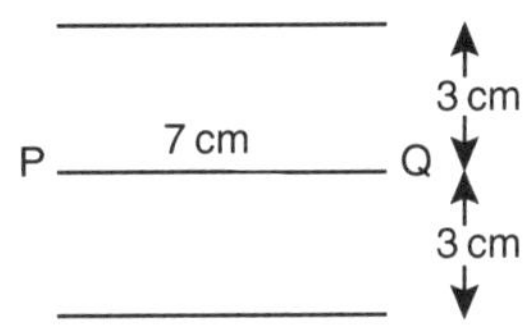

2 A sketch:

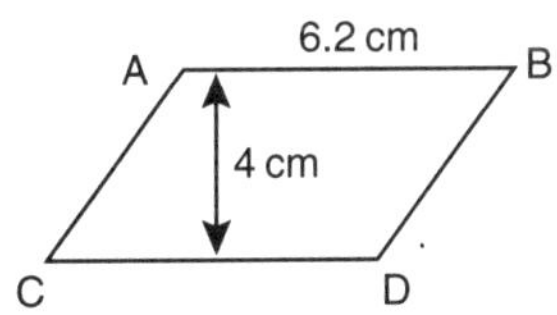

3 A sketch:

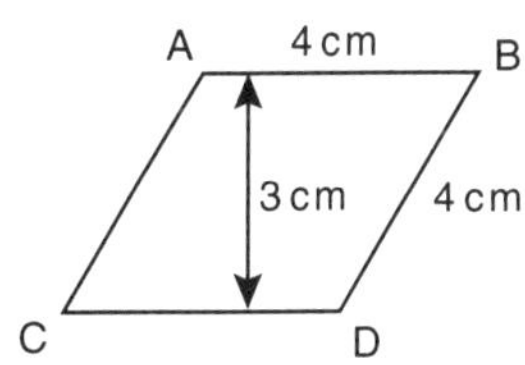

• Circle – a reminder

This section reviews earlier work on circles, their parts and how they can be constructed.

• Inscribed circle

For any triangle, it is always possible to draw a circle that touches its three sides. Such circles are called inscribed circles. It is explained in the textbook why the centre of the inscribed circle is at the point where the three angle bisectors meet: Points on an angle's bisector are the same distance from the two arms of the angle, so the point at which the three bisectors meet will be at the same distance from all three sides of the triangle.

The teacher should discuss this, as understanding it helps students to remember how to find the incentre.

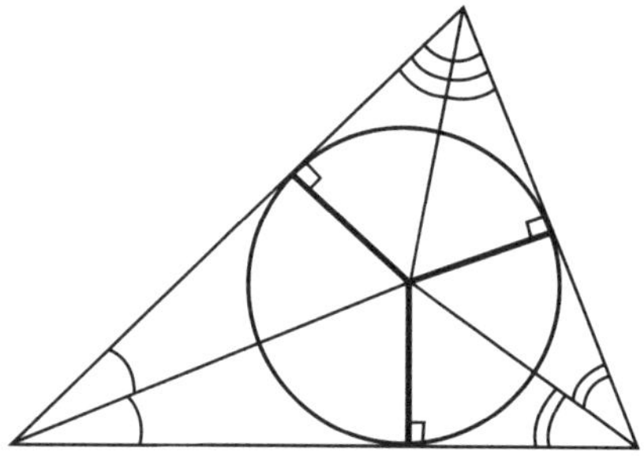

• Circumscribed circle

For any triangle, it is always possible to draw a circle that goes through all its three vertices. Such circles are called circumscribed circles or escribed circles.
It is explained in the textbook why the centre of the circumscribed circle is at the point where the three side bisectors meet: Points on the bisector of a line segment are the same distance from its two end-points, so the point where the three line segment bisectors meet is the same distance from all three vertices of the triangle. The teacher should discuss this, as understanding it helps students to remember how to find the circumcentre.

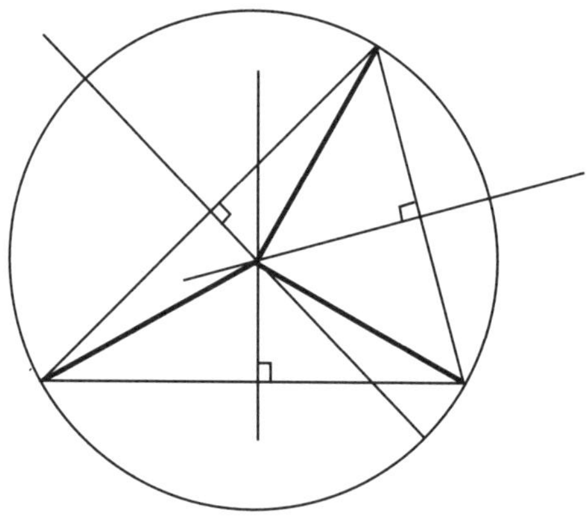

EXERCISE 12E

1 **a** A sketch:
Radius = 1 cm

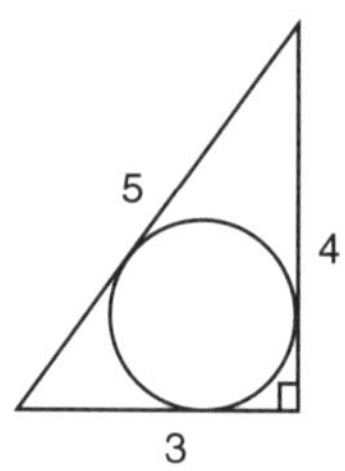

Note:
The *inscribed* circle in a right-angled triangle is interesting: The right-angled triangle below has sides BC = a, AC = b, and AB = c. The inscribed circle has radius r.

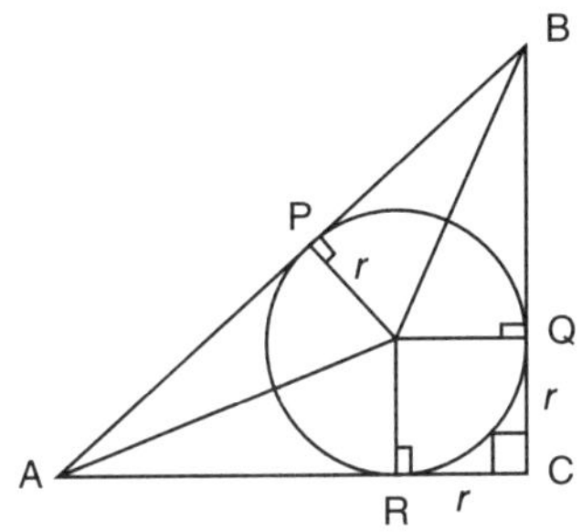

BC = a, so BP = BQ = $a - r$
AC = b, so AP = AR = $b - r$

But c = AB = AP + PB
so $c = b - r + a - r = a + b - 2r$

and $r = \dfrac{a+b-c}{2}$

The diameter of the *circumscribed* circle of any right-angled triangle is the hypotenuse:

Here $r = \dfrac{c}{2}$ and $c^2 = a^2 + b^2$

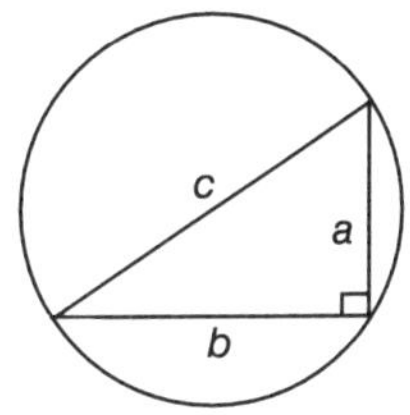

2 A sketch:
Diameter = 6.7cm

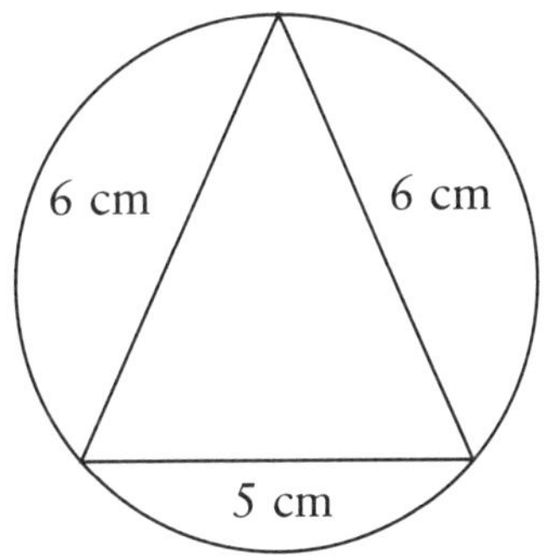

3 A sketch:
CP = 6.4 cm

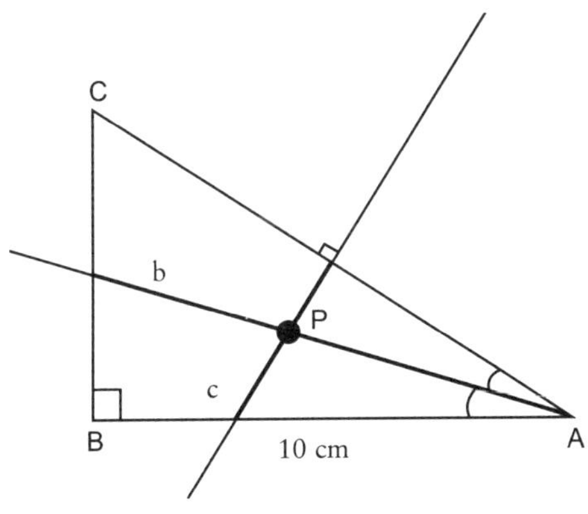

4 A sketch:

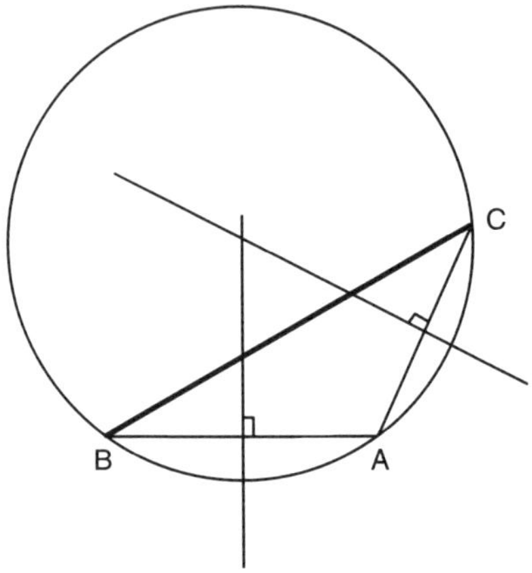

5 A sketch:
Distance between centres = 1.2cm

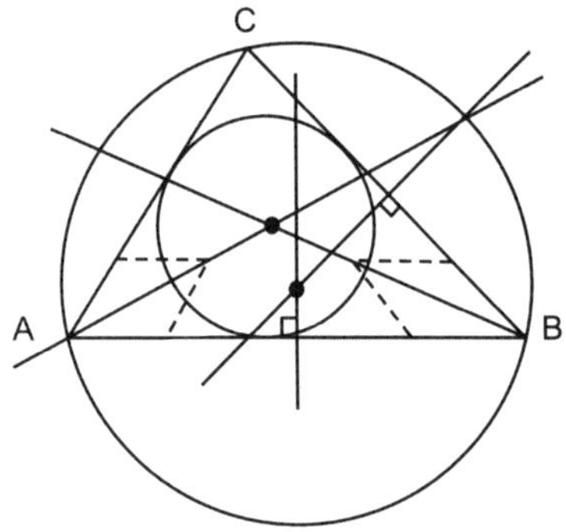

6 By drawing it is found that:
(i) The centre of the ladder moves a quarter circle, radius 5 m, centre the point where wall and ground meet, as shown on the diagram.
(ii) A point 2 m from the top of the ladder moves in a steep curve as shown on the diagram.

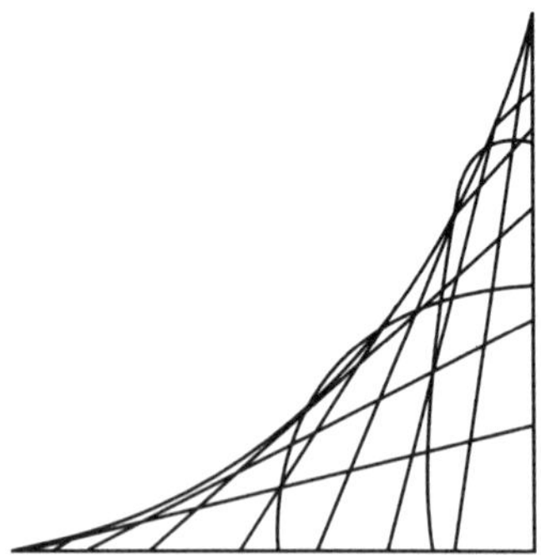

We can show (i) that if the ladder is x m long, then the centre is always

$\frac{x}{2}$ m from A, the point where wall and ground meet.

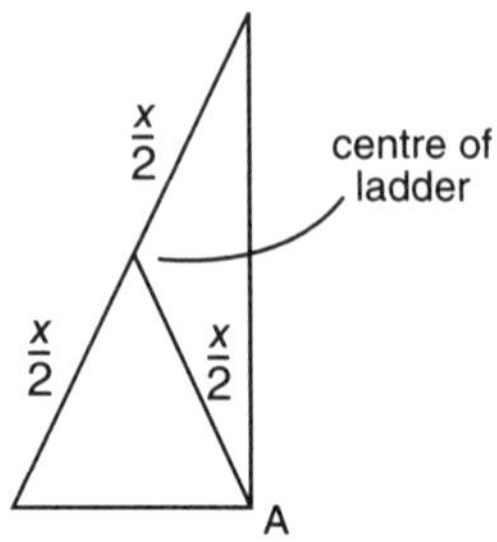

13 Algebra – expansion, factorisation and algebraic equations

• Aim of chapter

The aim of the chapter is to introduce the students to the factorisation of quadratic expressions, including the difference of two squares.

• Objectives

By the end of the chapter the students will be able to:

1 Multiply a bracketed expression by an expression
2 Subtract an expression in a bracket
3 Multiply two brackets together
4 Find the square of a bracket
5 Find the difference of two squares
6 Factorise completely linear expressions
7 Factorise completely quadratic expressions where the coefficient of x^2 is 1
8 Factorise completely the difference of two squares
9 Solve quadratic equations by factorisation.

• Brackets – algebraic expansion

The failure to understand the rule for multiplying out brackets is one of the commonest mistakes in mathematics. Teachers become very accustomed to seeing mistakes like $3(x+y)=3x+y$. It is not difficult to understand why students make this kind of mistake. If they are told to work out 3, add 4, multiply by 7, they will get the answer 49; but if we write this out in mathematical symbols as it sounds we get $3+4\times 7$ which becomes $3+28=31$ because of the mathematical convention that multiplication is carried out first. So the confusion is understandable. The students' attention has to be repeatedly drawn to the convention; the number or letter outside a bracket (whether at the front or the back) is multiplied with everything inside the bracket.

EXERCISE 13A

1 a $5a+10b$ b $7x-7y$ c x^2+xy
d $4x+8y$ e $10a-5b$ f $16c-8d$
g $ab+ac-5a$ h $4x+8y$ i $2b^3+4b^2-6b$
j $6x^4-8x^3+2x^2$ k $2x^3-2x^2+6x$

2 a $12x+7y$ b $4x+2y$ c $4c^2-c$
d x^2-2x e 18 f $x+3$
g $5a+b+5c$ h 0

• Subtracting brackets

The two sets of important rules relating to the subtraction of a bracket are developed in this section. The rules are:

$$a-(b+c)=a-b-c \qquad a-k(b+c)=a-kb-kc$$
$$a-(b-c)=a-b+c \qquad a-k(b-c)=a-kb+kc$$

These can be summarised as 'If there is a subtraction sign in front of a bracket, the operation sign inside changes when the bracket is removed'.

The rules are developed through examples.

EXERCISE 13B

1 a $x+3$ b $x-2$ c 3
d $x+8$ e $3b$ f $-x+10$

2 a -3 b $x+2$ c $x+18$
d $2x$ e $2a-b$ f $2x+13$

3 a $4x+1$ b $6x-11$ c $7x+18b$
d $9x+2y$ e $2a$ f $10y$

• Expansion – multiplying two brackets together

Rectangles are used to develop the identities

$$(a+b)(c+d)=ac+ad+bc+bd$$

and

$$\begin{aligned}(x+b)(x+a)&=x^2+ax+bx+ab\\&=x^2+(a+b)x+ab\end{aligned}$$

• Square of a bracket

The identity $(x+a)^2=x^2+2ax+a^2$ is a special case of the previous work.

• Difference of two squares

The difference of two squares identity $(a+b)(a-b)=a^2-b^2$ is an important special case of the rule for multiplying out brackets.

EXERCISE 13C

1 a x^2+2x-8 b $x^2+3x-28$
c $a^2+4a-45$ d $b^2-3b-28$
e $b^2+7b+10$ f $k^2-14k+48$
g x^2-4x+3 h x^2-4x-5
i $x^2+7x-44$

2 a $2x^2+7x+3$ b $6x^2+23x+20$
c $2x^2-25x+63$ d $3x^2-10xy-8y^2$
e $10x^2+x-3$ f $20x^2+x-1$
g $14x^2-x-3$ h $2x^2-5xy-7y^2$
i $6x^2-7x-3$

3 a x^2+2x+1 b $x^2-10x+25$
c $x^2+8x+16$ d $4x^2+4x+1$
e $9x^2-12x+4$ f $25x^2-40x+16$

4 a x^2-1 b x^2-9 c x^2-49
d $4x^2-9$ e $9x^2-1$ f $25x^2-16$

5 a $13x^2-2x+2$ b $5x^2-5$ c x^2+4x-6
d $8ab$ e $-x-3$ f $-5m^2-11mn+7n^2$

• Factorisation of algebraic expressions

Previously students learnt to multiply out brackets. Now they learn how to go in the opposite direction and express an algebraic expression as the product of simpler expressions.
In this first section, the expressions to be factorised are simple linear expressions whose terms have common numbers or letters that can be factored out.

EXERCISE 13D

1 a $5(a-5)$ b $2(a+2)$ c $2(x-4)$ d $2(3x-4)$
e $3(a-1)$ f $2(2a+3)$ g $5(2a+1)$ h $2(3a+2)$

2 a $5(a+2b)$ b $2(3x+2y)$ c $2(x-b)$ d $4(4x-3y)$
e $3(2x-3y)$ f $x(a+y)$ g $a(x+5)$ h $6(x-y)$

3 a $a(5a-b)$ b $2x(x+2)$ c $2(x^2-4)$ d $8x(1-x)$
e $3a(a-2)$ f $2b(2a+3b)$ g $5a(2a+1)$ h $a(a+b)$

4 a $5(2a+b-3c)$ b $2(2x-y-4)$
c $2x(6y-x+2)$ d $3a(2x-4y+3z)$
e $3(x-2y+3)$ f $x^2(x+y+4)$

• Quadratic factors

To factorise an expression such as $x^2+9x+20$, we have to find two numbers with a sum of 9 and a product of 20. These numbers are 4 and 5. We can immediately write down the answer $(x+4)(x+5)$. Once we have found the two numbers 4 and 5 we know the factors.
Some teachers expect their students to write

$$\begin{aligned} x^2+9x+20 &= x^2+5x+4x+20 \\ &= x(x+5)+4(x+5) \\ &= (x+5)(x+4) \end{aligned}$$

But the two middle lines are surely unnecessary; once the 4 and 5 have been found we can write down the answer without any further writing. The extra lines serve no useful purpose. They give the impression of being working needed to find the factors, but in fact they are a waste of time.

The work begins with practice at finding two numbers with a given sum and product. Students find problems of this type particularly difficult if one of the numbers is 1. In this first section all the signs are positive. In the next section more difficult problems which involve negative signs will be used.

EXERCISE 13E

1 a 1, 4 b 1, 1 c 3, 5 d 6, 2 e 1, 7
f 6, 6 g 6, 8 h 1, 19 i 4, 25 j 5, 8

2 a $(x+6)(x+1)$ b $(x+2)(x+5)$
c $(x+4)(x+2)$ d $(x+3)(x+5)$
e $(x+6)(x+2)$ f $(x+7)(x+8)$
g $(x+5)(x+4)$ h $(x+4)(x+25)$
i $(x+1)(x+4)$ j $(x+5)(x+12)$
k $(x+1)(x+17)$ l $(x+6)(x+6)$
m $(x+1)(x+19)$ n $(x+5)(x+8)$
o $(x+10)(x+10)$ p $(x+8)(x+6)$
q $(x+3)(x+12)$ r $(x+1)(x+36)$

When the expression to be factorised has negative signs in it, finding the numbers we require can be more difficult.

For example, in the expression $x^2-7x+12$ we are looking for two numbers with a sum of -7 and a product of 12. The product is positive so both numbers are positive or both numbers are negative. The sum is negative so both numbers must be negative. In this case the numbers are -3 and -4. The process involved here is not very different from finding the numbers we need when factorising $x^2+7x+12$, but when there is a negative sign in front of the last term, we are in effect looking for the difference between two numbers. For example, to factorise $x^2-6x-16$, we are seeking two numbers with a sum of -6 and a product of -16. Since the product is negative, one number will be positive and one number will be negative. We are in effect looking for two numbers with product 16 and difference 6. This is more difficult than the earlier examples.

• Applications of difference of two squares

Using the identity $a^2-b^2=(a+b)(a-b)$, many expressions can be quickly factorised. The students have to learn to see that the terms in the expression are both perfect squares and that the identity only works when the squares are being subtracted. a^2+b^2 cannot be factorised simply.

Questions **5** and **6** apply the difference of two squares identity to make some mental arithmetic quicker and more fun. These questions should only be attempted by the more able pupils. They are open ended in the sense that the ideas developed here can be taken much further.

EXERCISE 13F

1 a $-1,-4$ b $-1,-1$ c $-3,-5,$ d $-12,+2$
e $-4,-4$ f $-4,+1$ g $-5,+2$ h $-6,+2$
i $-5,+8$ j $-3,+4$

2 a $(x-4)(x-3)$ b $(x-3)(x-6)$
c $(x-4)(x-4)$ d $(x-7)(x-1)$
e $(x-5)(x-2)$ f $(x-6)(x-9)$
g $(x-3)(x-3)$ h $(x-5)(x-20)$
i $(x-7)(x-4)$ j $(x-3)(x-12)$

3 a $(x+9)(x-2)$ b $(x+2)(x-9)$
c $(x+8)(x-1)$ d $(x+3)(x-5)$
e $(x+6)(x-2)$ f $(x+2)(x-28)$
g $(x+5)(x-4)$ h $(x+9)(x-10)$
i $(x+7)(x-2)$ j $(x+4)(x-15)$
k $(x+11)(x-2)$ l $(x+2)(x-14)$
m $(x+12)(x-2)$ n $(x+5)(x-20)$
o $(x+19)(x-2)$ p $(x+3)(x-17)$

4 a $(x+6)(x-6)$ b $(x+10)(x-10)$
c $(y+1)(y-1)$ d $(x+12)(x-12)$
e $(2x+3)(2x-3)$ f $(x+3y)(x-3y)$
g $(2a+5)(2a-5)$ h $(4x+7y)(4x-7y)$
l $(3x+2)(3x-2)$ j $(2ab^2+3x)(2ab^2-3x)$

5 a $9+8=17$ b $41+40=81$
c $61+60=121$ d $101+100=221$
e $54+53=107$ f $1001+1000=2001$

6 a $39\times 41=1600-1=1599$
b $13\times 15=196-1=195$
c $24\times 26=625-1=624$
d $99\times 101=10\,000-1=9999$
e $28\times 32=(30+2)(30-2)=900-4=896$

This can be extended:
$33\times 27=900-9=891$, $34\times 26=900-16=884$,
$35\times 25=900-25=875$ etc.

• $a\times b=0$

One of the common errors that students make is to think that if, for example, $x^2+4x=x(x+4)=6$ then either $x=6$ or $x+4=6$
After all, if $x^2+4x=x(x+4)=0$ then either $x=0$ or $x+4=0$
The significance of 0 is that if $a\times b=0$ then either $a=0$ or $b=0$ (or both).

But if $a\times b=6$ then we cannot say that either $a=6$ or $b=6$. For a could be 3 and b could be 2, or $a=12$ and $b=0.5$, and so on. There are an infinite number of possibilities.

When a product is equal to 0 we know that one of the multipliers must be 0.
This property of 0 is crucial to understanding how to solve quadratic equations so this section examines it carefully.

EXERCISE 13G

1 Many possible answers, including:
a 3, 4; 2, 6; 1, 12 b 1, 41; 41, 1; 2, 20.5
c 1, 1; 2, 0.5; 5, 0.2 d 3,7; 7, 3; 1, 21
e 1, 0; 2, 0; 0, 5 f 1, 31; 31, 1; 10, 3.1

2 a $x=-5$ or 6 b $x=-3$ or 5
c $x=0$ or -7 d $x=0$ or 1.5
e $x=-7$ or 8 f $x=3$ or 4
g $x=-\frac{7}{3}$ or 1 h $x=-0.5$ or $-\frac{5}{3}$
i $x=0$ or 8 j $x=0$ or $-\frac{2}{3}$

• Solving $x^2+bx+c=0$ by factorisation

Quadratic equations of the form $an^2 + bn + c = 0$ in which the coefficient of x^2 is 1 are solved first because they are easier to do. To find the factors in this case, all the student has to do is to find two numbers whose sum is b and whose product is c. In the next section the coefficient of x^2 is more than 1 and the process is a little more complicated.

EXERCISE 13H

1	$x=-5$ or -2	2	$x=-8$ or -3
3	$x=-1$ or -6	4	$x=-4$
5	$x=2$ or 6	6	$x=4$ or 7
7	$x=3$	8	$x=1$ or 10
9	$x=-5$ or 2	10	$x=-5$ or 4
11	$x=-5$ or 3	12	$x=3$ or -8
13	$x=-3$ or 6	14	$x=15$ or -3
15	$x=7$ or -4	16	$x=-6$ or 8
17	$x=2$ or -6	18	$x=-2$ or -5
19	$x=3$ or -5	20	$x=13$ or -3

• ax^2+bx+c

The method used to factorise expressions of the form ax^2+bx+c is explained in detail. The method in the book is a reliable and fairly straightforward method to use. The method is justified in the textbook though students do not have to learn this justification.

EXERCISE 13I

1 a $(3x+4)(x+1)$ b $(4x+5)(x+2)$
c $(2x+1)(4x+3)$ d $(5x+3)(x+4)$

2 a $(7x+1)(x-3)$ b $(3x+2)(4x-3)$
c $(6x+1)(x-5)$ d $(3x+4)(x-4)$

3 a $(3x+4)(x-1)$ b $(3x-1)(2x+5)$
c $(2x-1)(4x+7)$ d $(3x+4)(x-4)$

4 a $(2x-1)(x-4)$ b $(3x-2)(2x-3)$
c $(4x-3)(3x-4)$ d $(3x-1)(2x-1)$

• $ax^2+bx+c=0$

The method used to factorise expressions of the form ax^2+bx+c is now used to solve equations of the form $ax^2+bx+c=0$.
The method is fully explained in the text-book. In the exercise, the first few questions are already factorised, in order to start the students off with easier examples.
The teacher should discuss with the students the difference between quadratic expressions and quadratic equations.

As well as problems of the form $ax^2+bx+c=0$ there are also problems with unknowns on both sides of the equation which have to be rearranged before they can be solved.

EXERCISE 13J

1 a $x=0$ or 3 b $x=0$ or -4
c $x=0$ or 1.25 d $x=0$ or $-1\frac{1}{3}$

2 a $x=-1.5$ or 4 b $x=-6$ or $-1\frac{1}{3}$
c $x=-\frac{2}{5}$ or $-1\frac{1}{3}$ d $x=-4$ or 2.5

3 a $x=0$ or 4 b $x=0$ or 1.5
c $x=0$ or -1.5 d $x=0$ or -2.5

4 a $x=-1$ or -1.5 b $x=-2$ or $-\frac{1}{3}$
c $x=-1\frac{1}{3}$ or -0.5 d $x=-0.5$ or -1.5

5 a $x=1.5$ or 1 b $x=2$ or $1\frac{1}{3}$
c $x=1.5$ or 0.8 d $x=1\frac{2}{3}$ or $1\frac{1}{3}$

6 a $x=2$ or $-1\frac{1}{3}$ b $x=3$ or -2.5
c $x=2.5$ or $-1\frac{1}{3}$ d $x=6$ or -2.5

7 a $x=-5$ or $\frac{2}{3}$ b $x=1.5$ or -2.5
c $x=-3$ or 0.25 d $x=-5$ or 2.5

8 a $x=3$ or -1.5 b $x=2$ or $-2\frac{2}{3}$
c $x=7$ or -2 d $x=-0.5$ or 0.75

9 a $x=-4$ or 1.5 b $x=6$ or 2.5
c $x=2.5$ or -0.5 d $x=-0.5$ or 3.75

• Problems involving quadratic equations

Quadratic equations can be used to solve real life problems. This section gives students some practical examples. Most students find word problems difficult. The teacher should help students to learn to read a question and identify important information that can be used to form a quadratic equation. Students should develop the skill of translating the given information mathematically.

EXERCISE 13K

1 8 cm

2 5 and 10 years

3 9 cm by 14 cm

4 5

5 4 and 13

6 9 and 12

7 8 cm
(The quadratic equation also gives 12 as a solution but in this case the other side of the rectangle would be 14 cm long and the question states that the longer side is 10 cm long.)

14 Ratio and proportion

• Aim of chapter The aim of the chapter is to extend previous work on ratio, including proportion and the unitary method.

• Objectives By the end of the chapter the students will be able to:

1 Solve simple ratio problems
2 Solve sharing problems using ratios
3 Increase and decrease amounts in a given ratio
4 Solve ratio and proportion problems involving more than one ratio
5 Find the scale or representative fraction of a map or scale drawing
6 Use the scale of a map to find the distance on the ground that any distance on the map represents
7 Use the scale of a map to find the distance on a map that would represent the distance on the ground between two places.

• Ratios This section should be largely revision. A ratio compares things. The things may be numbers, lengths, masses or amounts.

EXERCISE 14A

1 a 2:1 b 1:2 c 4:5 d 2:3
e 1:4 f 2:3 g 4:5:6 h 8:1
i 1:4 j 12:3:5 k 4:1:2 l 2:5

2 a 3:4 b 7:10 c 2:3 d 7:9
e 1:4 f 8:9 g 4:5 h 4:5

3 a 1:2 b 1:2 c 1:4

4 a 1:2 b 1:3 c 1:6

5 a 2:3 b 4:9

6 a 2:3 b 2:5

7 7:5

8 1:4

9 9:8:10

10 a 1:2 b 4:5 c 1:2

11 3:2

12 a 3:2 b 2:3 c 5:4

13 a 6:4:5 b 10:9:15 c 2:3:5

• Sharing

Sharing problems are a standard ratio problem. The crucial idea that, once understood, makes these problems simple is that if a quantity is shared in the ratio $a:b$, then the quantity is divided up into $(a+b)$ parts and the sharers get a and b parts, respectively.

EXERCISE 14B

1 a 18 sweets, 12 sweets b K400, K200
c 28 oranges, 56 oranges d K60, K90
e 20 bananas, 5 bananas f K600, K1400

2 22 boys, 18 girls

3 20 Chichewa books, 30 English books

4 80°, 60°, 40°

5 60, 40

6 42 kg, 18 kg

7 Mabangi gets K2400, Namatovu gets K3000

• Ratio problems

In this section more ratio problems are considered. The usual method is to use what is sometimes called the unitary method – find the cost, length etc. of a single item first. Notice that the calculation is carried out at the end. This is because numbers often cancel out and simplify the calculation considerably.

EXERCISE 14C

1 a 6 b 20 c 12
d 4 e 14 f 8
g $x=2, y=8$ h $y=10, a=15$ i $z=12, b=28$

2 a 25 km b K450 c 20 hours d 4.9 litres

3 a 25 kg b K2700 c 14 minutes d 2 km

4 a 18 b 44

5 12

6 63 kg

7 162 cm

8 80 ml of sugar, 400 ml water, 720 ml of lemon squash

9 K64

10 K19 800

11 K21

12 K125

• Direct proportion

In this section we look at ratio problems in which quantities are in direct proportion. Examples are discussed. Use local examples to introduce this topic.

EXERCISE 14D

1 15 hectares

2 1750 seedlings

3 36 minutes

4 a 205 km b 307.5 c 32 litres

5 K192

6 K33

7 K75

8 K36

• Inverse proportion

In this section we look at ratio problems in which quantities are in inverse proportion. Students often have difficulty deciding whether quantities are in direct or indirect proportion. When they multiply by a ratio, which way up should the ratio be?

They should think about whether the quantity should be increased or decreased. For example, if more men are employed to dig a trench then the length of time taken will decrease.

On the other hand, the more men there are, the more bricks can be made in a given period of time. It is always a question of applying common sense. If students do that they should be able to get sensible answers.

Some of the later problems involve both direct and indirect proportion. These questions can be very tricky. The method used in the text-book is the unitary method.

Advise the students always to put the quantity which is unknown on the right-hand side of the equation.

EXERCISE 14E

1 20 minutes
2 5 hours
3 16 minutes
4 360 km
5 12
6 22.5 hectares
7 2250 plants
8 18 postmen
9 9 hours

• Scales

An important use of ratios is in expressing the scale of a map. The ratios are always expressed in the form $1:n$. Ratios in this form are simpler for students to use than ratios like 5 : 3 or 7 : 4 which require much more tricky manipulation.

It is useful as a teacher to remember that 1 km = 100 000 cm so if a map has a scale of 1 : 100 000 then a distance of 1 cm on the map corresponds to a distance of 1 km on the ground. If the scale is 1 : 300 000 then 1 cm on the map represents 3 km on the ground. A scale of 1 : 1 000 000 means that 10 km are represented by 1 cm on the map.

In the text-book examples are used from Malawian atlases. It is much more interesting if you also take examples from the atlases that your pupils have.

The scale is expressed either as a ratio, as in 1 : 350 000, or as the 'representative fraction', 1/350 000. Students should be familiar with both. Sometimes on a map the ratio is not stated at all. At the bottom of the map there is a line showing the distance represented by a particular length. By measuring the length of the line in centimetres and comparing its length with the distance it is representing, it is possible to work out the scale of the map.

EXERCISE 14F

1 47.5 km
2 126 km
3 105 km

4 32 cm

5 17 cm

6 10 cm

7 1 : 2 000 000

8 1/400 000

9 147 km, 10.5 hours

15 Similarity

• Aim of chapter

The aim of the chapter is to introduce students to the basic concepts, skills and notation of positive, negative and fractional enlargements and the properties of the shapes and images resulting from enlargements.

• Objectives

By the end of the chapter the students will be able to:

1 Find the centre of enlargement, given an object and its image under an enlargement
2 Show that an object and its image under an enlargement are congruent
3 Find the scale factor of an enlargement
4 Find the image of a shape given the centre of enlargement and the scale factor
5 Compare the lengths, areas and volumes of similar shapes
6 Divide a straight line into equal parts.

• Recognising similar shapes

Bring many similar and dissimilar things into the class and let the students sort them out (leaves, photographs, boxes, ...).

• Centre of enlargement

In this section students find by drawing the centre of an enlargement when they know the shape and its image. All the lines joining points and their images are concurrent. Where they meet is the centre of enlargement.

This property makes the preparation of questions quite simple. Any two similar shapes have a centre of enlargement. It does not matter where the two similar shapes are drawn but lines joining corresponding points must always meet in a point, which is the centre of enlargement. This surprising result is useful but you still need to be careful that the centre of enlargement is not too far away and impossible to draw on the same sheet of paper. You can do this by drawing the shape and its image at an angle to each other.

EXERCISE 15A

1 a A′, B′ and C′

b

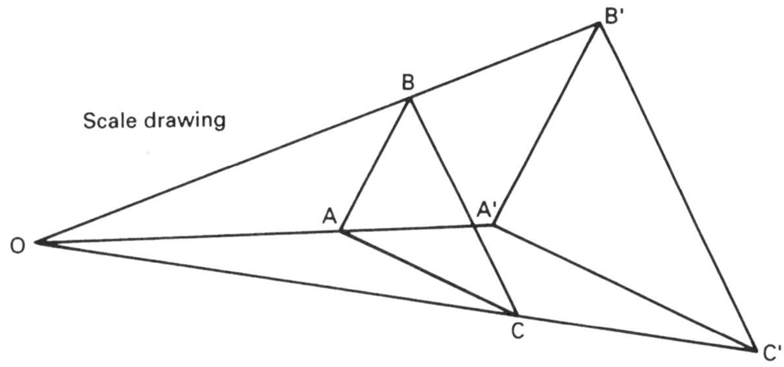

c Angle A = angle A′ = 85°, Angle B = angle B′ = 55°, Angle C = angle C′ = 40°.

2 a A′, B′, C′ and D′

b

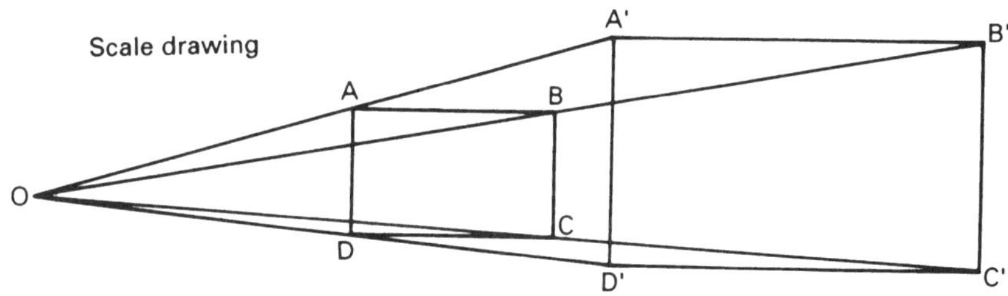

3 a A′, B′, C′, D′ and E′

b

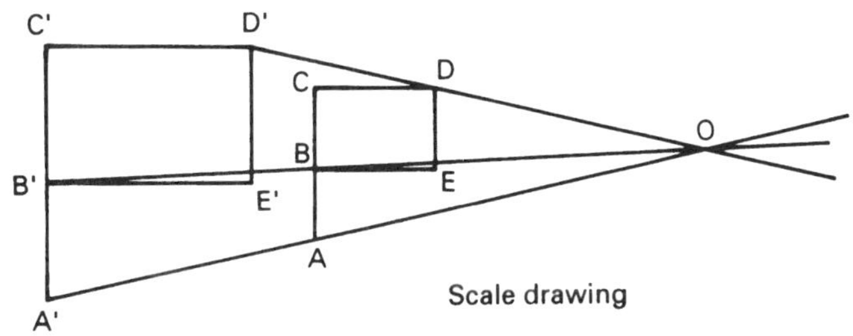

(It is only necessary to draw two lines to find the centre of enlargement. It is wise, however, to draw three to make sure you have not made a careless mistake drawing one of the lines.)

4 a P′, Q′ and R′
b

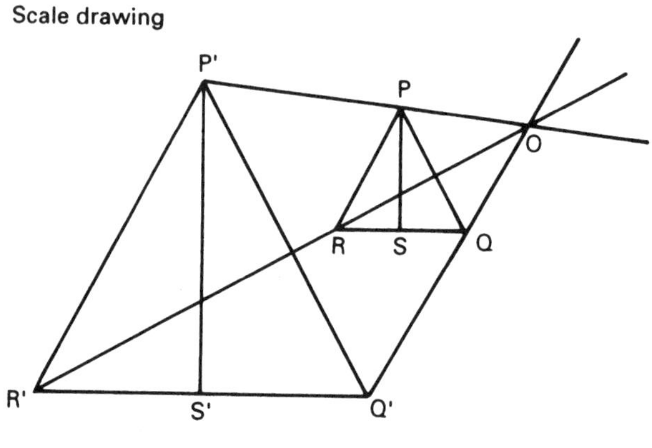

d Angle Q′P′R′

5 d The centre of this enlargement is C = (5, 7).

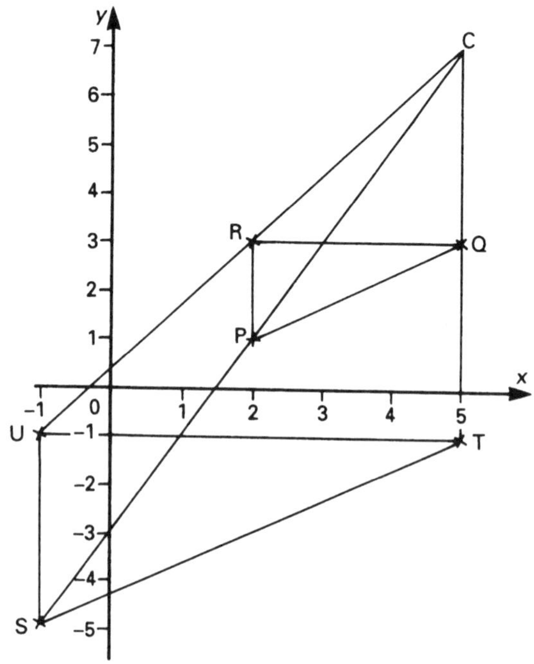

• Scale factors

The scale factor is the distance from the image of a point to the centre of enlargement divided by the distance from the point to the centre of the enlargement.

For example:

The scale factor is $\frac{OA'}{OA} = \frac{15}{10} = 1.5$.

Students tend to think that $\frac{OA'}{OA} = \frac{10}{5} = 2$, which, of course, is wrong.

The teacher needs to be on the lookout for this kind of mistake.

EXERCISE 15B

1 a 2 b 1.6 c 3 d 4

2

a
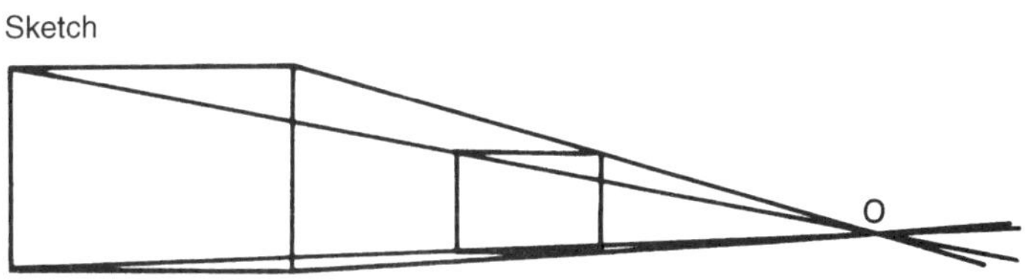

b
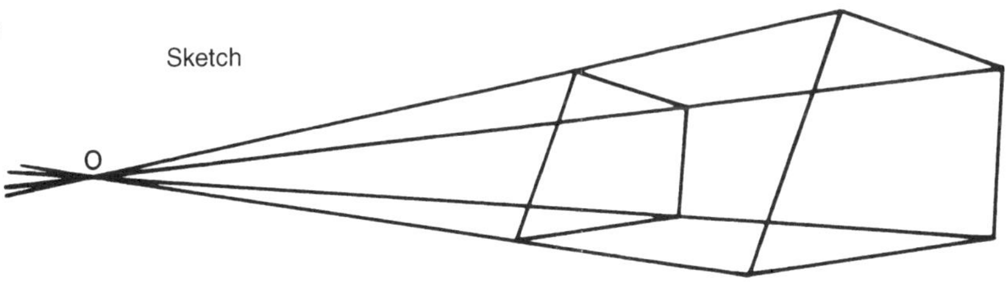

d
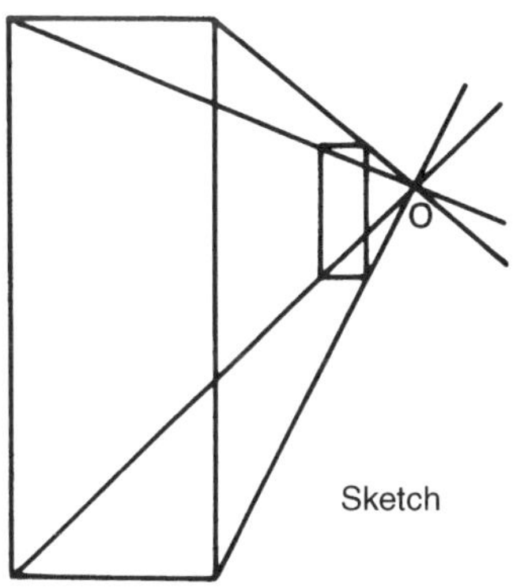

c
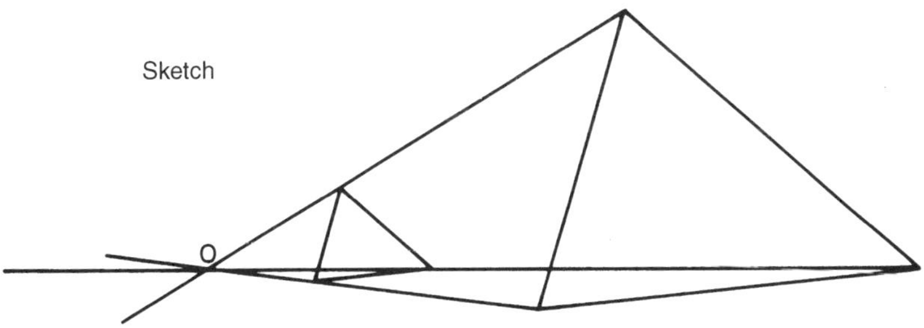

3 1.5

4 4.5

5 a 2 b 3 c 1.5 d 1.5

• Scale factors that are fractions or negative

A scale factor which is a fraction reduces the size of the object. In mathematics the transformation is still called an enlargement, even when the size is reduced, so we can talk about an enlargement scale factor a half; in ordinary English this would be called a reduction. A scale factor which is negative reverses the direction of the shape. The image is on the opposite side of the centre of enlargement.

EXERCISE 15C

1 a 3 b -2 c $\frac{1}{3}$ d $-\frac{1}{2}$ e $\frac{2}{3}$ f 1.5

2 a The centre of enlargement is the point R. The scale factor is $-\frac{2}{3}$

b 2

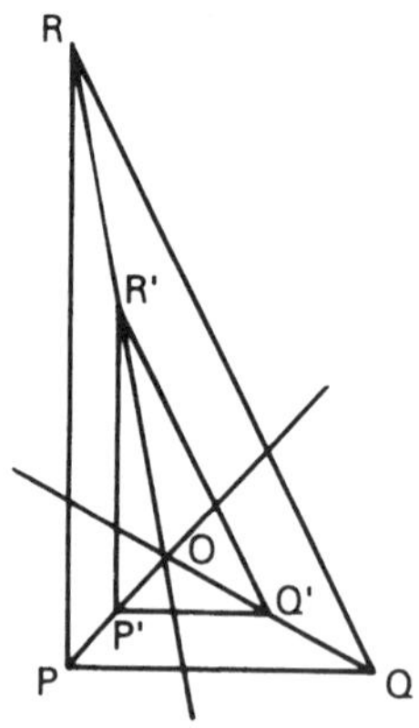

c -1

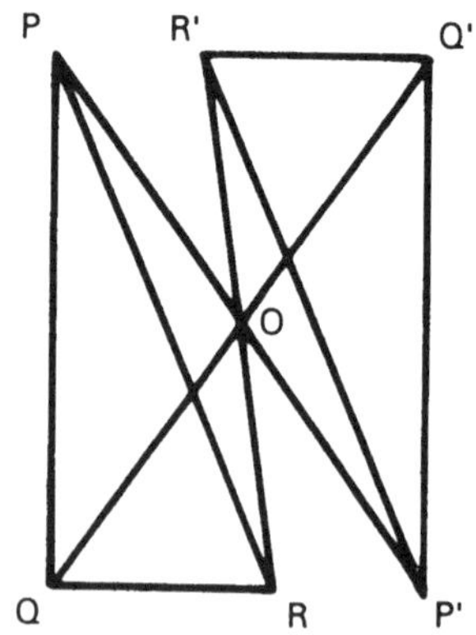

3 a centre: the origin, scale factor -2
b centre: P(2, 4), scale factor -3
c centre: (4, 10), scale factor 1.5
d centre: (8, 7), scale factor -2

4 a (9, 11) b (4, 1)

5 a $A'=(4,-3)$, $B'=(13, 3)$, $C'=(7, 15)$ and $D'=(1, 6)$
b $A''=(1, 1)$, $B''=(2.5, 2)$, $C''=(1.5, 4)$ and $D''=(0.5, 2.5)$
c $A'''=(-4,-2)$, $B'''=(-10,-6)$, $C'''=(-6,-14)$ and $D'''=(-2,-8)$

• Area of similar figures

This section teaches the important idea that if lengths are in the proportion $x:1$, then areas are in the proportion $x^2:1$ and volumes are in the proportion $x^3:1$. These properties are developed by using rectangles and right-angled triangles.

EXERCISE 15D

1 $54\,cm^2$

2 $192\,cm^2$

3 $648\,cm^3$

4 a Triangles ABC and A′B′C′
  b 2
  c (i) BC = 5 cm   (ii) AB′ = 16 cm
  d 90°
  e BC and B′C′ are parallel.
  f Triangle ABC has area $20\,cm^2$;
   triangle AB′C′ has area $80\,cm^2$.

5 a 3 : 1   b 3 cm   c 108 : 12 = 9 : 1

6 a $\frac{1}{2}$
  b 20 cm
  c $800\,cm^2$
  d AB and ED are parallel lines.
   Angle ABC = angle DEC
   Angle BCA = angle ECD
   Angle CAB = angle CDE

7 12 m

8 42 cm

• Dividing a line equally

This short section shows students how to divide up a line into equal parts when the length of the line is not an easy multiple of the number of parts.

EXERCISE 15E

1

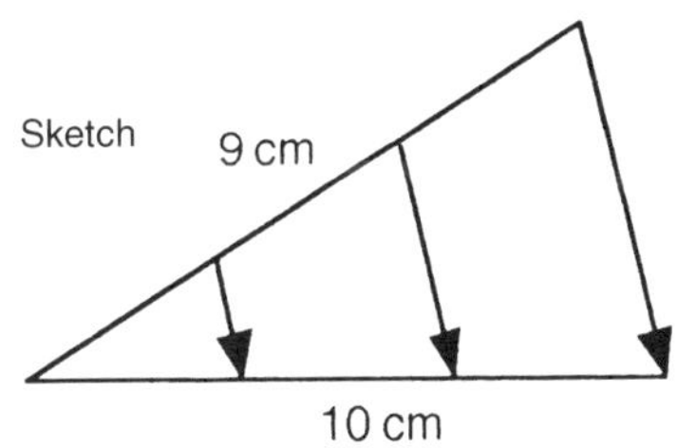

2

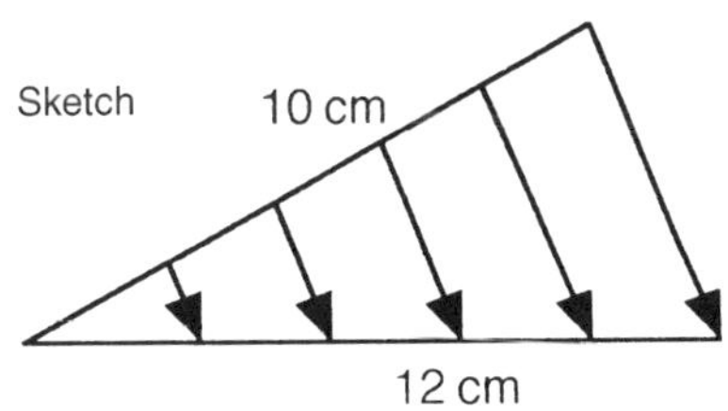

16 Probability

• Aim of chapter

The aim of the chapter is to introduce students to the basic ideas of probability.

• Objectives

By the end of the chapter, the students will be able to:

1 List possible outcomes of a probability experiment
2 Find the probability of a simple event
3 Represent probability as a number or as a percentage
4 State that the probability of an impossible event is 0
5 State that the probability of a certain event is 1.

• Chances

The chapter begins by looking at chances. Activities in our daily lives depend on chances. Using local, familiar situations, the teacher should discuss many examples with the students. These examples can include the weather, examination results, scores in sports events etc.

• Listing outcomes

In probability we look at the likelihood of a particular event occurring. For any event we can usually list all the possible outcomes. The outcomes which give the result we are interested in are called 'favourable outcomes.' Use coins, dice, playing cards and coloured beads in a bag to consolidate the concept of outcomes. Let students perform experiments and list the outcomes. Outcomes which have an equal chance of occurring are called 'equally likely outcomes'.

• Calculating probabilities

The probability of an event is a ratio. It is a comparison of the favourable outcomes and the total number of possible outcomes.

$$\text{Probability} = \frac{\text{Number of favourable outcomes}}{\text{Total number of possible outcomes}}$$

Emphasise that, in order to calculate the probability of an event, we first need to list all the favourable outcomes.

We can use shorthand to describe a probability. This saves us a lot of writing. For example, when a coin is tossed, the probability of getting a tail can be written as P(T).

• Certainties and impossibilities

Probability scales are used in mathematics to describe the likelihood of something happening.

The scale can be given as a number:

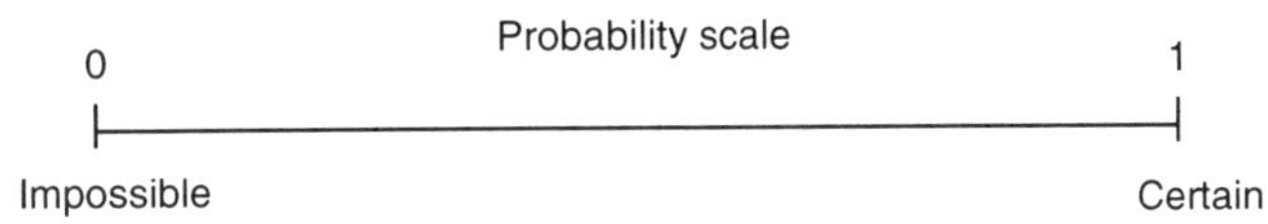

Or it can be given as a percentage:

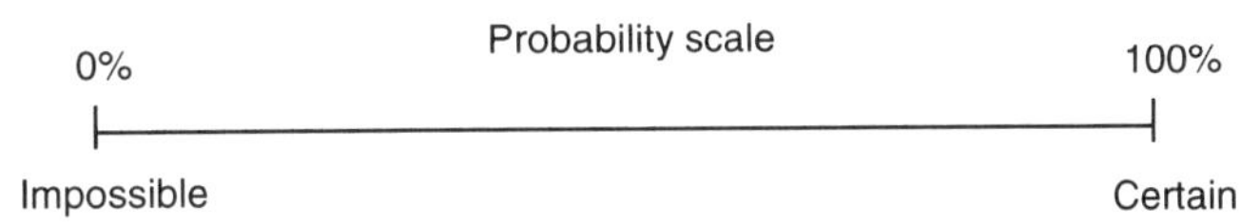

The probability of an event can have any value from 0 to 1 or 0% to 100%.

EXERCISE 16A

1 Saturday

2 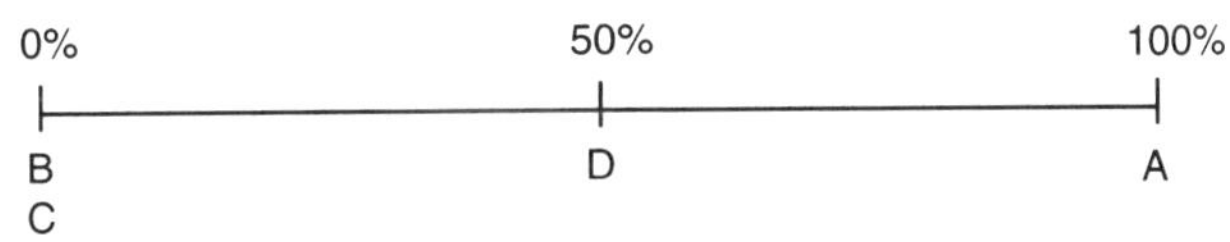

E will depend on the proportion of girls in the school.
F will depend on the proportion of Toyotas being driven.

3 a (i) Mlamba (ii) Usipa
b Usipa, Chambo, Mphuta, Utaka, Mlamba
c Could be over-fishing?

4 a $\frac{1}{2}$ b $\frac{1}{2}$ c $\frac{1}{3}$ d $\frac{1}{2}$ e $\frac{1}{3}$

5 a $\frac{1}{8}$ b $\frac{1}{2}$ c $\frac{1}{2}$ d $\frac{1}{4}$ e 0

6 a $\frac{1}{8}$ b $\frac{1}{8}$ c $\frac{1}{2}$ d $\frac{1}{2}$ e $\frac{1}{4}$

7 a $\frac{2}{11}$ b $\frac{2}{11}$ c $\frac{4}{11}$ d $\frac{7}{11}$

8 a $\frac{18}{29}$ b $\frac{11}{29}$

9 a $\frac{1}{13}$ b $\frac{1}{4}$

10 $\frac{1}{20}$

11 a $\frac{2}{3}$ b $\frac{5}{18}$ c $\frac{1}{18}$ d $\frac{13}{18}$ e $\frac{17}{18}$

12 a $\frac{7}{20}$ b $\frac{1}{4}$ c $\frac{1}{5}$ d $\frac{1}{5}$ e $\frac{4}{5}$ f $\frac{4}{5}$

17 Mensuration

• Aim of chapter

The aim of the chapter is to introduce students to the pleasure and skills of making models from nets.

• Objectives

By the end of the chapter the students will be able to:
1 Identify cubes, cuboids, pyramids and tetrahedra by name
2 Identify triangular and other prisms, and cylinders
3 Draw the nets of solids and construct models from them
4 Calculate areas and volumes of cylinders and pyramids.

• Solids

This chapter is practical, and it should make a good topic to end the year with. The students should make lots of attractive models.

This section reminds students about the names for some important polyhedra: cubes, cuboids, pyramids and tetrahedra.

• Prisms

Prisms have a uniform cross-section. The shape of the cross-section gives many prisms their name.

EXERCISE 17A

1 a and d
2 a cuboid b cylinder c pentagonal-based pyramid
  d tetrahedron

• Nets

Nets enable attractive shapes to be made from flat card. Old envelopes can be used if proper card is not available.

EXERCISE 17B

1 Different students can make different models.
2 a The faces of the completed model can be painted with different colours to make an attractive display.
  b The equilateral triangles must be carefully made the same size and shape.
  c Accuracy is especially important when making a net with so many faces.
  d A dodecahedron can be used to make a very attractive calendar. Each of the twelve faces can have the calendar for one month on it.

3 Students make a pentagonal pyramid using the net shown in their book.

• Volume and capacity

This section reviews volume and capacity and compares a volume of $1\,cm^3$ and a capacity of 1 millilitre. These two are equal.

• Volume of a prism

All prisms are of uniform cross-section. We can find the volume of any prism by multiplying its cross-sectional area (which is the same as the area of the base) by its height. This section starts by considering the simplest of prisms, the cuboid.

• Volume of a cylinder

The cylinder is a prism whose uniform cross-section is a circle. The area of the circle is πr^2, so the volume of the cylinder is $\pi r^2 h$.

Water pipes which are hollow cylinders are considered and the formula for their volume, $\pi R^2 h - \pi r^2 h = \pi(R^2 - r^2)h$ is derived.

EXERCISE 17C

1 a $480\,cm^3$ b $400\,cm^3$ c $198\,cm^3$

2 $500\,cm^3$

3 5 cm

4 $20\,cm^2$

5 $900\,cm^3$

6 a $21.56\,cm^3$ b $1\,232\,000\,cm^3$ c $272\,200\,mm^3$

d $43\,120\,cm^3$ e $197\,120\,cm^3$

7 a 22.7 m b 56.8 cm c 207.8 cm

8 a 32 *l* b 288 *l* c 8000 *l* d 32 *l*

9 a 6.52 cm b 2.24 cm c 3.16 cm d 26.9 m

10 a $2009.6\,cm^3$ b $125\,600\,cm^3$

• Surface area of a prism

There is no simple formula for the surface area of any prism in the same way that there is a formula for the volume of a prism. To find the surface area of a prism you have to work out the area of all the faces and then add these areas together.

The surface area of a cuboid is straightforward – there are two faces area $l \times b$, two faces area $b \times h$ and two faces area $h \times l$. So the total area $= 2(lb + bh + hl)$.

• Surface area of a cylinder

Most tins of vegetables or fruit have labels on them. These labels can easily be taken off and it is clear that they are rectangular. Ask the students to bring in old tins with labels (they must clean them). The height of the rectangle is the height of the cylinder, h, and the length of the rectangle is the circumference of the circular base of the rectangle, $2\pi r$.
So the curved surface is $h \times 2\pi r = 2\pi rh$.

The two ends are circles with areas of πr^2.
Students must learn to decide whether the ends of a cylinder are to be considered when working out the surface area. A pipe is not blocked at either end, a water container must be sealed at one end and a tin of food must be sealed at both ends.

EXERCISE 17D

1	a 592 cm^2	b 864 cm^2	c 132 cm^2	d 360 cm^2
2	a 94.2 cm^2	b 31.4 cm^2	c 1004.8 cm^2	d πa^2 cm^2
3	9 cm			
4	50 cm^2			
5	16.94 cm^2			
6	22.2 cm^2			
7	0.11 m^3			
8	a 14 800 cm^2	b 72 000 cm^2	c 180:37	
9	a 12 cm^2	b 240 cm^2		
10	a 2512 m^2	b 26 pots		
11	3234 mm^2			
12	160 m^3			

• Pyramids

Pyramids take their name from the famous square-based pyramids in Egypt. Other examples of pyramids are shown in the text-book. A triangular-based pyramid whose edges are all the same length is called a tetrahedron. It is one of the 5 Platonic solids (the others are the cube, the octahedron, the dodecahedron and the icosahedron).

All pyramids have a polygonal base and sides which meet at a point. A cone is similar to a pyramid; it has a point, just as the pyramids do. Its base is a circle. This section introduces important words such as height and slant height.

• Surface area of a pyramid

There is not a simple formula for the surface area of a pyramid. In order to calculate the surface area of a pyramid, we have to work out the areas of the faces and add them together.

If the base of the pyramid is an n-sided polygon, then the surface consists of the base and n triangles. If the pyramid is a 'right pyramid', all the triangles will be congruent isosceles. Examples of working out the surface area of pyramids are given in the text-book.

• Surface area of a cone

There is a formula for the surface area of a cone which is expressed in terms of the slant height. In the text-book, students are asked to derive the formula. The surface area is found by thinking of the curved surface as a sector of a circle. This leads to the simple formula πrl.

In these problems the important relationship between the vertical height and the slant height is used.
The slant height is longer: $l^2 = h^2 + r^2$

Students will find the derivation easier if the teacher gives each of them a cut-out paper circle and they then cut out a sector of the circle. When the two radii that were cut are brought together the paper looks like a cone. The larger the sector that was cut out, the greater the surface area of the cone it will make.

EXERCISE 17E

1 55 cm^2

2 692.8 cm^2

3 336 cm^2

4 273.2 cm^2

5 a 330 cm^2 b 440 cm^2 c 2.64 cm^2

6 616 cm^2

• Volume of a pyramid

A full proof of the formula for the volume of a pyramid is beyond the scope of this course. What the text-book does is to show the result is true for a few special cases. First, square-based pyramid ABCDV is shown to be $\frac{1}{6}$ of the volume of the cuboid and hence its volume is $= \frac{1}{3}$ area of base × height.
The volume of triangular-based pyramid ABDV in the same diagram is shown to satisfy the same formula.

The measurements are given for making a pyramid, six of which fitted together make a cube and so each has an area of one-sixth of the volume of the cube. The fit is quite good (the measurement of the sides of the triangles should be 8.66 cm to be more accurate, but we cannot expect greater accuracy than measurements to the nearest millimetre).

These and other examples are used to suggest the formula holds for other cases.

There are two worked examples using the formula. The first is a routine use of the formula for a pyramid whose base and height are known. The second example asks for the volume when the slant edges are known. To find the height of the pyramid so that we can apply the formula we have to use Pythagoras' theorem.

EXERCISE 17F

1 a 63 cm^3 b 324 cm^3 c 166 667 cm^3

2 240 cm^3

3 6000 cm^3

4 1000 cm^3

5 250 cm^3

6 24 cm^3

7 144.3 cm^3

8 126 m^3

9 2 637 376 m^3

10 16.9 cm^3

• Volume of a cone

Thinking of a cone as a pyramid with a circular base helps a students to remember the formula. The circular base has an area of πr^2.

So the volume is $\frac{1}{3} \times$ area of base $\times$ height $= \frac{1}{3}\pi r^2 h$.

EXERCISE 17G

1 a 1540 cm^3 b 1760 cm^3 c 205.3 cm^3
d 5.13 cm^3

2 a 6 cm b 3.46 cm c 7.07 cm

3 1232 cm^3

4 16π m^3

5 5.84 cm

6 12.8 cm

7 111.8 kg

8 a 65.9 m^3 b 67.5 m^2

18 Density and mixtures

• Aim of chapter

The aim of the chapter is to introduce students to the concept of density.

• Objectives

By the end of the chapter, the students will be able to:

1 Find the density of substances
2 Substitute in density formulas to evaluate unknowns
3 Calculate relative density
4 Find the density of blended substances.

• Which is heavier?

Most students associate heaviness with size. But it is not always true that the larger object is the heavier. Half a kilogram of feathers is much larger than a kilogram brick. The teacher should discuss with students more examples of this nature. After this discussion the students are introduced to the concept of density. Density is a ratio comparing two quantities with different units. It is defined by the formula:

$$\text{Density} = \frac{\text{Mass}}{\text{Volume}}$$

The idea of density is also used to compare populations. This topic is also discussed in the section. **Population density** is defined as the number of people per unit area. This can be the number of people living in a square kilometre or hectare. It can also be the number of spiders found in a square metre of woodland.

The unit of density we get from a formula depends on the units of mass and volume. If the mass is in grams and the volume in cubic centimetres, then the density is in g/cm^3.

$$1\,\text{kg} = 1000\,\text{g} \quad \text{and} \quad 1\,\text{m} = 100\,\text{cm}$$

If a substance has a density of 1 kg/m^3, it means that 1 m^3 has a mass of 1 kg.
This means that $100 \times 100 \times 100$ cm^3 has a mass of 1000 g
and 1 cm^3 has a mass of $\frac{1000}{100 \times 100 \times 100} = 0.001$ g.
So a density of 1 kg/m^3 is the same as a density of 0.001 g/cm^3.

EXERCISE 18A

1 0.9 g/cm^3

2 1.143 g/cm^3

3 675 g

4 900 kg

5 **a** 32 people/km^2 **b** Yes
c Poor sanitation, environmental problems etc.

6 **a** 0.1 snails/m^2 **b** 100 000 snails

7 **a** 20 ants/m^2 **b** 20 million

• Relative density

The densities of most substances are calculated relative to the density of water which is 1 g/cm^3.

Relative density of a substance =

$$\frac{\text{Mass of a given volume of the substance}}{\text{Mass of an equal volume of water}}$$

Relative density has no units.

EXERCISE 18B

1 8

2 0.67 to 2 decimal places

3 750 g

4 50 cm

5 **a** Yes (relative density $= 0.8 < 1$)

b No (relative density $= \frac{200}{196} > 1$)

c No (relative density $= \frac{1000}{3.14 \times 5^2 \times 10} > 1$)

• Mixtures Substances can be blended. The ratio in which the substances are mixed will determine the quality of the mixture.

EXERCISE 18C

1 1.23 g/cm^3

2 1.02 g/cm^3

3 0.55

4 660 litres

5 1 : 3

6 K19.88

7 8.04 g/cm^3

8 1.09

19 Applied arithmetic – miscellaneous applications

• **Aim of chapter** The aim of the chapter is to apply arithmetic to problems of everyday life involving money and percentages.

• **Objectives** By the end of the chapter the students will be able to:

1. Change percentages to fractions and decimals and vice versa
2. Express one quantity as a percentage of another
3. Find a percentage of a quantity
4. Find a new price when a percentage price increase is given
5. Solve discount problems using percentages
6. Solve commission problems using percentages
7. Calculate household budgets
8. Solve profit and loss problems using percentages
9. Solve simple interest problems using the formula
10. Solve compound interest problems (not by formula).

• **Percentages** Percentages are used a great deal to express price increases or decreases and interest rates in banks, so it is important that the student is familiar with their use before attempting calculations about money. Percentages are attractive as a way of expressing rates because the numbers used in percentages are more manageable than those used in fractions or decimals. If a bank said the interest rate was 0.09 or $\frac{9}{100}$, we would not be very impressed. 9 per cent sounds like so much more!

A percentage is quite simply the numerator of a fraction which has a denominator of 100. 35.2% means $\frac{35.2}{100}$. To change a percentage to a fraction we just write the percentage with denominator 100 and simplify the fraction.

We can change percentages to decimals even more simply:

$$64\% = \frac{64}{100} = 0.64$$

• Fractions, decimals and percentages

To change a fraction or decimal to a percentage, we first have to find an equivalent fraction with denominator 100:

$$\frac{3}{4} = \frac{3 \times 25}{4 \times 25} = \frac{75}{100} = 75\%$$

$$0.6 = \frac{6}{10} = \frac{6 \times 10}{10 \times 10} = \frac{60}{100} = 60\%$$

In each case we have to think what number multiplied by the denominator gives the result 100. This is quite easy for factors of 100 (which includes the decimals), but for other numbers it is more difficult. A simpler way of changing both fractions and decimals to percentages, which works in all cases, is to multiply them by 100% (which is equal to 1).

For example $\frac{3}{4} = \frac{3}{4} \times 100\% = 3 \times 25\% = 75\%$ and $0.643 = 0.643 \times 100\% = 64.3\%$

EXERCISE 19A

1 a $\frac{1}{2}$ b $\frac{1}{3}$ c $\frac{21}{25}$ d $2\frac{1}{4}$

2 a 0.75 b 0.562 c 1.3 d 2.83

3 a 80% b 40% c 185% d 125%

4 a 70% b 7% c 92.1% d 380%

• One quantity as a percentage of another

To find what percentage quantity A is of quantity B we divide A by B and multiply by 100. The common mistake people make is to forget to change A and B to the same units.

• Percentage of a quantity

This use of percentage is often met in everyday life. Prices are reduced to 80% of what they were, wages are raised by 20% of what they were and so on. Percentages are popular because they make a small number seem larger. The percentage is changed to a fraction or a decimal for calculation. Many calculators have a percentage button and the calculation can be done without this step being seen.

EXERCISE 19B

1 a 60% b 74% c 25% d 5%
 e 2.5% f 20% g 25% h 17.5%

2 a 20% b 5%

3 a 64 b 30 c 5.4 d 36
e K200 f 22 m g 0.36 l = 360 ml
h 36 l 1.44 j 12

4 a 55.6% b 66.7% c 57.1% d 72.7%

5 Chichewa – 65%, English – 70%. He did better in English.

6 16

7 K1269

8 429

9 408

10 vegetables – 4 hectares, sorghum – 9 hectares

• Increase per cent

Changes in the cost of items, rates of pay and so on are often expressed in percentages. This section looks at situations in which price rises are so expressed.

• Discounts

This sections looks at situations where prices decrease, such as when a shopkeeper reduces prices to sell items that are selling too slowly and wants room for new stock. The calculation is the same except that the change is subtracted.

EXERCISE 19C

1 a 720 b 960 c 1200

2 a 280 b 200 c 120

3 780

4 K5.60

5 K45

6 K62.50

7 20%

8 33%

9 a 33 000 b 36 300
(The increase is 10% of 33 000 = 3300;
33 000 + 3300 = 36 300)

10 14%
Woman's new earnings are K6000 + 10% of K6000 = K 6600
Husband's new earnings are
K4000 + 20% of K4000 = K 4800
New total earnings are K6600 + K4800 = K11 400, an increase of K1400.

11 K2990

12 a length 9 m, width 5.4 m b 19%

• Commission

Selling goods on commission is quite common – it encourages the seller to work hard as the more she sells the more she earns. In most cases it is usually simpler to work out the total selling price and calculate the total commission than to work out the commission on each item and add the commissions together.

EXERCISE 19D

1 K24.24 2 K8800 3 K160

4 $1855 5 K21.50

• Household budgets

Percentages can be used to compare parts of a budget spent on different items.

EXERCISE 19E

1 K97.25

2 loaves of bread at K18	36.00
1 kg of sugar at K20 per kg	20.00
250 g of margarine at K125 per kg	31.25
1 litre of milk at K10	10.00
	97.25

2 K6610

5 m of material at K600 per m	3000
2 paperbacks for K5 each	10
3 pairs of shoes for K1200 each	3600
	6610

3 a K234 b 32.5%

2 clusters of bananas for K40 each	80
2 kg of oranges at K12 per kg	24
2 cabbages for K10 each	20
3 kg of carrots at K8 per kg	24
2 kg of green peppers at K5 per kg	10
2 kg of fresh beans at K8 per kg	16
2 kg of dry beans at K30 per kg	60
	234

4 a K2440 b 41%

20 mathematical sets for K50 each	1000
72 exercise books at K15 per unit	1080
30 ball pens at K2 each	60
20 pads of paper for K15 each	300
	2440

5 K615

1 sack of charcoal for K50	50
500 grams of yeast for K15	15
2 pkt of baking flour for K160 per pkt	320
	385

• Profit and loss

Profit and loss are calculated as a percentage of the **cost price**. This is where many pupils go wrong – they work out the profit as a percentage of the selling price. There are several types of problem: finding percentage profit or loss when we know the cost and selling prices; finding the selling price when we know the cost price and the percentage profit or loss; and finding the cost price when we know the selling price and the percentage profit or loss.

EXERCISE 19F

1 25%

2 25%

3 a 20% b 25% c 25% d 11.1%
e 4.2% f 33.3% g 15.4% h 33.3%

4 96 kg

5 K900 000

6 height 154 cm, mass 66.5 kg

7 20%
(She sold 90 for 80t = K72.)

8 He expected 33.3% profit. He lost 8%.
(He sold 69 for K2 = K138, a loss of K12.)

9 25%

10 K7.50

11 K2530

12 K20

13

Cost price	*% profit/loss*	*Selling price*
a K350	20% profit	**K420**
b K480	10% loss	**K432**
c K8000	**20% profit**	K9600
d K1800	**16.7% loss**	K1500
e K12 per dozen	**20% loss**	80t each
f **K1000**	20% profit	K1200
g K5000	100%profit	**K10 000**
h K6000	**16.7% profit**	K7000

14 K36 800

15 K72 000
K64 800

• Simple interest

The method banks use to calculate interest is usually much more complicated than the simple interest method. Interest is often calculated on the daily balance and, in effect, compound interest is paid as the interest itself starts earning interest as soon as it is credited to the account. Simple interest is the simplest form of interest, so it is sensible to start with calculations using this.

The main terms the student needs to be familiar with are **interest** and **principal**.
The formula $I = PRT/100$ is developed first by considering the interest for one year and then several years' interest is considered.

EXERCISE 19G

1 **a** K300 **b** K645 **c** K76 **d** K2310
e K2040 **f** K1350 **g** K1400 **h** K30
i K650 **j** K900

2 K4000 K11 000

3 **a** 2.5% **b** 12.5% **c** 9% **d** 12%
e 15% **f** 4% **g** 10% **h** 20%
i 75% **j** 12.5%

4 4 years

5 **a** 1 year **b** 1 year **c** 11 years **d** 5 years
e 1 year 6 months **f** 4 years
g 6 years 3 months **h** 1 year 3 months
i 3 years 6 months **j** 5 years

6 K4800 K6000
(She invested K8000 thousand at 6% so I must invest K6000 at 8%.)

7 My aunt
(5% of K12 000 = K600, 7% of K9000 = K630)

8 K1320

9 K1200

10 Increase of K90
Interest in the first year is 7% of K3000 = K210.
In second year he invests K3000 + 210 − 710 = K2500.
Interest in second year is 12% of K2500 = K300, which is K90 more than earned in the first year.

• Compound interest

In compound interest the interest earned is reinvested. The first year the interest is unchanged, but thereafter the amount of money invested increases each year. Do not teach the formula; it is not required and the examples to be considered can all be handled quite easily by calculating the change year by year.

EXERCISE 19H

1	K6600	K7260	K7986
2	K4320	K4665.60	K5038.85 (to nearest tambala)
3	K63 000	K66 150	K69 457.50

4 This question compares compound interest and simple interest. It shows how money left in the bank to grow undisturbed at compound interest can mount up quite a lot.

K800 K864 K933.12 K133.12

20 Rotation

• Aim of chapter

The aim of the chapter is to introduce students to the properties of rotations and rotational symmetry.

• Objectives

By the end of the chapter the students will be able to:

1 Find the order of rotational symmetry of any shape
2 Find the angle of rotation of any negative (clockwise) or positive (anticlockwise) turn
3 Find the image of any shape under a rotation when the centre and angle of rotation are known
4 Find the image of any point whose coordinates are given under a rotation, centre the origin, and angle of rotation a multiple of 90°
5 Find the centre of rotation when a shape and its image under that rotation are known.

• Order of rotational symmetry

As suggested in the text-book, tracing paper or any paper that can be seen through is very useful for work on rotation. The tracing paper is put on top of the shape which is then outlined on the tracing paper. The tracing paper is then turned to see whether the drawing on the tracing paper will fit over the shape underneath. The number of ways the shape and the shape on the tracing paper fit is the order of rotational symmetry. Notice that no shape has order of symmetry 0. An irregular shape like the letter R has order of symmetry 1, because it fits its outline in one way.

• Centre of rotation – angle of rotation

This section introduces the concept of rotational symmetry. The order of rotational symmetry is the number of ways that the shape can fit in its outline when it is turned around (but not turned over).

EXERCISE 20A

1 2, 2, 1, 2

2	a 1	b 2	c 4	d 5
	e 4	f 4	g 3	h 1

• Angle of rotation – clockwise and anticlockwise rotations

The convention that a clockwise rotation is **negative** and an anticlockwise rotation is **positive** is unfortunate, for it would seem more natural if we could think of a clock as turning in a positive direction, but it has to be accepted.

EXERCISE 20B

1 a 90° b −270° c −90° d 135°

2 a South b West c West
d South West e North East

3 a −110° b 110° c 40° d 120°

• Images

The result of moving any shape under any transformation is called its image under that transformation. Under a rotation the shape and its image are congruent. Note that we can rotate a figure about any point, and we will get a different image for each point we rotate the shape about and for each angle of rotation.

EXERCISE 20C

1 4

2 6

3

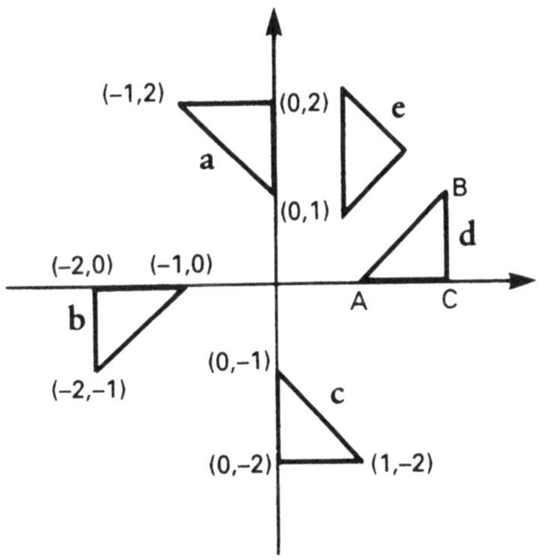

4 a P′ = (−2, 4), Q′ = (−2, −1), R′ = (0, 3)
b (1, 2)
c S = (4, −3)

5 a The image of P is (1, −2).
The image of Q is (6, −4).
b The image of P is (−1, 2).
The image of Q is (−6, 4)

• Equal rotations

This section shows that a clockwise rotation of $x°$ has the same effect as an anticlockwise rotation of $(360 - x)°$.

• Finding the centre of rotation

If a point A is rotated to point A′, then the points A and A′ are on the circumference of a circle whose centre is the centre of rotation. The line AA′ is a chord of the circle and its centre O will be on the perpendicular bisector of the chord AA′.

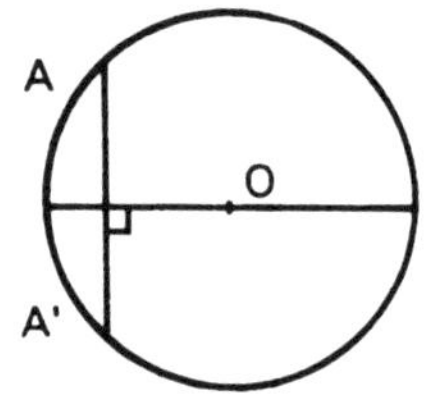

In order to find the centre of rotation we need another point and its image. If point B has image B′ under the same rotation, then the centre O will also lie on the perpendicular bisector of BB′. Where the perpendicular bisectors of AA′ and BB′ meet will be the centre of rotation.

EXERCISE 20D

1 The angle of rotation is 90°.

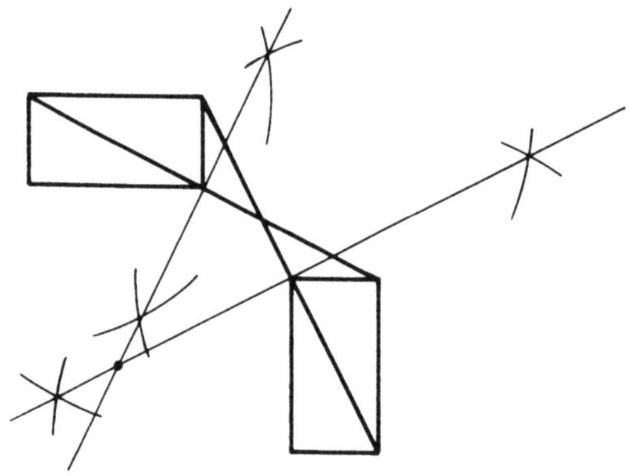

2

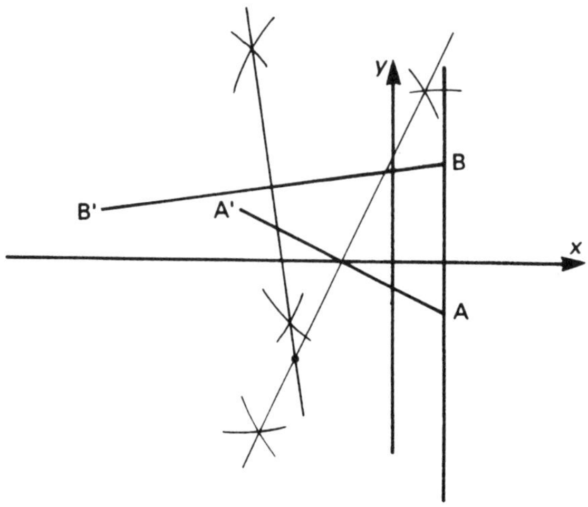

The centre of rotation is $(-1.5, -2)$.
The angle of rotation is 90°.

3 The centre of rotation is $(-1.5, 1.5)$.
The angle of rotation is 90°.

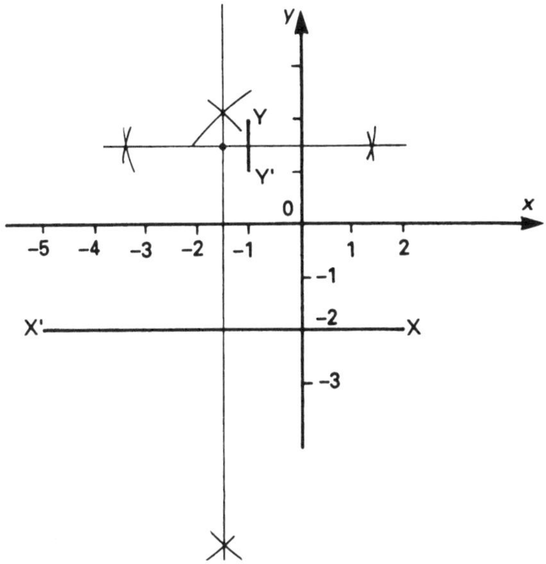

4 The centre of rotation is P.
The image of R is Q.
The angle of rotation is 90°.

5 a The centre of rotation is $(-0.5, 0.5)$.
b The angle of rotation is 90°.

6 The centre of rotation is $(-1, 0)$.
The angle of rotation is 180°.

7 The centre of rotation is $(-1, 1)$
The angle of rotation is 90°